Discovering
Argyll Mull & Iona

To Meagan
with best wishes
Willie On

Discovering
Argyll Mull & Iona

WILLIE ORR

JOHN DONALD PUBLISHERS LTD
EDINBURGH

To Jan
Iona and Morvern
and Liam

© Willie Orr 1990

ISBN 0 85976 269 6

Phototypeset by Newtext Composition Ltd, Glasgow
Printed in Great Britain by Martin's of Berwick

Acknowledgements

This book could not have been completed without the help of numerous individuals and organisations. I would like to thank the staff of Selkirk Public Library for their patience and cheerful assistance and also the staff of Oban Library for help in emergencies. The Nature Conservancy Council, particularly its Barcaldine office, provided a great deal of useful material and advice and the Forestry Commission helped with maps and data. The Crofters' Commission gave me some details of modern crofting townships and several firms, Foster-Yeoman of Glensanda, J. & A. Gardner of Bonawe, Tilcon of Lochaline and David McKee (Stockton) Ltd. at Strontian, provided a wealth of information on their operations, I would like to thank the salmon-farming companies, Marine Harvest, McConnel Salmon and Golden Sea Produce, for their frank discussions and Alison Ross of the Marine Conservation Society for her constructive comments on their activities. The staff of Rahoy Deer Farm and their College advisors were extremely helpful and allowed me to take photographs of the stags. Helen Grant, a native of Iona, lent me one of her father's books, which proved to be an invaluable asset, and Mairi MacArthur generously allowed me to read her thesis on the island. I will not forget the assistance of two gardeners whose enthusiasm for their plants was most infectious – Jim McKirdy of Crarae Gardens and Lt. Col. Campbell-Preston of Ardchattan Priory. I would also like to thank Mr. Cadzow of Luing and Lachie MacLean of Knock for their information on farming and Alasdair Campbell of Inverawe for tolerating my views while working in Inveraray Castle. The Duke of Argyll was kind enough to give me access to the family archives for previous research and his co-operation is much appreciated. Danny and Allison Kane of Laudale gave me shelter and sustenance when a storm demolished my tent, a kindness I can never repay.

I am grateful to Denis Hardley, Benderloch, for providing the colour photograph for the front cover, and to Jan Orr for the maps. I am also indebted to the following for permission to

Discovering Argyll, Mull and Iona

reproduce the photographs which appear on the pages referred to: The Royal Commission on the Ancient and Historical Monuments of Scotland, pp. 106, 123, 143, 168, 172; The National Library of Scotland, pp. 16, 120, 128; Harry Watson p. 30; *The Oban Times,* pp. 60, 99, 192; Iain Thornber, Lochaline, p. 47; Alex MacRae, Oban, p. 118; Sandy Orr, Kilmore, p. 72; Sally Orr, p. 175.

Contents

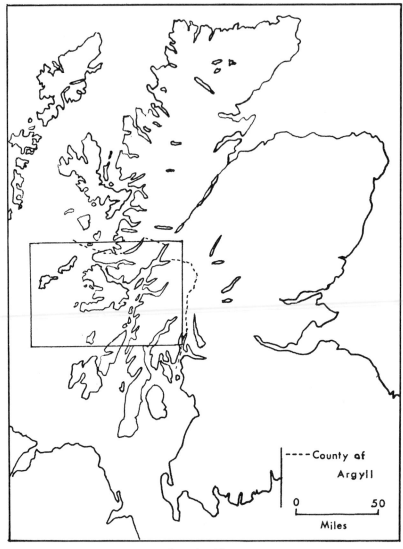

----County of Argyll

0   50

Miles

Location Map

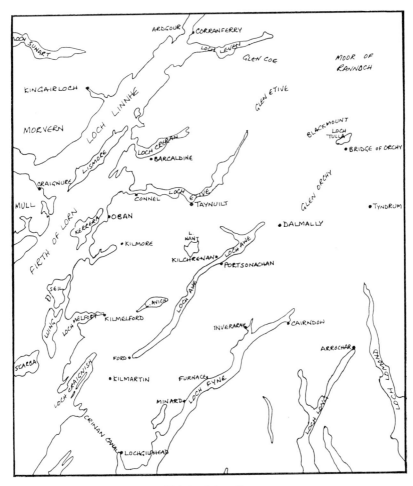

Mainland Argyll

Mull, Morvern and Ardnamurchan

Introduction

It is impossible to travel through North Argyll and not be curious about the primeval forces which shaped the remarkable landscape. The surface has been folded and twisted by movements of the earth's crust, blown apart by volcanic activity, carved by the glaciers of the Ice Ages and eroded by the storms of millions of years. The shape and character of the area was largely determined before man appeared on the earth.

Some of the oldest rocks in the world are to be found in the Highlands and, among these, the hard Lewisian Gneiss visible on the western shore of Iona protects the island from the Atlantic. These rocks are thought to be almost 2,000 million years old and contain no fossils. Even the 'younger' lava flows of Mull were laid down 60 million years ago. Man's impact on this ancient environment has been largely superficial. Granite has been quarried at Bonawe, Crarae and Bunessan and is currently being extracted on a massive scale in Morvern to supply construction projects like the Channel tunnel. Slate has been broken from the beds of Ballachulish and Easdale to roof the houses of Argyll and the tenements of Glasgow and Edinburgh. The white sandstone of Lochaline has been used to make glass. Barytes are mined and refined at Strontian. Lead has been mined in the quartz seams of Tyndrum, and now an Irish company is drilling for gold in the area. In spite of these operations, the landscape remains virtually unaltered since the last Ice Age, with deep glens and sharp mountain peaks in the north and gentle terraced hillsides round the plateau of Lorn.

Evidence of the forces which shaped the land are clearly visible throughout the area but it would be a mistake to imagine that the sides of a Highland Vesuvius can be discerned in the silhouette of the hills. Geologists estimate that the Mull lava beds are the remains of a lava pile which was once 2,200 metres deep, so the shape of the hills today bears no resemblance to the original landscape. Nevertheless, the legacy of volcanic activity can be seen clearly in the black lava sheets on the shores of Ardnamurchan, Morvern and Mull and in the columns of Fingal's cave on Staffa.

1

As the molten lava burst through the earth's surface – in Mull through the waters of a shallow lake – it naturally covered much older rocks and examples of these, some of them more than 800 million years old, can be found in the Old Red Sandstone of Kerrera, Mull and Oban and the white sandstone of Lochaline. Fossils of the creatures which lived above these sediments can be found at Carsaig Bay on Mull and on Kerrera. As successive eruptions spilled layers of lava over the earth, clear strata were laid down, the edges of which form the terraced hillsides of Mull, Morvern and Lorn. The main centres of volcanic activity in the area were on Mull and Ardnamurchan, but the force of the magma, squeezing into cracks in the crust or flowing across the surface, has affected the physical appearance of the entire district.

While the volcanic period threw up new mountains and folds in the earth's surface, the Ice Ages cut them down and gouged out great valleys through the rock. It is not difficult to envisage the Ice Age landscape. Anyone who has been on a Highland summit at dawn, when the glens are filled with mist and the tops of the hills seem to float like a fleet of ships in a white sea, will have seen the earth as it was then, and climbers who have crunched through the ice near the summit cairns or leaned into a blizzard on the narrow ridges have felt the residual breath of the Ice Age. Evidence of the great glaciers which filled the valleys and covered many of the hills is abundant in Argyll. The scores of the ice can be seen on the rocks; massive boulders have been carried from the hills to the coast and one of the rock lips, normally situated at the end of the glaciers, can be seen at the Falls of Lora near Connel. Outwash from the glaciers has narrowed Loch Linnhe at Corran, where the ferry crosses to Ardgour, and Loch Creran at Creagan. An ice-dammed lake covered the Loch Tulla Valley and five different water levels have been noted on the hillsides. Glacial debris formed the hillocks in Lorn, Mull and around Tyndrum.

When the ice retreated, the land, relieved of its burden, began to swell and rise above the sea. This movement produced the numerous raised beaches round the coast of Argyll, the most accessible example of which is in the gasworks car park in Oban, where the cliff-face formerly washed by the

Rannoch Moor, looking west to Clach Leathad.

sea overhangs the parking area. Archways worn through bands of rock which once reached into the sea can be found far from the shore in Appin and Morvern. The ice retreated between 6,000 and 8,000 years ago and those who claim that all these geological changes are irrelevant can be forgiven for their assertion, but the shape and the composition of the rocks determine the natural fertility of the soil and that, in turn, influences the tree cover, wildlife, farming, fishing and, indeed, the entire way of life.

The shape of the land has not changed substantially since men first arrived in North Argyll about 8,000 years ago, but its appearance has altered completely. When the caves around Oban were first inhabited, the entire area was covered in natural woodlands with Scots pine, juniper, birch, aspen, oak, rowan and hazel on the hills and willow and alder in the hollows. At that time wolves, wild oxen and beaver lived in the forests and men lived by hunting, gathering and fishing. However, as the tools and techniques improved, the forest began to recede. Trees were felled to make houses, enclosures, implements and weapons and to clear the land for planting.

Primitive Man, however, was not entirely responsible for the destruction of the Old Caledonian Forest – storms, lightning-fires, floods and wild animals hastened the process – but he was the most destructive agent. He cleared the land by felling and burning; he killed the predators of animals that devoured saplings, allowing the pernicious herds to increase; he protected animals which destroyed the forests. Yet, for centuries, most of the natural woodland survived. In the last two hundred years, however, the landscape has been transformed.

When the small Highland sheep were replaced by flocks of Cheviot and Blackface, the most effective deterrent to natural regeneration was introduced to the area. Not only do these animals destroy young trees directly but, because their grazing habits encourage the growth of coarse grasses which have to be burned off, their presence leads to the destruction of seedlings. Yet it is this form of husbandry which gives the hills of Argyll their character and leaves them open for climbers and hill-walkers. Sheep, therefore, have some advantages.

When the First World War revealed a serious shortage of timber in Britain, the Government embarked on a massive programme of replanting. The Forestry Commission was formed to purchase vast tracts of land and, with little consideration for the aesthetic and ecological consequences, covered the hills with regiments of alien conifers such as Sitka Spruce and Contorta Pine. The results of this policy can be seen throughout Argyll.

The Commission, however, did not pioneer the process of replanting. Some valiant efforts were made in the eighteenth century, when many landowners replanted their estates, occasionally using exotic and colourful species. They drafted regulations to eliminate the herds of goats kept by the small tenants and to make their people plant small areas of their holdings – the small clumps of pine or beech, which are scattered throughout the district, are the results of this policy. The lairds were assisted by the law, for a person could be deported for uprooting a sapling! When the iron industry was established in Argyll in the early eighteenth century, the fuel used to heat the furnaces was charcoal, which demanded extensive felling of the woodlands. The woods of Loch Awe, Loch Fyne, Glen Etive, Morvern and Mull were cut to satisfy this demand but the landowners controlled this exploitation with great care under a 'coppice' system so that the woods survived. The legacy of these 'improving' lairds is still apparent in the variety of trees surrounding the mansions and castles of Argyll – sequoia, Douglas fir, Japanese larch, cedar, cypress and Chile pine grow to a remarkable height in the district.

Apart from these woodlands, the scenery is generally the result of recent human activity. The open hills are usually sheep farms or former sheep farms, from which the flocks have been cleared to form deer 'forests'. The blanket of conifers, which covers many of the hills and often obscures the view, is the result of Forestry Commission activity and that of private forestry groups. In recent years some effort has been made to vary the altitude, shape and composition of these blocks and a good example of this more enlightened approach can be seen on the north side of the glen west of Tyndrum. The altitude of the tree line is not, of course, entirely determined by the foresters. The tops of the hills are often covered in snow in the winter and climatic conditions of this kind dictate the pattern of planting.

Forestry and hill sheep farming are not the only forms of land use in the area. There is also crofting. To many city dwellers this appears to be an idyllic way of life and indeed it has many attractions. It is a system of agriculture in which the occupier of a croft holds the arable land independently, while having access to pasture land held in common with neighbouring crofts. Crofts are usually very small, rarely providing a living to the occupant, who must therefore find a source of supplementary income, and they are collected in 'townships'. Crofting townships can be seen in Dalmally, the Ross of Mull, Ardgour, Sunart and Ardnamurchan. Strips of land laid out below a collection of small farm houses usually indicate a crofting township. Because they are often in areas of extraordinary natural beauty visitors are inclined to envy these communities but, in fact, it is a hard life with the tasks on the croft often attended to after a day's work in another job.

The larger farms also affect the scenery. Unlike those of central Scotland and the Borders, the farms in North Argyll grow little grain. Throughout the tourist season, therefore, the fields are green. It is essentially a livestock-rearing area, producing store lambs and calves for fattening in the South. Some lambs from the more fertile farms are sold for immediate slaughter and some farms grow rape to fatten them but the bulk of the animals leave the district to be finished elsewhere. North Argyll acts as a reservoir for southern livestock farms. Oban and Dalmally are the main auction centres where the stock is exchanged and a visit to either of the marts will provide a more accurate impression of the character of the people than that presented by some of the tasteless tourist shops which seem to flourish in Argyll. True, only a small proportion of people are engaged in agriculture but many of those employed in other activities are from a farming background and, if the area possesses a culture at all, it has its origins in the Gaelic-speaking crofting and farming communities.

Evidence of the latest industry to exploit the natural resources of North Argyll proliferates in the lochs. The square cages of fish farmers can now be seen in nearly every creek and inland loch. The sea cages are mainly for salmon and the inland ones for rainbow trout. Although the industry brings employment to remote areas and helps to keep young Highlanders at home, its long-term impact on the environment has not been assessed and its expansion is not sufficiently subject to control by residents of the area in which it is situated. So far, its intrusion has not destroyed the natural beauty of the lochs.

The history of Scotland is closely linked with that of Argyll, for the Celtic people, who gave their name to the nation, came from Ireland in the sixth century to establish a kingdom in Argyll, which they called Dalriada after their homeland. They brought with them their language, their traditions and their religion. Known to the Romans as Scotti, they referred to their new land as Erragaidheal – the March of the Gael – and they built a fortress at Dunadd near Lochgilphead. At their coronation ceremony their Kings sat on the 'Lia Faill', the carved marble Stone of Destiny, and placed a foot in a sole-shaped imprint in the rock. The Lia Faill is lost but the footprint is still there. The first king at Dunadd was Fergus, the son of Erc, who crossed from Ireland with his brothers, Aengus and Loarn, the latter giving his name to the area around Oban. One of their descendants, Kenneth McAlpin, became the first

King of Scotland in 843. Following Erc's sons, another Irish warrior prince, turning his back on temporal power, landed on Iona to found a religious community on the island. Columba and his disciples brought Christianity to the Picts and other pagan people. The Irish settlement in Argyll, therefore, had a profound effect on the rest of Scotland.

When the Viking longships sailed down the west coast, plundering the centres of religion and slaughtering the monks, they inadvertently helped to unite the people of Scotland. They established their sovereignty over the entire West Coast, including Kintyre. Their impact on the Gaelic culture was limited and their presence eventually led to a remarkable revival of Celtic tradition under the Lords of the Isles. The resistance began in Morvern, when Somerled or Somhairle led the men of Morvern against the Vikings in the twelfth century. Within a few years he had driven the Norsemen from the Hebrides and established a kingdom which stretched from Lewis to the Isle of Man. He was sufficiently astute to marry a Viking lady, Ragnhildis, daughter of Olaf the Red, thereby giving legitimacy to his claim to the Isles.

His son, Ranald, built Iona Abbey in 1203 and, two years later, finished Saddell Abbey in Kintyre. Under their patronage the Celtic Renaissance flourished and continued for two centuries under their descendants. Ranald's sons, Donald and Ruari, founded the lines of MacDonald and MacRuari and his brother, Dugall, the MacDougalls. The Lords of the Isles had their own bards or 'seanachies', their own Celtic medical practitioners and were crowned as 'Ri Innse Gall' – King of the Islands of Strangers – by a Great Council of the Isles. This Gaelic kingdom came to an end in 1493, when the King of Scotland finally asserted his authority over the clans.

In the seventeenth century, after the Union of the Crowns, Argyll was drawn into the Civil Wars fought to establish the sovereignty of the United Kingdom. The Duke of Argyll and the Campbells supported Parliament against the Crown, while the MacDonalds and MacDougalls supported the Stuart monarchy. The opposing forces swept to and fro across Argyll, burning the land, appropriating cattle and murdering opponents. The Earl of Antrim, supporting the Crown, sent his Irish troops under Alasdair MacColla Ciotach MacDonnell or

'Colkitto' to link up with the King's Lieutenant-General, the Earl of Montrose. The 2,000 'Irishes' landed in Ardnamurchan, taking Mingary Castle and Kinlochaline in Morvern. Having joined forces with Montrose, they attacked Argyll's stronghold in Inveraray in the winter of 1644/45 and laid waste the countryside. The Campbells regrouped in February but were defeated at Inverlochy near Fort William. Argyll, however, had his revenge two years later, when, after the Royalist forces were defeated at Philiphaugh near Selkirk, he pursued the Irish and their allies to Dunaverty in Kintyre and, after accepting an honourable surrender, butchered the 500 defenders. Argyll burned the MacLean lands on Mull and the MacDougall island of Kerrera. Several castles in North Argyll were reduced to ruins at this time but their crumbling battlements have survived as a reminder of those turbulent years.

In the eighteenth century the Jacobite Risings of 1715 and 1745 and the defeat of Prince Charles Edward Stuart at Culloden finally established the authority of the House of Hanover and the British Parliament in the Highlands. The subsequent peace and the rich pickings available on the forfeited estates of the Jacobite chiefs brought adventurers to the north to exploit the resources of the Highlands and, with them, came the flockmasters, offering rents far in excess of the modest sums generated by the Highland cattle trade. From 1760 Cheviot and Linton sheep began to replace the small, black cattle, which, for generations, had been the staple industry of the Western Highlands. Starting in South Argyll, the white tide reached Tyndrum and Glencoe before the turn of the century.

As rents increased, many 'tacksmen' – men who held tacks or leases – decided that it was time to leave. They were not the helpless victims portrayed in some accounts of the period but proud men of substance and status, the middle ranks of Highland society, who were sufficiently perceptive to realise that the traditional way of life was doomed. In some cases lairds pleaded with them to remain; in others, they actively tried to prevent them from leaving, but the tacksmen departed with their followers and their wealth to the shores of North America. The old system which they left behind survived in some areas for almost a century, to be described with disdain by southern 'improvers'. Based on cattle rearing, it provided salt beef for Nelson's navy, the great herds of black Highland cattle being walked first to Falkirk or Crieff Trysts and then to the fertile fields of Southern England for fattening.

It was not the stocksmanship of the Highland cattlemen that the improvers criticised, but their system of agriculture. The arable land was held in scattered, unfenced strips, which were regularly, sometimes annually, distributed so that no-one held the same piece of land for more than a few seasons. Referred to as 'run-rig', this system had been designed to ensure a reasonable distribution of wealth but, according to the improvers, it was inefficient and untidy. During the summer the entire community moved out to the hill pastures, where the sheep and cattle, thriving on the fresh grazing, produced a surplus of milk. The women milked the cattle and small sheep, which had been wintered in their houses, to make cheese. The men returned to the arable land occasionally to tend the crops of barley and oats. Each township had a traditional grazing area with a collection of huts, known as a shieling or airidh. This hill ground was vital to the community. Once it was let to sheep farmers, the township had a clear choice – either to live on the edge of starvation without their cattle or to leave the glen altogether. Many chose to leave and sailed for America where land was free.

The departure of the tacksmen and their followers caused some concern in Westminster, for it deprived the British Army of recruits and it involved a considerable loss of 'specie'. This concern increased to panic at the end of the century, when France was engulfed in Revolution and the contagion threatened to spread to Britain. The subsequent war against France stimulated the Highland economy in a dangerous manner. It inflated the value of kelp (an ash produced by burning seaweed, for use in the manufacture of soap and glass), it encouraged the cattle trade and it provided employment for young Highlanders in the armed forces. Some people used the additional cash to emigrate until the lairds, determined not to lose their kelp labour force, persuaded Parliament to pass the Passenger Vessels Act to stem the flow of Highlanders to America. Deprived of this outlet, the population soon reached a critical level and, as sheep farms displaced communities in the interior, the peripheral townships became perilously congested.

The first signs of crisis were apparent after the War, as cattle prices collapsed and servicemen were demobilised. A few years later kelp prices also fell, when Parliament reduced the import duty on a rival chemical, barilla, and the duty on salt. As the arrears of rent mounted, landlords realised that they were left with a 'redundant population'. The improvers claimed that the solution lay in the removal of the people, conversion of their grazings to sheep farms and relocation of the evicted communities either on the coast, as a labour force for new industries, or overseas to develop the New World. Many lairds adopted this policy and whole townships were removed. But the major catastrophe was still to come.

When the potato blight swept through the crops in 1846, turning healthy tubers to putrid hollows in the soil, it deprived the small crofters and cottars of their staple food. In some areas they were reduced to a diet of shellfish and water. Typhus spread through the debilitated communities and, as arrears accumulated, evictions increased. In spite of a massive famine-relief exercise initiated by the Free Kirk, which raised £250,000 and prevented mass starvation, thousands of people left the Western Highlands for America and Australia. Many departed voluntarily but many others were evicted. North Argyll is littered with deserted townships commemorating the tragedy – Auliston in Morvern, Shiaba and Ulva on Mull and Swordle in Ardnamurchan still stand as gaunt memorials to the Gaels who left on the emigrant ships.

The next major event in North Argyll was the arrival of the railway in 1880. Many of the Victorian houses and hotels were built after the steam locomotives brought crowds of tourists to the area. This was the first great 'leisure boom', when city dwellers of relatively modest means rented holiday accommodation in Oban and other Highland resorts, announcing their presence in the local newspapers. Queen Victoria's tour in 1847, during the first year of the famine, had conferred respectability on the area and, driven by a fascination for 'Celtic' legend and bucolic pursuits inspired by MacPherson's *Ossian,* Walter Scott and Edwin Landseer, wealthy industrialists, idle gentry, intrepid ladies, officers on leave and even members of the clergy, flocked north to sample the magnificent scenery and to observe the quaint specimens of humanity who inhabited the district.

The steamships, which had carried the tourists north initially, eventually crossed the oceans to return with the produce of the New World. Imported wool and mutton undermined the prosperity of Highland sheep farming and the flocks which had replaced black cattle earlier in the century began to depart. As they left, the pasture did not return to the remaining descendants of the people who had been deprived of it but was converted to deer forest for the amusement of the rich. The forests are still there – at Blackmount, Kingairloch, Laudale, Ben Hiant and Glenforsa – and contain some of the finest hill-walking routes in the Highlands.

There are two seasons in which North Argyll is at its best – neither of them in midsummer. When the bracken dies, its green turning to rust, and the first snow on the summits glistens in an autumn sunset, the colours are astonishing. In the late spring, on the other hand, when the hills are still white and the young, green shoots of the larches overhang the banks of primroses, there is an incomparable freshness about the district, the memory of which will revive any worn city-dweller in the dark evenings. There are times in winter, too, when a full moon illuminates the frozen ridges and the roar of a stag echoes in the silent corries, that will overwhelm the most insensitive observer. There are, of course, moments in summer which visitors will remember; the sun setting in Oban Bay behind the dark hills of Mull; the Atlantic swell breaking over Ardnamurchan point; dawn from the hills of Morvern with Loch Linnhe filled with mist and, most startling of all, the azure sea over the white sands of Iona.

It is a remarkable area and one for which I have a great affection. If I can convey this enthusiasm to others and encourage them to visit it and to linger a few hours or days longer than intended, I may be able to return part of what its land and its people have given to me.

CHAPTER 1

The Approaches

Tyndrum and Blackmount

Several towns in Scotland claim to be the 'gateway to the Highlands' but Tyndrum is the one which most merits this description. The road forks here – one route leading through the high pass above Auch to the Moor of Rannoch and Glencoe, the other to Oban and the Islands. The snow often lies at Tyndrum when the road through Strathfillan and the lands to the east are still clear. It is indeed a frontier settlement. One eighteenth-century traveller said of it that 'no-one would willingly go to Tyndrum a second time or remain there an hour', and Queen Victoria described it as 'a wild, picturesque and desolate place'. Although the Royal Hotel was obviously named to commemorate her visit, she did not actually sleep there. She stayed the night on her train in Tyndrum station. Her breakfast, however, was prepared in the hotel, though not by the local cook but by the Earl of Breadalbane's chef.

On old maps the village is called Clifton after Sir Robert Clifton, who started mining for lead in the quartz veins in the surrounding hills in 1739. Unfortunately Clifton was a Jacobite and, when the loyalist Argyll Militia passed through Tyndrum in 1745, they destroyed most of his equipment. However, mining continued till 1798. By that time 200 people lived in the village and the closure was a blow to the community. The mines were reopened in 1838, apparently under the direction of German miners, but closed again 30 years later, leaving 30 miners – a third of the male population – without employment. Fortunately the construction of the railway to Oban provided alternative employment on this occasion. Evidence of the mining operations can be seen through the pine trees on Meall Odhar above the Glencoe road, on Beinn Chuirn behind Cononish farm and at the foot of Beinn Laoigh. Around these excavations it is possible to pick up pieces of quartz laden with lead or zinc ore and some extraordinarily clear quartz crystals. The seams have recently attracted the attention of an Irish

Tyndrum. A view taken in the 1930s.

mining company, which has been drilling to establish the amount of gold in the quartz, and its preliminary investigations indicate that there is a sufficient quantity of the metal to warrant commercial extraction. The effect on Tyndrum could be dramatic. There is already a housing shortage and existing businesses already depend on neighbouring villages for their staff.

Even now there are signs of expansion. A new half million pound tourist complex, with caravan stances, a swimming pool, bunk house and restaurant has been built on the eastern approach to the village and a fast-food restaurant has opened beyond the Royal Hotel. Tyndrum used to resemble a Swiss mountain village, with the larger buildings concealed behind rows of trees, but the trees have gone and, if development is not controlled, it will lose its character completely. It is still an attractive settlement, providing some admirable tourist facilities, which do not intrude on the environment. There is an excellent craft complex with a restaurant and a shop which sells outdoor equipment – a useful service for travellers who have overlooked vital clothing or equipment in their rush to escape from the south.

The West Highland Way, which starts near Glasgow and leads to Fort William, passes through Tyndrum and the new bunk house is designed for walkers on this route. The Glasgow to Oban railway forks at Crianlarich, the upper line to Fort William also passing through Tyndrum. The village, therefore, has two railway stations and it is possible for walkers who wish to miss out part of the Way to join it or leave it at this point. The upper railway also offers a superb day trip to Fort William for visitors based in the area, travelling through some of the most impressive scenery in Scotland. There are several walks in the district which are not too arduous but very rewarding.

Leaving Tyndrum, the A82 climbs towards the county boundary above Auch, where Perthshire meets Argyll. Auch was part of a Royal Forest, providing stag hunting for the Kings of Scotland, and James IV stayed for a week here in 1506. Auch farm is situated in a hollow below the steep slopes of Beinn Dorain, where one of Scotland's finest Gaelic poets worked as deer forester to the Earl of Breadalbane. Born on the shores of Loch Tulla in 1724, Duncan Ban MacIntyre died in Edinburgh, far from his native hills, in 1812. His songs and poems show clearly the nostalgia which afflicted him in the city and the remarkable knowledge of the hills which he retained.

A memorial cairn has been raised to the bard at his birthplace on Drumliaghart, west of Loch Tulla, by members of Le Comunn Gaidhlig (Gaelic Society) of Inverness. Unfortunately the hillside has been ploughed for afforestation, which will eventually obscure the monument and the ruins of the township where he spent his youth. In the meantime however, it can be found fairly easily by following the new forestry road, which scars the ridge between Inveroran and Victoria Bridge.

Drumliaghart is part of the great Blackmount deer forest, which belongs to the Fleming family. To reach the estate it is necessary to take the A8005 at Bridge of Orchy. This is a single-track road, which crosses an eighteenth-century bridge and passes through the pine wood of Doire Darach. This woodland has been fenced off to encourage natural regeneration and there is a memorable sign, reminding visitors of the dangers of fire – 'That which burns never returns' is a statement which has more impact than the usual command 'Do not start fires'. Yet even this courteous reminder has been insufficient. Two large plantations were destroyed recently by fires started by careless visitors.

Beyond the pine woods there is a magnificent view of the mountains above Loch Etive – Stob Ghabhar, Stob Coire nan Albanaich and, in the distance, Ben Starav.

Blackmount is one of the oldest deer forests in Scotland. In 1622 King James VI, hearing that a white hind had been seen in the forest, sent his forester, John Scandoner, to capture it. He did not succeed and had to leave without the prize. The word 'forest' can be misleading. It may convey the impression of woodland with green glades, but the forests, in fact, were areas of jurisdiction with their own forest courts and foresters appointed by the Crown. In many cases they consisted of open hillsides and mountain ranges. Although the lower slopes of Blackmount were once covered in trees, the hills were much the same as they are today. Many of the ancient forests disappeared during the Napoleonic Wars, when they were converted to sheep farms, and Blackmount shared the same fate. Duncan Ban MacIntyre was so incensed by the change that he wrote in his 'Song to the Foxes':

> On the foxes be my blessing
> For they the silly sheep are chasing.

Indeed it may well have been this conversion that forced Duncan to leave the district.

After the War, in 1820, the ancient deer sanctuary of the Corrie Ba was restored to its original status by the Earl of Breadalbane's son. The sheep were removed, deer foresters employed and trees planted to provide shelter. It was to become one of the most famous forests in Victorian Britain. Landseer was a frequent visitor and his 'Stag at Bay' is based on an incident on Loch Tulla, when a stag, pursued by the hounds, ran down from Ben Taoig and turned to face the dogs in the loch. In those days the rifles were neither powerful nor accurate enough to kill a stag at a distance, so deer hounds were used to run down the chosen animal and bring it to 'bay'. These hounds, which were massive creatures with deep chests and shaggy coats, were said to be descended from the hunting dogs of the legendary Fingalian warriors, who lived in Glen Etive and Glencoe, and were given names like Bran and Fingal. They appear in several of Landseer's paintings. Sir Edwin's interest in the Highlands encouraged other eminent Victorians to visit the area.

Deer hounds bring down a stag – the Victorian view.

Blackmount is still run as a sporting estate and, during the stalking season (from August to February), it is always safer to consult the keepers before crossing the land. In the summer the deer are mainly out in the high corries, unless severe weather drives them down to the loch, so tourists are unlikely to see them by the roadside. The stags are culled once their antlers have shed their 'velvet' and have hardened. They cast their antlers every year in the late spring and grow a new set, which, in the early stages, are covered in a nutrient skin called velvet. The old antlers are often chewed or eaten by the herd to provide extra nutrition. When the velvet dies on the new ones it peels off, occasionally giving the stag the appearance of a moving washing line. When the velvet disappears, the stalking begins and lasts till October. Red deer are social animals, moving in groups or great herds across the forest but, for ten and a half months of the year, stags and hinds live in separate groups. In late September the breeding season or 'rut' begins and the groups of stags split to mix with the hinds. The roar or 'belling' of the stags echoes through the corries as they challenge their competitors for possession of a few hinds. The big stags, their manes black with peat and their jaws white with froth, are a fearsome sight. The young stags are driven off and can often be found grazing alone. The mature ones rarely eat during the rut and are lean and exhausted by October. In spite of the sharp antlers – or perhaps because of them – disputes seldom end in a battle and, when fights do occur, they are rarely fatal. The calves are born in the early summer and are hidden in the bracken or long heather. With their dappled coats and instinct to lie still when danger approaches, they are very difficult to find. In spite of the attention they receive from their mothers, 40% of them do not survive. The long, cold nights of winter are a critical time for the whole herd. Lean stags, caught above forestry fences, perish in the snow. Old hinds, lacking the strength to cross swollen burns, are carried away. Young hinds, descending to the roadside to escape blizzards, are struck by careless motorists. In spite of these fatalities, the numbers must be controlled, if the herd is to survive. Thus the hinds are culled between October and February, the old, sick or lean ones being shot by the stalkers.

There is superb hill walking round Blackmount. The summit of Stob Ghabhar can be reached by taking the road to Clashgour, turning north at the bothy and climbing the southern ridge. The old forest fence, erected in 1853 to keep the Clashgour sheep out of the deer sanctuary, follows the ridge. In the winter, ptarmigan, in their white plumage, can be seen here below 600 metres. Beyond the summit cairn lies the long, green ridge of Aonach Mor leading towards Glencoe. Ravens nest in the cliffs above the Corrie Ba and a cornice of snow sometimes hangs above the precipice till July. If you leave the ridge and follow the River Ba towards the West Highland Way, you can see, on the river bank, the massive stumps of the pine forest which was stripped in the eighteenth century. The path from the corrie joins the Way at Ba Bridge and, turning north, the route leads past the ruins of Ba cottage towards King's House and Glencoe. On the shoulder of Meall a Bhuiridh, near the path, there is a monument to the author and traveller, Peter Fleming, who took part in an expedition to the Amazon and travelled through the Far East, describing his adventures vividly in *Travels in Tartary*. He died while shooting on Blackmount in 1971. His brother, Ian Fleming, was also an author and created James Bond. Turning south at Ba Bridge, the route follows the old military road back to Loch Tulla.

There are less strenuous walks in the forest. It is possible, for example, to walk or cycle from Blackmount to Glen Etive through Glen Kinglass or walk over Gleann Fuar to Glen Strae and there is level ground for a tent near Inveroran Hotel. This hotel was one of the old droving inns with a stance for the great herds of black cattle to rest on their way to Falkirk or Crieff Trysts. When the Earl of Breadalbane, anxious to minimise the disturbance of the deer in his forest, tried to close the stance in 1844, the drovers took their case to the Court of Session, maintaining that the stance was indispensable to their trade. The Court found in their favour but the Earl took the case to the House of Lords, where he received a sympathetic hearing, and the stance had to be moved to Tyndrum. It was in the old inn at Inveroran that Duncan Ban MacIntyre met the girl who was to become his wife, Mhairi Bhan Og, the daughter of the innkeeper, Nicol MacIntyre; and James Hogg, the Ettrick Shepherd, stayed there in 1803. Dorothy Wordsworth, in the same year, described the scene in the kitchen:

> About seven or eight travellers, probably drovers, with as many dogs, were sitting in a complete circle round a large peat fire in the middle of the floor, each with a mess of porridge, in a wooden vessel, upon his knee; a pot, suspended from one of the black beams, was boiling on the fire.

Today the hotel supplies bar meals for walkers on the West Highland Way and full accommodation for other travellers.

On the east side of the A82 stands the shell of Achallader Castle, where, in June 1691, the Earl of Breadalbane met some of the Jacobite chiefs to bargain for their allegiance to the new monarch, King William III. The Earl had been granted £12,000 by the Crown to secure their loyalty and managed to negotiate an arrangement, which gave the chiefs six months to declare their allegiance. It was MacIan's failure to comply with this by 1 January 1692 that led to the Massacre of Glencoe. In fact Breadalbane's loyalty was as questionable as MacIan's for he revealed his willingness to join in a Jacobite rising to General Buchan, King James's commander in the Highlands. The slippery Earl had hedged his bets. Achallader was traditionally the seat of the Fletchers, who claimed that they were the first 'to light fire and boil water' in Glenorchy and that, according to Celtic custom, the land belonged to them in perpetuity, but the Campbells eventually obtained possession of the lands, and Sir Duncan Campbell built the tower, which stands today, in 1600 to protect the lands. It was burned in 1689 by a Jacobite force, which included Camerons and MacDonalds of Glencoe.

Anyone travelling to Oban with a little time to spare should consider a diversion through Glenorchy on the B8074. It is a single-track road, which winds along one of the finest salmon rivers in Lorn. There are several deep pools, where the fish can be seen suspended like airships in the still water as they gather their strength to leap the falls. The Orchy in spate is an amazing sight. A band of slate and quartzite crosses the glen, forming steps, terraces and chasms in the river, through which the water has to twist and toss on its way to Loch Awe.

About a mile above Catnish there is a bridge leading to one of the most pleasant walks in the district. There is a padlocked gate, so cars have to be left at the bridge. The forestry road climbs north through a conifer wood, where, if visitors walk quietly, they can see roe deer among the trees. Where the road ends there is a magnificent wood of Scots Pine, which, fortunately, has been protected by the Nature Conservancy Council. If Allt Broighleachan is followed to the pass between Glen Orchy and Glen Strae there are some well preserved foundations of old shielings below Beinn Mhic Mhonaidh at Aridh Cailleach. Before the small tenants of Glenorchy were removed to make way for sheep, these hill pastures provided summer grazing for their cattle and sheep and these buildings were their temporary homes.

Returning to the Orchy, the ruins of Larigs can still be seen among the conifers north of the river. This was a shepherd's house with two storeys and, as it is surrounded by the ruins of much older buildings, was probably built during the transition from cattle to sheep. Near the bridge, on the south side of the road, among the ruins of Tom na Gualain there is an immense, stone-lined grain dryer, an indication of the amount of corn grown on the holding before the fields were abandoned to sheep.

There is a Forestry Commission picnic site below Catnish, near the footbridge, and several clearings on the banks of the Orchy where there is room for a tent. The south end of the glen is very different from the north. On the west side there is open farm land with scrub oak and alder on the river bank. The east side, unfortunately, has been ploughed recently for planting, clearly upsetting the balance of land use in the glen. The road joins the A85 at Inverlochy.

Glenlochy

The main road from Tyndrum to the west coast crosses the Regional boundary about half a mile from the junction with the Fort William road. This is indeed an ancient 'march' or boundary, thought to be the dividing line between the kingdoms of the Scots and the Picts and the site of the last great battle between the two races. Twenty years ago the hillsides of Glenlochy were mainly reserved for sheep, herded by three shepherds. The shepherds have gone and there are no farms in the glen now. The land has been ploughed and planted with trees. The different approaches to planting can be seen very clearly in the patterns of afforestation. On the north side the monotonous blanket of conifers reflects the insensitive policies of the post-war decades. After prolonged pressure from ecologists and the public, the Forestry Commission responded with a more enlightened approach, leaving spaces and varying the line and altitude of the trees, and the result of this change is evident on the south side as far as Beinn Dubh, where the old method again becomes apparent.

The loch in the hollow below the road – Loch na Bi – is occasionally frozen in the winter but it provides good trout fishing during the season. Halfway through the glen the former farm house of Arrivain or Airidh Meadhon (The Middle Shieling) stands in a conifer plantation beside the road. Arrivain existed as a 'merkland' holding in 1550. In 1784 it and the neighbouring farm of Arnabea were given to 6 tenants, probably as a sheep farm, and it remained as such till the early 1970s. The flocks on the south side of the river had to be gathered and driven across the railway to the old fank (handling pens) at Arrivain. The gatherings were social occasions, when all the neighbouring shepherds, sometimes as many as ten, assembled to help. When the work at Arrivain was finished, all the men would move on the following day to the next farm. The men had to be fed and the shepherds' wives had to cater for all the shepherds and any other assistants who might appear – sometimes up to a score of people. This system led to considerable social cohesion and provided support for every individual in the herding community.

When some of the hills were cleared for afforestation, the 'neighbouring' system collapsed and the resilience of the entire community diminished. In this respect at least, tourist development, because of its seasonal and ephemeral nature, can never compensate for the decline of hill farming.

The hills above Glenlochy are steep and their summits are often covered in snow for several months, thus providing some superb snow and ice climbing. There is a car park below Beinn Laoigh from which it is possible to reach the hills, although the railway and the River Lochy have to be negotiated first. The easiest access is from Tyndrum by the Cononish road. Beinn Laoigh is not only the highest mountain in the district, it is also the most fascinating. The central gully on the eastern face contains the longest snow route in Argyll and is normally capped with a deep cornice. Conditions on the top in winter can resemble those of the polar ice caps and, even in summer it can be dangerously cold. In the late spring, on the other hand, there is an array of wild flowers as varied as that of Ben Lawers, including wild thyme, saxifrages, milkwort and bog orchids. Beinn Laoigh is a National Nature Reserve, along with the neighbouring hills of Beinn a Chleibh, Beinn Oss and Beinn Dubhcraig, but they are also part of the sheep farm of Cononish and visitors should not take dogs to the reserve, unless they are on a leash. Even the presence of dogs disturbs the sheep. In the spring, when they are heavy with lamb or have young lambs at foot, frightened ewes may try to cross drains and fall in or leap across, leaving their lambs to drown in their attempt to follow. Dogs should really be left at home in the spring.

Dalmally

As the A85 leaves Glenlochy to descend Strone Brae the whole Strath of Orchy, with its woodlands and fields and unmistakable skyline, comes into sight. It is a remarkable view. Unfortunately there is no safe parking place or viewpoint here, so motorists must enjoy the scenery from their cars. There is a place to park about halfway down the hill and, from this point, it is possible to reach a beautiful natural oakwood on the banks of the Succoth burn.

Dalmally is the first village encountered after leaving Tyndrum. It contains the only crofting township east of Loch Awe and some of the most fascinating walks in the district. The crofting township, which is on the B8077 marked for Stronmilchan, was formed in 1784 'for ye accommodation of Soldiers and such as could not be otherways provided'. It was laid out in 20 to 30 crofts. Ten of these have survived, although little of the land is ploughed. The original eighteenth-century houses, now unoccupied, can still be seen above the road. Unfortunately the appearance of the township has been altered by a clutch of modern bungalows but it is still an attractive area.

The road to Stronmilchan turns north at 'Bruce's Stone' opposite Dalmally Hotel. Near this junction the octagonal church stands on an island formed by the Orchy, where, apparently, the Druids used to hold their ceremonies. This unusual building was completed during the Napoleonic War in 1811 and its timbers, which have just been replaced, were supplied by tenants from different parts of the estate. In Glenstrae the last of the old pine forest was felled for the church. The building was designed by James Elliot of Edinburgh and its construction supervised by the architect of Taymouth Castle. The manse behind it was built by John Stevenson of Oban for £750 shortly after Admiral Nelson fought the Battle of Trafalgar in 1805. In those days errant members of the congregation could be summoned before the Kirk Session for their misdeeds. In 1837, for example, three men were called before the elders for 'profanation of the Sabbath', the latter complaining that 'the said individuals had taken hire from some tourists, who were at said day at the Inn,

Dalmally Church, prior to recent renovation.

for rowing them down to Lochawe'. Even in a year of scarcity such enterprise was not tolerated on the Sabbath. Most of the session's business at that time dealt with the iniquities of the congregation, much of it in efforts to establish the paternity of 'natural' or illegitimate children.

The church is well worth a visit. There are several medieval tombstones – of Fletchers, MacIntyres and MacNaughtons – in the graveyard, and a nineteenth-century mortsafe.

Beyond the church there is an elegant bridge over the Orchy, built by Lewis Piccard in 1781. On the far side of the bridge a road leads east along the river bank to Craig Lodge, which was once a shooting lodge and is now a popular Catholic retreat with handsome gardens. A hundred years ago there was a deer forest of 40,000 acres with the lodge, providing 20 stags and let for almost £3,000. At that time there were fallow deer in the woods and the game bag included woodcock and partridge, species which no longer exist in the area. At the beginning of this century Craig Lodge and forest were rented by a Mr William Niven, who occasionally brought his baby son, David, later to become a film star, to stay in Dalmally. In 1967 the estate was sold to the Forestry Commission and, since then, the farm has been administered by the Department of Agriculture.

On the hill above Stronmilchan there is a good example of a volcanic dyke, intruded from the eruptions on Mull. It stands out as the sharp points of Creag Mhor, from the summit of which there is an excellent view of the whole strath and the head of Loch Awe. This is part of the common grazing of the Stronmilchan crofts, divided from the deer forest by a high fence running across the hill. Stags often lie on the heather knolls beyond the fence, particularly in a south-west wind, and, in the late spring, the discarded antlers can be found beside their resting places. On the western shoulder of the hill the ruins of Tigh Mhor, the stronghold of the MacGregors, can be discerned among the heather.

About halfway along Stronmilchan the White House, once the residence of the Breadalbane's ground officer, stands in the trees on the river bank. It is now owned by the Buchanan-Jardine family of Castlemilk estate, Lockerbie, whose predecessors founded the great Jardine-Matheson shipping company in the Far East. Some distance beyond the White House, where the road crosses the River Strae by an old stone bridge, there is a monument to Duncan McLaren, a leading Edinburgh radical, who was Lord Provost of the capital from 1851 to 1854 and a Member of Parliament for 16 years from 1865.

Glenstrae, of course, was the home of the MacGregors. The clan lost control of the lands in the fourteenth century, when Ian of Glenorchy was captured by Edward I at Dunbar and, in his absence, Neil Campbell arranged a marriage between his son and Ian's heiress with the title to the lands as her dowry. Glenstrae is a tranquil valley now. The MacGregors and the Campbells have gone and only one family lives in the glen, which at one time could raise six or seven score of fighting men. It is a pleasant walk to the top of the river or, for enthusiastic hillwalkers, over the pass of Meall Copagach to Glen Kinglass.

The hills behind Castles farm, on the west side of the Strae, provide superb hill walking and climbing. In summer it is possible to cover all the peaks of Cruachan in a day without too much difficulty. A road belonging to the North of Scotland

Duncan Morrison of Glenorchy shinty team in action, 1989.

Hydro-Electric Board climbs round the shoulder of Beinn Eunaich and Beinn a Chochuill. This is to service the catchment channels and tunnels feeding Cruachan Dam but it is of great assistance to hillwalkers. From the summit of Beinn Eunaich there is an amazing view of Loch Etive and Blackmount forest but there is a steep drop below the cairn and, in winter, the descent to Meall Copagach often needs crampons.

Visitors who do not take the Stronmilchan road at the hotel will pass the auction mart and shinty pitch. From August to October the auctioneers travel from Stirling to sell cattle and sheep from the west coast and the islands in the Dalmally ring. Part of the mart buildings is used as a changing room for the shinty players, when there is a home match. Glen Orchy fields one of the best shinty teams in the Highlands and every visitor to the West should make an attempt to see them play this extraordinarily skilful and peculiarly Celtic game. Every year, at the beginning of September, the local Agricultural Show is held beside the shinty pitch, an event which attracts livestock, crafts, garden produce and even art from the whole of Lorn.

The old road to Inveraray, marked for Monument Hill, leaves the village near the railway station. Although it is

Blackface lambs at Dalmally Mart.

possible to drive to the summit, the public road ends there, and it is much more rewarding to walk. The banks on either side of the road are covered in wild flowers – bog orchids, scabious, meadow sweet, milkwort, butterwort, lousewort – and, in the hollows, the bog myrtle, which, when crushed, emits a pungent scent like eucalyptus. Peregrines occasionally nest in a quarry halfway up the hill and, in the evenings, owls hunt among the young spruce, gliding silently over the trees like phantoms in the dusk. Hen harriers have also been seen here and siskins have returned to the conifer woods. At the top of the hill, on the site of an ancient fort, stands another monument to Duncan Ban MacIntyre. This edifice, unfortunately, is something of a monstrosity. Built in 1859 of granite quarried in Appin and constructed in what was described as the 'Druidic' style, it squats malevolently on the hillside, dominating the landscape. There is, however, a magnificent view of Loch Awe and the entire strath from the site. According to Dorothy Wordsworth, it was this panorama that inspired her brother's 'Address to Kilchurn Castle'. Descending towards the village from the monument, it is easy to imagine the district as it was at that time, for the pattern of the old crofts in Stronmilchan is very clear on the opposite hill.

There is another interesting walk through the plantation south of the village. Beside the railway bridge a forestry road leads to Barr nan Eireonnach, locally known as 'Paddy's Point', and a track to the ruins of Barr a Chaistealain. This collection of deserted houses was the home of the MacNabs, the hereditary armourers to their clan chief. It is said that one of them helped to supervise the rebuilding of Kilchurn Castle in the fifteenth century. In 1645, when Montrose passed through Dalmally, he ordered the smiths at Barr a Chaistealain to sharpen the pikes of his foot soldiers. The last of the family to live at Barr a Chaistealain died in 1823. On the east side of the Teatle Water near Barran there are some slag heaps from old iron workings, suggesting that the MacNabs not only fashioned their weapons and other ironware but also made their own metal.

Barran is one of the best places in the district to see red deer, particularly in the winter. The land is part of one of the last sheep farms in Dalmally, the property of the Crerars, a family which has farmed in the parish since the early nineteenth century. Near the Crerars' farm house at Brackley the ruins of the old village of Auchtermally (Uachdar Mhaluidh) stand above the railway line. Several old lime kilns in the settlement show that the inhabitants knew enough about good husbandry to apply calcium to the land and thus counteract its natural acidity. It is said that the people of Auchtermally were renowned for their skills in horn carving and weaving.

Dalmally today really consists of three distinct communities – the old township of Stronmilchan, the new council housing behind the police station and the collection of houses which grew up round the railway station. There is an excellent craft shop in the latter hamlet, which specialises in fishing equipment and from which fishermen can obtain permits for the Orchy.

Leaving Dalmally, the road to Oban passes the small, but challenging, golf course and the entrance to Kilchurn Castle. The five-storied keep of Kilchurn was built by Colin Campbell in 1440. Quite a remarkable man, Colin visited Rome three times and was made a Knight of Rhodes. In 1655 another Campbell, the Marquis of Argyll, was besieged in Kilchurn by Royalist troops. From the battlements he watched them burn

Kilchurn Castle, Loch Awe, formerly a Campbell stronghold. The EIB/CMC carved above the doorway stands for John, Earl of Breadalbane and Countess Mary Campbell, married in 1678.

and pillage the countryside and finally gather for an assault on the castle. Fortunately some of General Monck's troops arrived to save the garrison. The castle, however, must have fallen into disrepair, for, in 1685, John Campbell, Earl of Breadalbane, who hoped to establish a great Highland militia under his command, began to reconstruct the building as a base for this force. Had the Government permitted him to realise this ambition, the Jacobite rebels would have had a ready-made army in the Highlands. Breadalbane swore allegiance to King William but his Jacobite leanings are well documented. However, the castle was used as a garrison by Hanoverian troops in 1745. In 1770 the roof was removed to slate houses and other buildings in the area – some of the stones from a spiral stairway were used as lintels in Drishaig cottage. Kilchurn remained in Breadalbane hands until 1986. It is one of the most picturesque and well-preserved castles in Argyll.

Loch Awe

Beyond the long bridge over the Orchy lies the village of
Loch Awe, which is essentially a product of the railway
developments of the late nineteenth century. Loch Awe hotel
was built to attract tourists from the railway, having its own halt
on the line. A pier was built near the platform so that goods
and passengers could travel on the regular steamer services to
Ford and Port Sonachan. The *Marchioness of Breadalbane*
provided this service from 1936 to 1951. Recently an
enterprising individual from the Clyde has revived the
tradition with a small steam vessel, offering cruises round the
islands and up the Orchy to Kilchurn.

In the village there is one of the most extraordinary churches
in Argyll. Built in 1886 by Walter Campbell of Blythswood,
who owned the neighbouring island of Innis Chonain, it
contains a bizarre mixture of styles selected from different
periods and schools of architecture which may astonish the
casual observer. In spite of the strange details, the interior is
refreshingly plain with the wooden communion table bathed in
a well of light from the chancel windows and the rooflights
above. Seen through the shadows of the nave and the dark,
ornate choir stalls, the chancel seems to shine on the most
overcast morning. Fragments from the abbey on Iona have
been incorporated in the wall of the south aisle and a window
from Saint Mary's parish church, Leith, lights the Bruce
Chapel, where there is an effigy of Robert the Bruce with an
ossuary containing a bone of the monarch. Campbell also
collected a bell, originally forged for Skerryvore Lighthouse in
1843, and placed it in the chapel. The first part of the church
to be completed was the nave but this was extended in the
twentieth century to include the rest of the building. After
Campbell's death in 1914 the work was continued by his sister,
Helen, and the church was finally dedicated in 1930. Walter
Campbell was also responsible for the mansion on Innis
Chonain, a beautiful wooded island at the west end of the
village containing an Italian terraced garden and a variety of
trees which adds brilliant colour to the loch in all seasons.

A few miles beyond the island the modern buildings of
Cruachan Power Station and Visitor Centre stand between the

Lady Rowena, a small steam vessel, offers summer cruises on Loch Awe.

loch and the railway line. Cruachan is a pump-storage Hydro-Electric scheme in which water from a dam high in the corrie above falls through the turbines to Loch Awe to generate electricity during the day; at night the turbines can be reversed, using power from the national grid to pump water back up to the dam. The turbines are located in a vast hall deep in the hillside which is open to visitors during the summer. The hall is so far from the surface that tourists have to be conveyed by mini-bus through the access tunnel from the Visitor Centre. Tours are well organised and most informative. The dam, which is 1,200 feet above sea level, can be reached by a path above the Visitor Centre or by a Hydro Board road from Loch Awe village. It blends with the hill surprisingly well and attracts several species of wild birds, including Canadian snow geese. Hydro-Electricity is one of the cleanest forms of energy but only a very small part of Scotland's requirements is provided by schemes of this kind. The network of dams throughout the Highlands is a fitting tribute to the most vigorous Secretary of State to represent Scotland at Westminster. Tom Johnston, the Labour M.P. for Stirlingshire, was appointed to the position during the last war and it was his ambition to regenerate the Highland economy by providing a cheap source of power to every community. In spite of bitter opposition from sections of the 'landed interest' the North of Scotland Hydro-Electric Board was established in 1943. Now it seems that Cruachan is to be offered for sale with the South of Scotland Board when the industry is 'privatised'. Control of this asset, like that of so many enterprises in the Highlands, will move south, a situation which Tom Johnston tried to reverse but one which now occurs with monotonous regularity.

West of Cruachan the loch flows out through the steep, narrow Pass of Brander. This gash in the mountains is caused by a geological fault which divides the granite of Beinn Cruachan from the lavas of North Lorn, forming the soft scree beneath the precipices on the south side of the pass. This weakness was exploited by the great mass of ice which covered the area during the glacial period and squeezed through the crack to form the ravine. Until the late eighteenth century there was no road through the pass, the old track being more than 1,000 feet up on the shoulder of Cruachan. Dorothy Wordsworth used the new road along the shore in 1803, vividly describing her route in her journal. Centuries before her visit, in 1308, Robert the Bruce lured his old adversary, John MacDougall of Lorn, into an ambush here. Despatching James Douglas and his archers to outflank the enemy by climbing the shoulder of Cruachan, he met the MacDougalls in the pass where, under a hail of arrows from above, they broke ranks and fled westward. At a narrow, wooden bridge over the Awe they were drowned and slaughtered as they fought with each other to cross the river. John MacDougall, however, escaped in his galley from Bonawe. The name of the pass in Gaelic is appropriately 'am Brannraidh' – 'place of ambush'.

At the western exit there is a dam across the river with a tunnel leading to a generating station near Loch Etive. This barrage has raised the level of the loch considerably and, although it is controlled by heavy gates capable of releasing a massive volume of water during a flood, delay in opening the gates often raises the level and floods the croft land on the banks of the River Orchy. This is not surprising as, in the early nineteenth century, the bed of the river in the pass was lowered to help the Orchy crofts. When the gates are opened the huge mass of water, cascading down the Awe, is an impressive sight and, when the flood subsides, salmon gather below the dam before they use the lift. They can be seen from the bank leaping from the water to clear the sea-lice from their scales. The lift, which works like a canal lock, allows the fish to reach the spawning beds in the rivers feeding the loch.

In the settlement west of the dam called Crunachy or Bridge of Awe there is a spacious caravan and camping site beside the river and, beside the road bridge, an old stone one spanning the Awe.

Directly opposite the old bridge a road leads north to Inverawe and Loch Etive. About a mile down this route the crow-stepped gables and square tower of Inverawe House can be seen through the trees. Built about 1850, the building was altered extensively by Sir Robert Lorimer in 1913 for James Currie of the Currie Shipping Line and changed again in 1953. Since the sixteenth century, however, the estate had been the seat of the Campbells of Inverawe, who were connected with one of the most celebrated Highland ghost stories. In the eighteenth century one of the lairds, Duncan Campbell, opened his door to an exhausted individual, who, fleeing from armed pursuers, begged protection. Campbell took him in, giving his word that he would not be harmed, only to discover that the man had murdered his foster-brother. His oath, however, was sacred and the murderer remained in the house unscathed. At night apparently Campbell was visited by his foster-brother's spirit demanding revenge but Campbell would not comply. Three times the wraith appeared and three times he resisted its demand. On the third occasion it disappeared, ominously whispering that they would meet again for the fourth and last time at a place called 'Ticonderoga'. Some years later, in 1758, while serving with his regiment in North America, Campbell was involved in an attack on one of the French forts. During the evening before the assault he casually asked his commanding officer the name of the fort. Aware of the prophecy, his superior gave him the French name, Fort Carillon. Mortally wounded in the assault the following day, Campbell discovered that the Indian name of the place was Ticonderoga and, as his strength waned, the spirit of his foster brother appeared by his bedside for the last time.

Beyond Inverawe today there is a salmon farm and smokery with a nationwide reputation, where visitors are welcome. The road ends on the shores of Loch Etive, which reaches north into one of the most beautiful glens in Scotland.

Taynuilt and Loch Etive

It was to Glen Etive that the legendary Deirdre and the three sons of Uisnach fled from King Conchobar of Ulster. When she was born it was prophesied that she would be the most beautiful woman in Ireland and that she would unwittingly destroy the House of Ulster. The King, hoping to save the dynasty by taking the girl as his wife, had her concealed from the eyes of the court. The child grew into a beautiful girl – 'Deirdre of the fair skin, whose locks were more yellow than the gold of the summer sun'. Unfortunately she met and fell in love with Naoise, one of the sons of Uisnach and, to avoid the wrath of Conchobar, they fled to Scotland with Naoise's brothers. They settled with their retinue of 150 warriors at Dalness in Glen Etive, hunting with their great Irish hounds in the deer forest and raising cattle on the sweet pasture on the banks of the river. The Gaelic verse, in which the story is told and which contains some of the most poignant lines in Irish literature, described Dalness:

> Lovely its wood in the smile of the early morning,
> A cattle fold of the sun is Glen Etive.

King Conchobar eventually discovered Deirdre's refuge and sent an emissary to tell the sons of Uisnach that he had forgiven them and that they could return to Ireland safely. Deirdre had a dream in which she saw birds flying from Erin to Scotland with honey in their beaks but returning covered in blood. She knew that it was a bad omen and tried to persuade Naoise to remain in Glen Etive. But the men longed for their native land and reluctantly she sailed to Ireland with them. Conchobar, consumed with passion for Deirdre, had the brothers executed. Deirdre of the Sorrows, devastated by the loss of her Naoise, died of grief. In her grief she constantly sought solace in memories of their idyllic years in Argyll:

> Glen Etive! O Glen Etive!
> There I built my first bower.
> Glen Mason! O Glen Mason!
> High its herbs and fair its boughs.
> Glen da Rua! O Glen da Rua!
> My love on all whose mother thou.

Somehow a trace of her longing still lingers in the air of Glen Etive, and legend it may be but a tree in her orchard at Cadderlie survived till the sixteenth century. Eilean Uisneachan contains a circular ruin where one of the brothers is said to have built a lodge, and a ruin near Dalness may well have been her 'bower'.

It is possible to take a boat trip up Loch Etive from the pier at Taynuilt and any visitor to the area should not miss the opportunity to sample the atmosphere of the glen and, on the way, watch the colonies of seals or see the eagles soaring above Glen Noe. There is no public road along the lochside, the only access of this kind being from Glencoe, so the boat trip is of considerable benefit to elderly people who might not be able to walk in.

For those who are fit the glen provides some superb hill-walking. Beinn Starav is a majestic hill and, in the winter, the ridge walk from its summit across to Stob Coir an Albannaich is quite remarkable. On the west side Beinn Trilleachan not only provides a quick afternoon walk from Glen Etive with clear views of the woods of Glen Ure but it also offers some unusual climbs on the great slabs on its eastern face. From Inverawe it is possible to walk to the head of the loch or through Glen Kinglass to Blackmount. The farm road, which leads to Ardmaddy, is spectacular with some steep drops to the loch immediately below the edge.

Beyond Glen Noe, Glen Kinglass stretches through to Blackmount and, at the mouth of the river, the meadows of Ardmaddy provide pasture for the red deer in rough weather. Near the keeper's cottage the remains of the first iron furnace in Lorn have been exposed by archaeologists. This enterprise was started in 1723 by two Irishmen, Arthur Galbraith and Rodger Murphy of Dublin, who were granted the right to 'cut, coall, cord and carry away' all the firs and oaks in the Barony of Glenorchy, except the firs of Glenstrae and Corriveran and all trees over two feet in circumference. It is significant that Murphy was a tanner, for the sale of bark for tanning was more profitable than the sale of timber. Murphy and Galbraith were joined by another two Irishmen and they began to extract timber from Drumliaghart at Blackmount, floating it down the rivers. The Earl of Breadalbane visited the forest shortly afterwards and was appalled at the devastation. 'They have not left one standing oak tree in the countrie,' he wrote, declaring his intention to end their contract. Yet the extraction continued and, in 1728, the small tenants of Drumliaghart, complaining that they were being oppressed by the Irishmen, told the Earl that the company were still destroying the woodlands, felling trees reserved for preservation and all the alder, birch and hazel. Fortunately for them, the company ceased operations two years later when there was a depression in the iron trade and Murphy was hanged for murder in Ireland! The damage had been done, however, and hundreds of acres of woodland at Blackmount destroyed. The Earl learned from his mistakes and subsequent contracts were carefully worded to guarantee proper management of the forests.

The second iron furnace, which was established at Bonawe below Taynuilt in 1752, is remarkably well preserved and has been restored by the Department of the Environment. It is open to the public with leaflets explaining its operations. The ironmasters who founded the Lorn Furnace Company, Richard Ford of Grisedale and Michael Knott of Rydall, imported their ore from England and used local charcoal to heat the furnace. The vast, echoing space of the restored charcoal store gives an indication of the immense quantity required. It has been estimated that at least five tons of wood were needed to produce one ton of iron. By the 1840s Lorn was sending 25 to 30 tons of iron per week to Wales for making tin plate – this would have involved about 60 hectares of forest annually. The furnace drew on the woods of Loch Etive, Loch Awe, Morvern and Mull. Yet the exploitation of the forests was carefully controlled. This is very obvious in the contracts which have survived and which contain rigorous conservation measures. The woods on Loch Etive, for example, were to be cut three times between 1752 and 1810 and firs or oaks which were

Bonawe Iron Furnace, established 1752.

The strict rules contained in the contracts are largely responsible for the survival of the woodlands in the area. At a time when the high rents offered by flockmasters were tempting proprietors to convert their pastures to sheep walks, many of these woods would have disappeared had they not been protected by charcoaling leases.

The Lorn Furnace continued to produce iron till 1875, surviving innovations in technology such as coke furnaces and the hot blast in the 1830s. It was, therefore, a remarkable enterprise, producing high-quality iron which sold at four times the usual price. The workers in the early stages were mainly from England and they erected the first monument in Britain to Admiral Nelson, which still stands in a field behind the church in Taynuilt.

As the main road approaches Taynuilt, the great scar of Bonawe Quarry can be seen on the wooded hillside on the far side of Loch Etive. Just before Nant bridge the road to Kilchrenan turns sharply away south towards Glen Nant, where there is a Nature Reserve and nature trail in the oak woods. Taynuilt itself is easily recognised by the old coaching inn which stands at the crossroads. Described by a traveller in 1824 as 'a vile pot house', it has been extensively modernised since then but the original stable and laundry at the back of the building reflect its antiquity. Immediately opposite the inn the village, concealed from the main road, is easily missed. Visitors who choose to pass it are missing, not only the services available in the main street, but also a magnificent view of Loch Etive from the old pier and the chance of a sailing trip into Loch Etive.

Tucked away behind the main street, the parish church of Muckairn stands on a hill near the school. Completed in 1829 to Thomas Telford's design, it is on the site of a much older place of worship, the ruins of which can be seen in the graveyard. Originally called Killespickerill – the Chapel of Bishop Harold – it was once the seat of the first Bishop of Argyll before it was transferred to Lismore in 1236. The first building has disappeared and the ruins behind the church today are sixteenth century. High on the south wall of the present church there is an extraordinary female figure known as a 'Sheela na Gig' or, in Gaelic, 'Sìle na gcioc', a medieval fertility symbol possibly from the thirteenth century. The only other figures of this kind in Scotland are to be found in Iona and Rodel, Harris. The Georgian manse below the church, also built to Telford's design, was occupied in the early twentieth century by one of the most radical ministers in Argyll, Malcolm MacCallum, who stood for Parliament as a Labour candidate, worked closely with the Crofters' Commission in defence of tenants' rights, became a County Councillor and published a book entitled *Religion and Social Justice*.

Passing the station, which is a splendid example of late Victorian railway architecture, recently converted to a brewery and taphouse, the road to the pier crosses a bridge and descends to the river. On the left at this point a gateway leads to the games field where, at the end of July every year, athletes, dancers and pipers gather – rather too often in the rain – to take part in the Taynuilt Highland Games. Crossing the Nant and turning sharply up a hill past the Catholic church, the road eventually reaches sea level near the iron furnace. With the shore on one side and level pasture marked with the ridges of old plough rigs on the other, this is the most attractive part of the parish. The entire iron works, including the blast furnace, ore sheds and charcoal stores, have been restored and the surrounding grounds maintained immaculately. Sitting on the grass under the great oak trees with only the distant drone of traffic on the Oban road to break the silence, it is easy to forget that the site once reverberated with the rhythmic thunder of the blast or the roar of steam as cold water poured over the white-hot metal in the cooling troughs.

Passing the old pier, known as Kelly's pier after the furnace manager, Alexander Kelly, the road leads to the quay from which the *Anne of Etive* leaves for Glen Etive. There are some splendid places for picnics on the soft turf of the shore and spectacular views of Loch Etive, its dark waters reflecting the wooded slopes and sometimes snow-capped peaks of Beinn Cruachan and Beinn Starav. A walk up the bank of the River Awe may bring a glimpse of a salmon, lying almost motionless behind a rock or leaping in a flash of silver out of the water as it returns from the Atlantic. There was a salmon fishing station at the mouth of the Awe in the eighteenth century, the fishermen taking advantage of the ore ships to send their catches to England. The Corfe House was the centre of the industry, where the salmon were cooked in great boilers and packed in ice ready for shipment. The ice was broken from ponds at Lochandhu in the winter, carried by pony to the ice house beside the Corfe and packed tightly in the underground chamber.

On the south side of Taynuilt an alternative and much more attractive route to Oban leaves the main road at the inn, heading towards Glen Lonan. The road climbs up to Barguillean through a birch and hazel wood. It is a single-track road and mainly unfenced, so motorists should look out for sheep and cattle. Barguillean, renowned for its Blackface sheep stock, has been run by the MacDonald family for three generations. The present proprietor has diversified into horticulture and has established a successful nursery garden, which is open to the public from April to October. Specialising in azaleas, flowering trees and shrubs, it supplies plants to markets all over the UK and Ireland. Beside the nurseries a track leads north to Balindore (Baile an Deoir), once a well-populated township, from which, according to local tradition, the grandfather of

Robert Burns fled to Ayrshire to avoid prosecution for murder, changing his name to Burnhouse – the literal translation of 'Taynuilt'.

Beyond Barguillean Glen Lonan opens out into a most picturesque high valley with tall conifers on the slopes and flat marshland round a loch in the centre. Reminiscent of the American mid-west before the buffalo hunters arrived, with green pasture land in open spaces beneath the trees and steep rock faces above them, it is a landscape rich in colour and varied in form. The hill on the western side of the strath, known locally as 'G Height', is in fact Deadh Choimhead – the Outstanding Watchpoint – and a climb to the summit will reveal the origin of its name, for it provides an extraordinary panorama of North Lorn. There are only two houses in the strath and, near the second of these, Clachadhu, there is a ruined byre with the old 'crucks', which supported the roof timbers, still in place.

West of Taynuilt the A85 crosses the railway and, passing the former Free Church and manse, built in 1860, rises to the hill above Airds Bay and continues through the oakwoods of Muckairn towards Oban.

Arrochar

Another approach to Lorn is across the narrow neck of land separating Loch Long from Loch Lomond at Tarbet, turning west at Tarbet hotel on the A83. The distance between the two lochs is negligible and, before the military roads joined this area to the south, it was not uncommon for boats to be hauled from one piece of water to the other. In 1263, during King Hakon's raid on the Clyde, sixty galleys under Magnus, King of Man, sailed up Loch Long to obtain provisions for the Norwegian force. They drew the ships across the isthmus into Loch Lomond and created havoc round the shores, carrying away hundreds of cattle. On their return journey ten of their ships were lost in Loch Long but the rest reached the Clyde to take part in a skirmish with the Scots at the 'Battle' of Largs. Today the road joining Tarbet and Arrochar passes under the Glasgow to Fort William railway line in the middle of the isthmus and, as it approaches Loch Long, gives an impressive view of what Scottish climbers call the 'Arrochar Alps'.

This range of hills, with its distinctive silhouette resembling a cobbler crouched over a lapstone, was the nursery for many eminent Scottish climbers and, being close to Glasgow and therefore providing a haven for unemployed industrial workers in the 1930s, gave Scottish climbing its radical character. Unemployed shipyard workers and engineers escaped to the 'Alps' by train, bus, bicycle or on foot, remaining for a few days in the hills until they had to return to the city to 'sign on'. They stayed in bothies, caves or under shelter stones like the one in the high corrie of the Brack.

Beneath the Cobbler is the Royal Navy torpedo base, from which unarmed torpedoes were tested in Loch Long, and further south the Coulport base for Trident missiles. The materials for the construction of the latter are being driven in on a temporary road through Glen Douglas, which will be removed when the base is complete. One day, perhaps, money will be found to build proper roads to remote parts of Argyll which will not need to be demolished after a few years. In the meantime the sinister shapes of submarines can be seen gliding through the dark water of Loch Long, somehow more menacing than the stark precipices of the mountains above them.

Beyond the Youth Hostel and caravan site on the western side of the loch lies Glen Croe, one of the most dramatic valleys in the district. The new road climbs gradually towards the summit, while its eighteenth-century predecessor follows the river far below until, at the head of the glen, it has to snake up the steep hillside. Remembering that it was used by horses pulling heavy wagons, it is easy to understand why the summit was called 'Rest and be Thankful'. When J. E. Bowman travelled through the glen in the winter of 1826, there was a semi-circular seat of turf at the summit with a stone bearing the inscription 'Rest and be thankful. 1748. Repaired by the XXIII Regiment 1767'. The stone survived but not the seat. Like many of the roads in the Highlands, this was built by the Government to facilitate troop movement and thus exercise control over the unruly clans. Indeed, when Bowman reached the summit, he encountered a contingent of military engineers living in a caravan, who had been given the task of maintaining the road. There is a magnificent view from the top looking east down the glen to Loch Fyne. Just beyond the car park Loch Restil fills a small hollow left by the glaciers. In the winter its surface is often frozen and the black rocks of Beinn an Lochain above it are covered in sheets of ice.

As the road descends towards Loch Fyne it passes the lonely and sunless shepherd's cottage of Butterbridge before it reaches Cairndow. At this point it is joined by the A815 from Dunoon and Cowal. In Cairndow there is another octagonal church like the one in Dalmally. Built in 1816 on the site of a medieval chapel, it is well maintained and its white, pinnacled tower is clearly visible from the road. There is an inn in the village in which the Wordsworths spent the night of 29th August 1803. They breakfasted on herrings fresh from the loch but 'were completely out of patience' because they had risen at seven to find the staff still asleep. Similar displays of impatience with the Highlander's casual approach to business still surface occasionally among frustrated visitors who cannot sympathise with the Gaelic saying that 'when God made time, he made plenty of it'. Yet it is this approach which makes a holiday in the West so relaxing. Above the village the gardens of Strone House are open to the public from April to October and contain one of the finest collection of pines in Britain, including the nation's largest Abies Grandis, which is more than 200 feet tall. On the south side of the river lies Ardkinglas estate, the seat of Lord Glenkinglas, formerly the Secretary of State for Scotland, Michael Noble, and M.P. for Argyll until defeated by the Scottish Nationalist, Iain MacCormick.

On the far side of the loch Dunderave Castle stands in the trees below the road. Built in 1596 for the 12th chief of the MacNaughton clan, it was extensively reconstructed in 1911 by Sir Robert Lorimer, who had completed the renovation of Ardkinglas House four years previously. It is said that the last chief of the MacNaughtons absconded to Ireland with a daughter of Campbell of Ardkinglas and settled at a place in Antrim which is still called Dunderave. More recently it was the setting for 'Castle Doom' in Neil Munro's novel.

Inveraray

The road follows the shore round Loch Fyne and, passing
through several miles of oak woods on the west side, crosses the
River Shira below the Dubh Loch. At the foot of the glen there
is a level piece of ground where a camp was built to house the
men working on the construction of Shira Dam. Several of the
workers were killed in the tunnels and on the site and their
sacrifice is remembered in a song called 'Shira Dam', composed
by Helen Fullerton, who used to run a mobile shop to the
camp. A couple of verses convey the spirit of the camp:

> I workit in the tunnel and I workit in the shaft
> And then I poured the main dam, it was there I did me graft.
> The nipper makes a fortune a-stewin' up yer tea,
> I think he boils his underwear, for it tastes like that to me.

> And when ye're doon the glen again ye join the dinner queue
> And at the end a grisly lump – I heard them ca' it stew.
> McKay's fat dog it gets the meat and the milk it's watered sair
> And the soup comes up in the same old pail that's went tae wash
>   the flair.

> The swan it cries on Lochan Dubh and the seagull on the sea
> And city lights and clachan lights are burning merrily.
> The Shira Dam's a bonny dam and nothing more remains
> Of the lads who died a-buildin' her – I could gie ye a' their names.

The public road in Glen Shira ends at a locked gate near
Elrig but it continues as an access road for the Shira hydro-
electric dam at the head of the glen. The name Elrig has been
given to several places in Scotland and refers to a medieval
device for killing deer; it consisted of a long wall against which
the deer were driven by a team of servants and gradually
herded into a pen at the lower end. The deer drive, known as a
'tinchel', was a means of providing the townships with venison.
Above Elrig the ruin of Rob Roy's house is still discernible at
the foot of Beinn Bhuidhe. The Duke of Argyll, possibly
hoping to annoy the Duke of Montrose whose lowland tenants
had suffered from Rob Roy's 'protection' schemes, offered the
house to the outlaw after the Battle of Sheriffmuir in 1716.

Inveraray from the north.

According to local tradition Rob Roy was a well-known figure in Inveraray and a popular guest at weddings.

The main road enters the Royal Burgh of Inveraray by an elegant, but narrow, bridge over the River Ara or Aoradh. From the parapet there is a clear view of Inveraray Castle. Built between 1744 and 1790 with the help of the distinguished architect Roger Morris, it has been damaged by fire and restored twice in 1877 and in 1975. The third storey and the conical turrets were added after the first fire. The effect is impressive rather than pleasing. The interior, however, possesses all the elegance and grandeur one would expect of the period. Decorated by Robert Mylne and completed under the supervision of William Adam, the father of John and Robert, it is like a different building inside. Intricate French tapestries and paintings by Gainsborough, Batoni and Raeburn cover the walls, and pieces of delicate period furniture fill the rooms. Clusters of antique weapons decorate the hall and examples of Japanese Imari ware are displayed with the furniture. The castle is open to the public between April and October.

Inveraray and Loch Fyne from Bell tower; a wartime view. Note warship in the background. The foreground spire on the church has since disappeared.

The town, which was originally located near the mouth of the river, curves round a small bay with a wide green between the houses and the shore. It should be an attractive town but, because the Duke of Argyll had it crowded on to a headland to keep it away from the Castle, it is slightly unbalanced. Most of the buildings on the front, including the Argyll Arms Hotel, were completed in mid-eighteenth century to the design of Robert Adam and the screen of arches linking the buildings was completed between 1788 and 1790 – just after the French Revolution. In 1787 Robert Burns stayed at the new inn, scratching on one of the windows,

> There's naething here but Highland pride
> And Highland scab and hunger.
> If Providence has sent me here
> 'Twas surely in an anger.

The old town had consisted of a few fishermen's cottages, built of wattle and clay or turf, with thatched roofs, and a fortified house belonging to the Campbells of Argyll. In 1432 Sir Colin Campbell had built 'the town and house' of Inveraray and the 'large tower' with battlements. About twenty years later the first Earl of Argyll abandoned the traditional family seat at

Inveraray Castle, home of the Dukes of Argyll. Open to the public April to October.

Innis Chonnail on Loch Awe and made Inveraray the centre of his administration. Visitors from the Court began to frequent the village and, in 1533, James V stayed with the Earl. Thirty years later Mary, Queen of Scots, half-sister to the Countess of Argyll, visited Inveraray in July 1563. Attired in Highland costume, she proceeded through the burgh accompanied by members of the Privy Council and remained in the area for three days before riding to Creggans for the ferry to Strachur.

On more than one occasion the town suffered the consequences of its association with the Campbell laird. In 1644 it was laid waste by Montrose and Colkitto MacDonald, who, descending from the north, burned houses and steadings, stole the cattle and imposed themselves on the terrified inhabitants over Christmas. The noble Earl had fled on a herring boat down Loch Fyne, leaving his people to their fate. When the Royalist forces left in January, the villagers patiently rebuilt the houses. In 1685 the 9th Earl tried to raise an army in Argyll as part of a rebellion against the Stewart dynasty but the attempt failed and, once again, the Royalist clans descended on the Campbell lands, hanging, burning and looting. Several Campbells were hanged on the Gallows Foreland on a spot now

THE GREAT HALL, INVERARAY CASTLE

Interior, Inveraray Castle.

marked by an obelisk in the garden of what is now the Bank of Scotland. Millstones and fishing boats were broken, nets and woodlands burned. More than 34,000 trees were carried away. The Duke of Atholl, who had commanded the raid, destroyed every building which he thought might be used in subsequent rebellions. Eventually the Privy Council intervened, ordered restraint and replaced the Duke of Atholl. Yet the burgh and the surrounding countryside had been devastated and never really recovered from the assault.

No sooner had the inhabitants repaired the damage than the 3rd Duke swept the old town away and began to build the new burgh on the headland. Between 1746 and 1785 the old buildings were gradually demolished and new ones constructed at Arkland and Relief Land. For some time the inhabitants were without a church and had to worship in two adjoining houses which now form the George Hotel. The new church was built between 1800 and 1805 and originally contained separate chambers for the English- and Gaelic-speaking congregations. A new Town House, which served as a court house and prison, was built on the seafront in 1775, the old one evidently having fallen into disrepair, for, when James of the Glen was tried in Inveraray for the Appin murder in 1752, the English Church in the square was used as a court house. The old court house near the river had seen the trial of 'Half Hung Archie', who, having been condemned to death for murder, was hung at the Crags. As his relatives ferried his body across Loch Fyne towards Strachur, they noticed that there were still signs of life and managed to revive him. Archie survived and was allowed to remain at liberty but his head was permanently twisted to one side from his suspension on the gibbet. By 1805 the magistrates declared the prison in the Town House to be inadequate and a new jail and court house was eventually built in the square in 1816. This was opened as a museum of crime and punishment in 1989 with nineteenth-century prison conditions and activities faithfully reproduced in the cells.

The motto of the burgh, 'May the herring always hang from your nets', indicates the former importance of fishing to the community. In 1796 there were no fewer than 500 boats employed in the herring fishing with 100 'busses' and larger vessels from other parts of Britain and Ireland. In 1853 more than 4,000 people in the district were employed in the fisheries, and one traveller in 1871 described Inveraray as 'that most depressing of fish-smelling Highland towns'. By 1939, however, both herring and white fish had largely disappeared from Upper Loch Fyne and the fishing was abandoned. Only the motto remains to remind us of the trade which once provided work for fishermen, gutters, curers, boat-builders and net-makers. Today fishing trips can be arranged from the pier, in season offering the opportunity to catch mackerel, cod, saithe, haddock and skate.

One of Scotland's leading novelists was born in Crombie's Land in 1864. Neil Munro, author of the *Para Handy* tales, *John Splendid* and *The New Road,* worked as a junior clerk in Inveraray before leaving to join the staff of the *Falkirk Herald.* He died in 1930 and was buried in the old Inveraray graveyard beyond the castle. A monument was erected to the author at the head of Glen Ara, overlooking the home of his ancestors. The decline of the Gaelic language, which would have been lamented by Munro, is particularly evident in Inveraray, where a quarter of the population still had the language in 1931; by 1961 less than 4% were fluent in the tongue.

Like Glenorchy, Inveraray has a strong shinty team. Even the Argyll family have been known to participate in the sport, Lord Archibald Campbell leading the Inveraray Estate team in 1865 against Ardkinglas Estate. On that occasion the game was played in the traditional Celtic manner with sixty players on each side! In January 1879 the ice was so thick on Loch Fyne that a match was played on the frozen surface of the bay. There is a theory that ice hockey originated in games of shinty played by Highland emigrants on the frozen lakes of North America.

During the Second World War Inveraray became the centre of Combined Operations, the headquarters of which was in the Loch Fyne Hotel on the Lochgilphead road. In 1941 Winston Churchill visited the burgh to inspect Naval and Military Units in the area, conveying his appreciation to the council for its patience and support. Half a million troops trained in the district for the Normandy landings. A fascinating record of these events has been compiled in the Combined Operations Museum at Cherry Park in the Castle grounds.

The Coffee House near the pier was built by the 8th Duke in memory of his Duchess in 1880 as a public reading room and social centre for the local fishermen. The bell tower of the Episcopal Church, built in 1886 for his second wife, contains the finest collection of bells in Scotland and, for a small charge, visitors can climb to the top of the tower to obtain an uninterrupted view of the burgh. In July Inveraray Highland Games bring athletes from all over Britain and Campbell 'clansmen' from all over the world. The Duke of Argyll also provides accommodation for a craft fair shortly after the Games, horse trials in May in Glen Shira and an Antiques Day at the Castle in June.

North of Inveraray, on the A819 to Oban, Glenaray Fish Farm is open to the public between April and October and visitors can feed, watch or catch fish in the numerous ponds and lakes. From the summit of the hill above Loch Awe there is a magnificent view of the Cruachan hills and the hydro-electric dam, which nestles unobtrusively between Beinn a Rhuiridh and Meall Cuanail.

On the road south there is a riding centre at Dalchenna with special facilities for disabled people and, in the same area, a wildlife park containing one of the most complete collections of Canadian geese in Europe. The remarkable aspect of this reserve is that the multitude of wild fowl settling on the ponds and in the enclosures – geese, swans and ducks – are free to leave at any time. Rather than depart, they choose to remain and attract other wild birds: eider duck, for example, which are all too often shot by mussel farmers, settle by the shore. Only the ravens and the extraordinary collection of owls are in cages. The reserve also contains wild boar, wallabies, deer, goats, dog foxes and wild cats. The paths round the enclosures are firm and level, convenient for disabled people and young children, and there is a small restaurant and information centre near the gate.

Among the trees south-west of the town, the remains of the old nickel mine can still be seen on the hillside. Opened in 1852 and worked by English miners, it produced about nine tons of copper ore and 400 tons of nickel between 1854 and 1867. Some local men were employed, including some miners from Strontian, but the skilled men were all from Cornwall or Cumberland. The mine was mainly open-cast but several small shafts were sunk, and traces of the minerals can still be found in their vicinity. There was also a small lead and silver mine just south-west of Clachan Beag at the head of Loch Fyne, which apparently yielded two ounces to the 'long ton', but it is very difficult to find.

CHAPTER 2

Oban and North-West Lorn

Oban

Oban is the hub of North Argyll and the southern Hebrides. Roads converge on the town from Fort William, Tyndrum and Lochgilphead. Ferries sail from its piers for the islands of Mull, Colonsay, Tiree and Coll, Lismore, Kerrera and Barra. A railway connects Oban with Fort William, Glasgow and the South. It is, therefore, a busy tourist resort. Lying in a crescent-shaped hollow beneath steep hillsides, it is sheltered from the cold east winds but, because the area of flat land is limited to the sea front and riverside, it has become seriously congested. Nevertheless the first glimpse of Oban Bay from the pass of Bealach an Airigh above the town is most impressive, particularly at night, when the harbour lights are reflected in the sea and the fishing fleet is tied up at the Railway Pier.

It is impossible to describe all the facilities available in the town, as it offers almost every service a visitor might need, but several of these particularly merit attention. At the far end of the town, for example, Caithness Glass is manufactured in a small factory at Lochavullin Estate and it is possible to visit the premises to watch the glass blowers at work. Not far from Lochavullin, on Soroba Road, there is a woollen mill which not only sells tweeds and tartans but also offers demonstrations of handloom weaving. On the north pier there is a remarkable display of 'A World in Miniature', a collection of settings with tiny furniture and fittings. Attached to the Corran Halls on the Esplanade there is a small museum and library run by the District Council. As the road enters the town, passing numerous 'bed and breakfast' houses, the Highland Discovery Centre and Theatre is on the left. Here visitors are offered what is described as an 'audio-visual experience', covering the history of the area and a tour of the islands. The town also has a swimming pool, a leisure centre, a golf course, numerous woollen and tweed shops, Celtic jewellers, an antique shop, an art gallery, a small craft shop supplied and run by local

Oban in the storm of 1989.

craftsmen and an art shop owned by an Oban artist who
exhibits his work on the premises.

Oban has become a major yachting centre, with a ships'
chandler's in Argyll Square and boat repair yards on Kerrera
and at the south pier, and has its own coastguard station and
sea rescue service. It provides a safe anchorage but is rather
exposed to south-westerly gales. Boats can be hired beyond the
south pier and there is an excellent fishing tackle shop near the
centre.

Oban has retained much of its Victorian character. Many of
the buildings were completed when the railway opened just
over a hundred years ago and their sandstone facades resemble
those of many Victorian watering places. The town was to have
had its own 'Hydropathic Institution', like those of Peebles,
Crieff and Strathpeffer, situated on a cliff top above Argyll
Square. The Oban Hills Hydropathic Sanatorium Company was
formed in 1881, a year after the railway opened, and a rail
track was laid through the town to convey materials from the
station to the site. A year later the company was in difficulties
and, with the walls completed and the roof almost finished,
work on the 137-bedroom hotel had to be abandoned. In spite
of raids on the building by local contractors, part of the shell

still remains as a monument to Victorian enterprise and to its architect, J. Ford MacKenzie. This building is not to be confused with McCaig's Tower, the circular granite structure which dominates the Oban skyline. Built by an Oban banker, John Stuart McCaig, a native of Lismore, as a memorial to his family, it is almost 200 metres in circumference and provides a superb view of Oban Bay, especially on a summer's evening when the sun sets over the hills of Mull. McCaig spent £5,000 on the monument, employing masons in winter when wages were low and work was scarce. Like the Hydro, the Tower was abandoned before completion when McCaig died in 1902.

The opening of the railway in 1880 had a major impact on the town but its population had already reached 4,000 before this first tourist boom as it had been growing steadily as a port of call for steamships. In 1818 Henry Bell's *Comet* started a regular service between the Clyde and Oban. Other steamers followed and a regular tourist trade developed.

When Queen Victoria sailed slowly across Oban Bay in August 1847, it was packed with steamers, small craft and the barges of the gentry. The Earl of Breadalbane, one of the Oban landowners, had his barge painted in the Queen's colours for the occasion and a tartan canopy fitted for his guests. In her journal Victoria described the town as 'one of the finest spots we have seen'. At night the town was brightly illuminated, 'presenting a flood of light that sparkled on the warm sea, with circles of coloured lamps arranged in tasteful forms and in words of loyal welcome, while, high up, two magnificent bonfires lighted the remote distance like planets of some other sphere'. Unfortunately this was the first year of the potato famine and the town had not recovered from its effects. One of the ministers had reported in January, 'I have never seen Oban in such a state as it is at present. I have within the past week given bread and meal to whole families that have been without food for two days'. The Queen's visit may have seemed slightly irrelevant to the poor under the circumstances.

However, Her Majesty's tour of the West promoted an interest in the area which brought further trade. By 1855 the King's Arms Hotel in George Street was open and this was followed by the Great Western in 1863 and later the Alexandra, Marine and the Columba. By 1855 George Street had taken shape, with a number of shops on the ground floor of the buildings. The Cumstie family had one of these, as well as shops in Argyll Square and Shore Street, and, near Peter Cumstie's store in George Street, the merchant, John Stevenson, had a house with stables, barn and byre.

These two families – the Stevensons and the Cumsties – could claim much of the credit for the development of the town from a trading station to a major port. The Stevenson brothers, after whom Stevenson Street is named, are said to have arrived in Oban with their widowed mother in the early eighteenth century to live in extreme poverty at Ardconnel Mill. One of the boys became a mason, eventually accumulating enough capital to take the lease of Glencruitten farm and a spirit store. The other served his time as a carpenter and, in partnership with his brother, started a small shipyard, hoping, no doubt, to profit from the fleets of ships passing through Oban on their way from the Baltic and to supply local fishermen with boats. By the end of the century their sons virtually monopolised the trade of the town. Hugh Stevenson was not only a merchant with a thriving tannery but was also the Collector of Taxes. Thomas managed the slate quarries on the island of Belnahua. John seems to have been a merchant too, for, in 1812, he placed an order with a wholesalers for '40 ells Officers Kilts 42nd (Regiment); 40 ells fine hoses; 30 ells Officers Plaids 42nd; 18 pair fine stocking hose', probably for the regiment of Black Watch billeted on the town during the French War.

Hugh died in 1820 and his side of the business was taken over by his nephew, who had returned from Peru, bringing with him a herd of llama for his farm at Soroba. These strange creatures from the High Andes seem to have settled remarkably well in the wet climate of the West Highlands and could be seen grazing with Stevenson's milk cows in the shelter of Soroba hill. The young man's return, however, did not prevent the business getting into difficulties in the depression which followed the collapse in kelp prices in the 1820s. By 1829 the entire business was insolvent and was forced into liquidation. By then the family assets included two steamships, Belnahua slate quarries, Oban distillery and the stock of two farms. The Stevensons, as the author of the Old Statistical

Account suggested, were the 'founders' of Oban.

In 1833 Oban became a Parliamentary Burgh with a council of six, elected by the 34 citizens entitled to vote. The first senior Baillie was William Cumstie, an itinerant merchant from Dromore, County Down, who had settled in Oban in 1823 to establish a drapery business and grocery in George Street. In 1836 he built a large schooner, the *William Campbell*, to expand his trade with America in association with another trader, J.W. Campbell. The business prospered and eventually Cumstie's son took over Stevenson's distillery, an enterprise which is still thriving today.

In the early nineteenth century communication with central Scotland was maintained by horse-drawn coaches. One commentator remembered that 'a blue coach, driven by a man in a brilliant coat, began to arrive daily in the summer time from Glasgow, sweeping in splendour down by Dunollie Road to the accompaniment of a bugle horn'. The main route led from Oban to Taychreggan ferry and, from there, across Loch Awe to Cladich and Inveraray. At that time the streets were still poorly lit at night, for gas light did not come to the burgh till 1863, when 'Villagers turned out into the front street and gathered in groups at McCaig's and Cumstie's shop windows to gaze at the new and (as it was thought then) wonderful light'. The gasworks, which had supplied the town with heating since 1848, were in Tweeddale Street but were recently demolished to provide an invaluable car park close to the town centre.

In the eighteenth century the Salt Laws, passed by the London Government to help pay for its wars, inhibited the fishing industry in the West Highlands by confining the general supply of salt to issues from Government depots. Oban, however, benefited from the legislation, as it was designated as a customs station in 1761. Fishermen from all parts of North Argyll and foreign fishing 'busses' had to put in to the village to obtain salt. By 1790 the population had reached 586. David Dale, who had founded New Lanark cotton mill, started a small weaving mill in Oban. At New Lanark his initial labour force had consisted of emigrant Highlanders, whose ship to America had been forced into the Clyde by bad weather. Dale, having persuaded them to remain in Scotland and work for him in New Lanark, had been so impressed with

West Highland Week, Crinan-Oban 1983. *Photo by A. MacRae, Oban.*

their skills that he evidently decided to experiment with the production of coarse muslin in Oban. Unfortunately, the enterprise suffered from 'dearth of fuel' and had to be abandoned. In spite of this disappointment, Oban continued to grow and attract visitors from the south. Johnson and Boswell stayed at a 'tolerable inn' in October 1773 on the south side of the Black Lynn. The inn was subsequently demolished and its site is now uncertain but it is thought to have been in Argyll Square. Boswell House, which, on its ground floor, accommodates the Tourist Information Office, was built roughly on the same site. One of the few buildings to survive virtually unaltered from the eighteenth century is the Manor House Hotel, which was built as the Duke of Argyll's dower house in the year of the French Revolution.

There are several buildings of historical interest in the town. On the south pier, for example, the small, whitewashed building is the pier master's house, completed just before the end of the Napoleonic Wars in 1814 at the same time as the south pier. This was the only jetty in Oban till the Marquis of Breadalbane laid the foundation of the north pier by buying the hulk of an American ship, the *B.C. Bailey,* which had foundered off Lismore, and sinking it on the shingle beach below the distillery. The most interesting Victorian building is the Free Church on Rockfield Road near the Gasworks car park which was built in 1846 to the design of David Cousin of Edinburgh. The cathedral of Saint Columba on the Esplanade is not, as its appearance might suggest, a Victorian building but was completed in 1952. Started twenty years previously with financial help from émigrée Catholics whose predecessors had been forced to leave Argyll and the Isles, its exterior is not particularly impressive but it is remarkably spacious and elegant inside.

Along the shore, beyond the cathedral, the walls of Dunollie Castle stand on a rock overlooking the bay. First recorded in the seventh and eighth centuries, this was the stronghold of the Lorn kings in North Dalriada. Apparently burnt by the Irish in 698, it was rebuilt by Selbach of Dalriada to become eventually the seat of the MacDougalls. In 1321 it was given to Arthur Campbell after Robert the Bruce deprived the MacDougalls of their lands for their opposition to his cause. John MacDougall had not only opposed Bruce but had defeated him at Tyndrum, snatching the king's brooch from his shoulder as he fled from the field. The Brooch of Lorn still remains in the hands of John's descendants. The MacDougalls remained in the castle, however, for, within its thick, impenetrable walls, Christian, John's widow, was incarcerated by her son, who suspected her of forming an undesirable relationship with Colin Campbell of Lochow. The resourceful lady managed to escape and fled to Loch Awe.

By 1385 the castle was officially restored to the MacDougalls and remained in their hands till it was abandoned after the 1715 Rising, through which the family, being staunch Jacobites, once again lost their lands. Ian Car MacDougall had fought under the Earl of Mar at Sheriffmuir and was presented with a medal for his loyalty by James Stuart. He remained in hiding for 12 years until he was pardoned, meeting his wife secretly in her cottage on Kerrera. He died in 1737, just before the last Jacobite Rising, the estate being transferred two years later to his son, Alexander. The latter did not join the rising, his participation being prevented, it is said, by his wife, a Campbell of Barcaldine, who poured boiling water over his feet to keep him at home. Two years later Alexander abandoned the castle, building a more comfortable home at Dunollie House, which is still occupied by the clan chief, Madam MacDougall. Still standing four storeys high, the ivy-clad walls of the old castle make it almost invisible from the sea.

On the roadside below the castle there is a strange pinnacle known as Clach a Choin – the Dog Stone – to which the legendary Ossian is said to have tethered his hound, Bran. The shallow channel round the base is supposed to be the mark of his leash.

As the great ice sheets, which covered Lorn more than 10,000 years ago, retreated, Mesolithic man settled in the caves on the shore. Thick woodlands of birch and pine covered the hills and swamps filled the valleys. The primitive Highlanders lived by hunting and gathering nuts and berries in the woods and by fishing in the shallow waters. Their implements were spears tipped with splintered bone or flint and axes bound to hazel shafts. For centuries their artefacts lay concealed in the caves until, in 1869, one of the entrances was discovered at the north end of Breadalbane Street in Oban. A passage more than nine feet long led to a large chamber about 11 feet high. There the amazed Victorians found the skeletons of a man and a child and, scattered on the floor, flint implements with the bones of deer, oxen, foxes, otters, pine marten, goats and water rats. In 1890 another cave was discovered behind Oban Distillery, which contained skulls, tools of deer horn and flakes of flint; on one of the skulls the frontal bones receded sharply from a point above the orbits. The most interesting discovery occurred four years later in the MacArthur Cave in Nursery Lane, just beyond Hamilton Park Terrace. This cavern was 25 feet long and contained two long-headed skulls, bone implements, including fish-spears, and deer-horn harpoons. The bones of a badger and a dog were found on the floor along with the remains of shellfish. This debris lay among natural shell beds, which suggests that the cave was occupied while the entrance was still at sea level. If this is the case, it would place the Oban settlers in the category of Azilian Man of 7,000 to 10,000 years ago. One of these caves – the one at the Distillery – can still be seen by arrangement with the management.

Thirty years ago Oban was still essentially a market town with a busy fishing pier. Cattle and sheep from Barra, Mull, Coll,

Morvern and Colonsay arrived at the piers and were driven through the streets to Corsons Auction Mart. After the October sales special trains carried the cattle to Stirling and the south. The ram sales lasted two days and, on the first night, a ceilidh was organised in the Columba Hotel.

Shepherds, stocksmen, farmers and flockmasters gathered from all parts of Argyll and the southern Hebrides to listen to the Gaelic music and trade tales in the bars. Far from home and among friends whose discretion was unquestionable, inhibitions slipped away as the evening progressed. Normally restrained and respectable Gaels abandoned their reserve and performed like regular reprobates in the bars. A few secrets of the 'tupp sale ceilidhs' will, no doubt, never be revealed. As the evening turned to early morning, those who remained gradually sank into nostalgic silence, soothed by the haunting melodies of 'An t-eilean Muileach' or 'Fagail Liosmor' or, the most poignant of all, 'Mo Run Geal, Dileas'. I can still hear the voices, swelling with that inexplicable longing which afflicts the Gael, echoing in the night air.

Since then, Oban has changed dramatically, with the growth of the housing estates at Dunbeg and Soroba, the latter known as 'The White City'. This influx of people has altered the character of the town and the secondary school has had to adjust to the change. It has been forced to abandon its 'grammar school' identity and become completely comprehensive, catering for the needs of the whole community. It is, indeed, one of the few truly comprehensive schools in Strathclyde, as all children, regardless of creed, join the roll. Oban High School has one of the largest geographical catchment areas in Britain. Children travel from the remote islands in the west, staying in hostels run by the Education Authority, and from Glen Orchy in the east. Built in 1877 to house a few hundred pupils, it has had to expand to find room for more than 1,300. It has a strong Gaelic department and a Gaelic choir which has won a multitude of prizes at the National Mod, the Scottish Gaelic festival. Three former pupils form the core of Capercaille, a Gaelic group with whose music every visitor should become acquainted, and other distinguished former pupils include Anne Lorn Gillies, the Mod Gold Medallist, James Hunter, the most eloquent Scottish historian, and Lorn MacIntyre, the journalist and author. Its staff has provided two of Argyll's MPs – the Nationalist Iain McCormick and John J. MacKay, who stood first as a Liberal and then won the seat as a Conservative.

In spite of the efforts of the Gaelic department and the local Gaelic Society, which organises the Provincial Mod in the town at the end of May or beginning of June, the proportion of the population speaking the language is declining. In 1931, 30% of the residents were Gaelic-speaking; by 1951 this had fallen to less than 19% and ten years later to 17%. This decline is not helped by the flow of immigrants from south of the border. In 1911, 2.9% of the people in Argyll had been born in England (which does not make them non-Scots, of course); by 1951 this figure had increased to 4.4% and by 1981 to 9%.

Figures from the Highlands and Islands Development Board indicate that between 1971 and 1976 there was a net inflow of 1% per year (3,300 people) into Argyll and Bute. Yet the dilution of the language is not a new phenomenon. It was noted at the end of the eighteenth century: 'On account of their frequent intercourse with the Low Country, they very soon learn the English language, insomuch that most of them speak it tolerably. But it is to be regretted that they adulterate their native forcible language with Anglicisms, which produce a disagreeable medley'. Hopefully, the decline will be arrested, if not reversed, by the growth of Gaelic broadcasting, the emergence of Gaelic folk-rock groups like Run Rig and Capercaille, the establishment of Gaelic playgroups and the encouragement given to the language in schools.

Behind Oban High School, at Mossfield Park, the Argyllshire Highland Gathering takes place on the last Thursday in August. The Highland Games are followed by the Gathering Ball, an event which attracts young aristocrats and gentry from all over the Highlands. Started in the nineteenth century by the Lorn Ossianic Society as an annual exhibition of Celtic sports and handicrafts, Oban Games has become a major event in the West Highlands. The local shinty teams also use Mossfield and occasionally shinty finals are held in the park. Beyond the games field there is a challenging 18-hole golf course.

Parade to the Argyllshire Gathering, 1988.

Glenlonan

The narrow road, which winds up the steep hillside behind the Games field, eventually leads to Connel or, through Glenlonan, to Taynuilt. A couple of miles beyond the golf course the Oban Rare Breeds Farm, recently established by a local vet, has a restaurant with one of the finest views in the district. Its large windows face north-east towards the Cruachan hills and Glen Etive. The park, set in natural birch and rowan woods on the edge of a burn and provided with gravel paths, contains red and roe deer, 12 breeds of sheep, pigs, goats, rabbits and several breeds of cattle, including Longhorn, British White, Highland, Dexter and Belted Galloway.

East of the Rare Breeds Farm there is a junction, where the Glencruitten road joins the route from Kilmore to Connel. About half a mile south of this another narrow road turns off for Glenlonan. As this passes through Strontoiller hill farm and is unfenced, motorists have to drive carefully, especially in the late spring when startled lambs are inclined to run towards any moving object such as car wheels. Just beyond the farm gates there is a tall standing stone, said to mark the spot where Diarmid O'Duine, a legendary Celtic warrior, died after a boar hunt in the ninth century.

Throwing the Hammer, Argyllshire Gathering, Oban 1989.

Ganavan, Dunstaffnage and Connel

Oban is not blessed with good beaches, for the shore is steep and the distance between the sea front and the tide is rarely more than a few metres. However, there is a broad, sandy beach within walking distance of the centre, north of the town at Ganavan, where there is a car park, a pavilion and tearoom, a children's playground and a donkey park. This area can be very busy in summer but, beyond it, a track follows the shore under the cliffs to Dunstaffnage and, as few people seem to venture beyond the Aonadh Mor, it provides a quiet walk with an uninterrupted view of Lismore and the Sound of Mull.

The main road north out of Oban also gives access to Dunstaffnage through Dunbeg. This housing estate was once known as 'Boom Town' because it was originally a settlement for servicemen connected with boom defence and English workers employed in the floating dock anchored in Dunstaffnage Bay during the last war. It is not a very picturesque estate but there are several places of interest in the area. The Marine Research Laboratory, which is linked with Stirling University, overlooks the western shore of the bay.

Biologists here are engaged in monitoring changes in marine life in the deep water of the Rockall trough and in investigating the formation of organic sediments closer to the shore. With the rapid expansion of marine fish farming on the west coast and its unpredictable impact on the environment, the research undertaken by Dunstaffnage is of inestimable value. Yet, since 1979, the station, which is largely funded by the Department of Education and Science, has suffered from increasing financial restrictions, leading to a 28% reduction in staff. To restrict funding, when the marine environment is subject to so many pressures, is surely an act of incredible folly.

Behind the laboratory, the tower of Dunstaffnage Castle rises from trees on the headland. Thought to have been built by Duncan of Lorn, the founder of Ardchattan Priory in the thirteenth century, it was given to Arthur Campbell after the MacDougalls were defeated by Robert the Bruce in the Pass of Brander in 1309. In the fifteenth century it was held by John Stewart of Lorn, who made the mistake of allowing one of his daughters to marry the Duke of Argyll, thereby giving him a claim to the estate. However, John also had a 'natural' son and, in order to protect his claim to the Lordship of Lorn, decided to marry the boy's mother. On the wedding day, as the party crossed the green from the castle to the small chapel, it was attacked and John was mortally wounded. Thinking that he was dead, the assailants withdrew but John was carried to the chapel, the wedding ceremony was completed and his son's claim to the estate assured before he died. The walls of the old chapel can still be seen about 150 metres south-west of the castle, its north wall and magnificent Gothic windows still intact. About thirty years after John's murder James IV came to Dunstaffnage to assert his authority over the western clans, who, he noted, still spoke 'the language of savages'. By this time the Earl of Argyll had gained control of Lorn, eventually installing an hereditary guardian in the castle, known as the 'Captain' of Dunstaffnage, a title which still exists today. Because of its Campbell stewardship it was attacked and taken by Alasdair Colkitto MacDonald during the Civil War but it did not remain in Royalist hands, for, by 1654, it was garrisoned by Government forces. In spite of Colkitto's assault the castle has survived to be held by the twentieth century 'Captains of Dunstaffnage'.

Dunstaffnage Bay provides a superb anchorage and is now crowded with yachts and pleasure craft in all seasons. It contains a marina, which offers boat charters, water-skiing and windsurfing.

The Falls of Lora, which lie beneath Connel Bridge, are formed by a lip of rock left by the edge of a glacier more than 10,000 years ago. In spring tides, when a huge volume of sea water pours over the lip from Loch Etive, the effect can be quite dramatic. Just above the 'falls' the old ferry pier, which was still used this century, reaches into the tide from the south bank. The small village of Connel contains several hotels, an extremely well stocked shop and a railway station, still known as 'Connel Ferry'.

About three miles east of Connel the gardens of Achnacloich estate are open to the public from April to the middle of June. In the early summer the display of azaleas, rhododendrons and huge magnolias is well worth the diversion from the A85, and the walk round the point from the old pier provides some remarkable views across Loch Etive.

Lerags and Kilmore

The main road south of Oban climbs out of the town towards Soroba. Soroba House, which was destroyed by fire in 1981 and subsequently rebuilt, was one of the finest Georgian houses in Oban. Young Lord MacAulay, whose grandfather had been minister of Lismore, stayed there in 1813 and Marie Corelli, the romantic novelist, lived at the lodge in the 1870s, contributing regularly to the *Oban Times*. This local newspaper has a considerable circulation in Canada and Australia, an accomplishment which is largely due to the efforts of Duncan Cameron, its editor in the 1880s, whose fearless support for the crofters against their landlords in the 'Crofters' Wars' won him the respect of the Gaels in the crofting communities. Sadly, his editorial policy was not maintained – indeed, for many years it was reversed – but his successors have benefited from his radical approach.

As the A816 begins to descend again, a road turns west towards Lerags and Kilbride. The ruins of an eighteenth-century chapel west of the junction mark the site of older thirteenth century buildings which gave their name to the Oban parish of Kilmore and Kilbride. The eighteenth century church of Kilbride was completed in 1706, a year before the Act of Union, but had to be restored in 1842. Within the ruins the table tomb of John MacDougall of Lorn (Iain Ciar), whose estate of Dunollie was forfeited in 1715, is covered in moss. Since 1737 successive MacDougall chiefs have been buried in the small graveyard. By the roadside near the chapel a green schist medieval cross bears the legend 'Archibald Campbell of Lerags caused me to be made in the year of Our Lord 1516'. Cast down and broken by the fanatics of the Reformation, it was re-erected in 1926. Archibald Campbell was also the keeper of one of the last crannogs in Argyll being paid for 'keeping the Isle of Loch Nell'.

The lands of Ardoran, on the eastern side of the bay, were given to the O'Conachers, the hereditary 'surgeons' in Lorn in the sixteenth century. John M'Conacher was 'churgeon' here in 1560 and Duncan O'Conchohair, who tutored Angus Beaton of Mull, was given Dunollie Beg in 1612 and, some time later, Ardoran. The John O'Conocher captured in Kerrera by the Marquis of Argyll in 1646 and executed in Inveraray may well have been the last of the Gaelic practitioners in Lorn. Today there is a marine sports centre at Ardoran pier, which offers windsurfing, boat hire and yacht launching facilities.

The walk from Lerags farm over the hill to Gallanach reveals some of the most impressive scenery in the Oban area. In the late spring, when the air is heavy with the scent of whins and the banks are coloured with trefoils, it is difficult to leave the peace of Tom nam Buachaille and return to the town. Standing on the high cliffs on a calm day overlooking the Sound of Kerrera, it seems as if every bank of weed and barnacled rock can be seen through the clear water of the sea below, while, in the west, the blue islands seem to melt in the haze. In spite of its proximity to Oban, few people seem to visit this shore, so its undisturbed beaches provide an abundance of interesting flotsam for aspiring beachcombers.

South of the Lerags junction the A816 descends through the trees to Cleigh or Clyschombie, where a narrow road turns east for Kilmore and Connel. This back road to Connel, which, for a time, follows the shore of Loch Nell, provides a much more interesting route to Oban than the main road. There are several Bronze Age cairns by the roadside at the south end of Loch Nell and one of the best examples of a prehistoric 'snake mound' in Europe. Loch Nell or Loch nan Eala – Loch of the Swans – contains two crannogs, one of which was inhabited till the sixteenth century. Just before the loch, however, a narrow side road turns south for Kilmore and the remote sheep farm of Musdale in Glen Feochan. The old church of Kilmore is now a ruin but, when Mrs. Grant of Laggan arrived to worship there in 1773, there was a substantial congregation. She was fascinated by the costume of the elderly ladies who wore 'gaudy coloured plaids fastened about their breasts with a silver brooch like the full moon in size and shape . . . round their heads is tied the very plain kerchief and on each cheek depends a silver lock'. After the service the entire congregation repaired to a public house for 'refreshments' while waiting for the horses. The fifteenth- or sixteenth-century building was already 'almost ruinous' by then. According to the minister in 1791, the old church was built in 1490 and had been a cathedral – a bishop's seat – during the 'Episcopacy', falling into disrepair before the Reformation. It had been rebuilt but was again 'badly in need of repair'. There were about 700 'souls' in Kilmore, many of whom were forced to seek work in the lowlands as the small farms were taken over by flockmasters as grazing for sheep. It was not, therefore, a wealthy parish and the church was not repaired till 1838, a year after the first great crop failure in the West Highlands, but it was used as the parish church till 1876 when a new place of worship was built at Cleigh. Oban, of course, was in Kilmore parish but it had its own church from 1822. The old building, some of its medieval windows and arches still intact, stands behind the farm house at Kilmore.

South of Kilmore road-end the A816 follows the shore of Loch Feochan to Kilninver and, a couple of miles further on, another minor road turns east, parallel to Glen Feochan, to Loch Scammadale. Here there is a caravan park, which is closed in winter, on the south side of the River Euchar and plenty of camping ground further up the glen. On the hillside opposite the park some green mounds mark the site of the

Sabhal nan Cnamham – the Barn of Bones – where Alexander
Colkitto MacDonald is said to have collected all the Campbells
in the glen into the barn and burned them alive.

Glen Scammadale is a most attractive area, with magnificent
waterfalls and crags above the loch. The road follows the shore
to Bragleenbeg, passing Shellachan and Scammadale farms. In
the eighteenth century Scammadale belonged to Colin
Campbell, who had tacks from the Duke of Argyll for three
farms on the Ross of Mull and whose descendants still live in
the glen at Bragleenmore. The family used to have
Bragleenbeg, a Victorian mansion, part of which has been
converted to holiday flats. Until 1906 it was a modest building
but it was altered and extended substantially to assume its
present character. The road ends at Bragleenmore but the old
drove road, the 'Sreang Lathurnach' or String of Lorn, leads
over the hill to Loch Awe. On this route, near Loch na Sreinge,
Sir Colin Campbell of Lochawe was killed by the MacDougalls
of Lorn in 1294. Sir Colin's son, Neil, was wise enough to
support Robert the Bruce and, as a reward for his fidelity, was
given most of the MacDougall lands. A cairn, Carn Cailean, still
marks the spot where Colin was slain.

Kerrera

The island of Kerrera, which can be reached by a regular
ferry service from Gallanach, provides a fascinating area of
exploration for geologists, naturalists, historians and even
casual visitors. The foundations of the island were laid down
some 400 million years ago, when an accumulation of mud
formed under the primeval water. Over millions of years the
pressure of subsequent sediments and the heat of molten lava
changed the dark mud to slate. On top of this layer red
sandstone was formed as mountains of Lewisian gneiss were
eroded and the sediment settled on the mud. The cliffs of
sandstone and shale at the south end of the island contain
fossils of primitive marine life but also show cracks made by the
sun as the water over the sand evaporated. Clear layers,
showing the strata of slate and red sandstone, can be seen near
Gylen Castle. About 50 million years ago, when the magma of

Oban from S.W.

Oban in the nineteenth century, with steam yachts in the bay.

the earth's core burst through the surface on Mull, fracturing the surrounding rocks and forcing molten lava into the cracks, a layer of basalt, some of it more than 1,000 metres thick, was laid down. Then came the ice, carving its way through the basalt and, with its immeasurable weight, depressing the land. As it departed, the earth, freed of its burden, rose slowly from the sea, leaving marine cliffs and beaches far from the water. Most of the eastern shore of the island consists of such raised beaches.

Kerrera is, on the whole, a fertile island with several good farms. The western shore, facing the Isle of Mull, is quiet and virtually uninhabited. In the eighteenth century cattle from Mull and the remote islands were landed at Barr nam Boc and Ardmore and drove roads from these landing places still provide routes across the island. Until 1824 it was the practice to swim the beasts from the north end of Kerrera to Dunollie. This route, however, passed through some of the best arable land and the drovers were inclined to let the herds stray into the cornfields, so a new route with a ferry was opened from Port Kerrera to Gallanach. This is the regular ferry route today.

The green field south of the ferry is known as Dalrigh – the

Field of the King – and is named after Alexander II, who, in an effort to establish his sovereignty over the Hebrides, had collected his forces and travelled to Oban in the summer of 1249. The King, however, contracted a fever and, after receiving the last rites, died on the island. His body was borne across the sound to Scottish soil, Kerrera being Norwegian territory, and was taken to Melrose.

Fourteen years later a great fleet of 100 Viking ships sailed into Horseshoe Bay. The tall prow of the leading vessel, shaped like a dragon's head, was covered in gold, and rows of shields along the gunwales flashed in the sun. King Hakon of Norway had arrived. Weary of the complaints of his Jarls in the Hebrides about constant raids on their property by the Thane of Ross and other Scots, who not only burned their houses and churches but slaughtered their women and children, Hakon had gathered his forces in Bergen for an assault on the Scots. From Kerrera he sailed south to reclaim Arran, Bute and the Cumbraes. Attempting a landing at Largs, his ships were driven back to sea by a sudden storm before disembarkation was completed and the men on shore were attacked and defeated by the Scots. Dispirited, Hakon turned his fleet for home, lashed by a storm of such ferocity that the sails could not be hoisted. A broken and demoralised force anchored again in Horseshoe Bay, very different from the proud fleet which had sailed from the north a few months previously. On the way back to Norway Hakon, like Alexander II, died of fever, receiving extreme unction in Orkney on Saint Lucia's day 1263. After his retreat the Hebrides were ceded to the King of Scots.

More than four and a half centuries later another ship anchored in the bay, carrying, as a prisoner, a young lady who had assisted Prince Charles Edward Stuart to escape to France after Culloden. Flora MacDonald, described by the captain of the *Furnace* as a 'pretty young Rebell', was taken to Dunstaffnage Castle to await transport south for trial. Horseshoe Bay also provides evidence of a direct trade in tobacco with America by Highland entrepreneurs, for, in 1736, a ship called the *Diamond,* laden with tobacco from Virginia, put in to the Bay to shelter from a storm. Unfortunately her anchor cable parted, she was driven on to a shoal and the precious cargo was wasted. The extent of this trade is difficult to ascertain but a 'General Tobacco Company' was formed in Argyll before 1731, one of the partners being Colin Campbell of Inveresragan near Ardchattan. One of the owners of the *Diamond* and a partner in the trade was an Oban merchant called John Nicolson.

At the south end of the island Gylen Castle stands on the edge of a cliff overlooking the Firth of Lorn. Set in a magnificent position with a clear view of the islands of Seil, Luing and Scarba, it is the most impressive fortification in the Oban area. Built of local stone by Duncan MacDougall of Dunollie in 1582, it is very well preserved, with its windows and huge, arched fireplace still intact. Below the intricately carved oriel window are carved the words – now almost illegible –

> Trust in thy God and sin no more,
> My son, do well and let them say . . .

In 1647 it was attacked by General Leslie and the Covenanting army. Inside was young John MacDougall, who had seen his father and 500 other men cut down after surrendering honourably to Leslie and the Marquis of Argyll at Dunaverty. It must have been with great trepidation that John surrendered Gylen and with great sorrow that he watched it burn. He was spared but he was forced to hand over the Brooch of Lorn and, to secure the safety of the widows and children of the men who had perished at Dunaverty, the Baillieship of Lorn to the Marquis of Argyll. Argyll had already attacked the island the previous year, murdering 14 islanders and carrying off another six to Inveraray to hang them there. The Marquis also burned the land and carried away the 'haill bestial, goods, corne and plenishings' of the islanders. Kerrera, like the castle, was reduced to embers. The island recovered but Gylen, in spite of rescue attempts in the 1850s and during World War I, remains much as Leslie left it.

Near the shore at Slaterach an eighteenth-century mill still stands as a reminder of the acres of corn once grown on the island. All the tenants were obliged to have their corn ground at the mill, which continued to operate till the early nineteenth century, closing shortly after the drastic crop failures of 1836/37. Beyond the mill there is a row of ruined houses known as the Leac, which were abandoned in the 1870s after

A Catalina of 210 Squadron based on Kerrera during the War.

two of the young men were drowned in the Sound. South of
the Leac there are two deep caves in the cliffs of the raised
beach at Rubha na Lice. The walk round this western side of
the island is superb, with constantly changing scenery and an
extraordinary variety of seabirds wheeling round the cliffs.
Seals bask on the rocks and occasionally the almost human cry
of a young seal echoes round the shore.

The north end of the island is busier and more inhabited.
There is a small ship repair yard and a fish farm. On the point
a monument to David Hutcheson, who brought his steamer to
Oban in 1835 to establish the regular service later taken over
by his partner, David MacBrayne, overlooks the narrow
entrance to Oban Bay. During the last war Ardentrive was used
as a base for Sunderland and Catalina flying boats, which were
eventually augmented by a Norwegian squadron of Fokker
T8W seaplanes.

In spite of – or perhaps because of – its proximity to Oban,
the population of the island has declined from 187 in 1841 to
60 in 1951 and to 27 in 1971. Yet it is a beautiful island, not as
green nor as gentle as Lismore, but, with its lava plateaux and
views over the Firth of Lorn, just as impressive.

CHAPTER 3

North and East Mull

Craignure

'It is a detestable island; trackless and repulsive, made without beauty, stormy, rainy and dreary. All this is true of the interior at least; the shores, in several places, afford striking objects.' That was how one jaded traveller saw Mull in 1824 but nothing could be further from the truth. 'Mull of the cool, high bens', with its dark, slender lochs, gentle, open hillsides and infinite variety of colours and shapes, is one of the most fascinating islands on the west coast.

When we first went to live there in 1964, there was no car ferry. Our belongings were shipped from Oban on a converted fishing boat. Today furniture vans can drive on to the *Isle of Mull* in Oban and unload anywhere on the island. The route is so busy in the summer that it is advisable to book with Caledonian MacBrayne well in advance. From the deck of the ferry passengers can obtain an exceptional view of Oban and Dunollie Castle. As it approaches Lismore lighthouse, the outline of Duart Castle can be seen against the hills of Mull. The highest of these is Dun da Ghaoithe (pronounced 'Gu'), the Hill of the Two Winds, on the eastern flank of which a track winds up to the TV mast. The next mountain to the south is Beinn Bhearnach, the Jagged Hill, where the red deer calve in the high corries in early summer. These hills are part of Torosay estate.

Just before Lismore light there is a black rock known as Lady's Rock, where, in the 1520s, Lachlan MacLean of Duart, wishing to marry another woman, chained his wife and left her to drown. But the lady was rescued and Duart was murdered by her brother, Campbell of Cawdor, in 1523. Nearer the shore there is a stone tower erected to commemorate William Black, a Victorian author. As the ferry passes beneath Duart Castle, it is easy to see why the clan chiefs chose the site. It is in a commanding position with a clear view of the Sound of Mull and the Firth of Lorn.

Duart Castle from the Mull ferry.

Duart is the home of the MacLeans. The late Sir Charles MacLean was Chief Scout and Lord Lieutenant of Argyll. His family have been connected with the estate for centuries, the earliest surviving charter to Duart being dated 1396. The MacLean Clan was a rich and powerful dynasty until the end of the seventeenth century. In 1400 Hector MacLean commanded a great fleet of galleys off the Irish coast and defeated the English king; landing his troops, he placed Dublin under tribute and carried fire and sword into the country. Hector also commanded the right wing of the Highland army at Harlaw in 1411, where 900 clansmen, including MacLean, were slain. At Flodden, where the flower of Scottish nobility and between 10,000 and 12,000 Scots were slaughtered by an infinitely superior English army, so many of Lachlan MacLean's islanders died protecting the standard and the body of their chief that the English soldiers encountered a wall of corpses on the hill. Such loyalty was part of the clan tradition. When David Leslie invaded Mull during the Civil War, MacLean of Duart, recognising that resistance would be futile, ordered his people to remain at home. The islanders, obeying their chief, did not take up arms. Leslie's troops swept through the island, committing fearful atrocities. By this time Duart's power and influence had started to decline.

In its ascendancy in the sixteenth century the family held numerous titles to land in Mull, Morvern, Coll, Tiree and Iona. Fortunes began to change in Tudor times when Lachlan Mor MacLean contacted Sir Robert Cecil and offered to help the English Crown quell Tyrone's rebellion in Ireland, raising a vast army in anticipation of the invasion. The army was never used. Instead of leading his men to Ulster, MacLean was killed in a fracas with the MacDonalds in 1598 and the expense of raising and maintaining the army burdened the estate with debt from which it never recovered. In 1674 Campbell of Argyll obtained letters of ejection against Duart for debts (claimed to be fictitious by the family) and was given 500 troops by the Government to enforce the order. With this force and 1,800 of his own men, Argyll invaded Mull, took Duart and Aros castles and turned his troops loose on the countryside. After Argyll's invasion the castle became virtually uninhabitable. In 1692 Sir John MacLean, a leading Scottish Jacobite, surrendered it to Argyll in return for a promise of safe conduct to the Court of King William III, where he acknowledged the new regime. It remained partly ruinous, although occasionally used as a barracks, till 1911 when it was restored by Sir Fitzroy MacLean.

Although difficult to reach, it is well worth a visit. The castle contains a dungeon in which the officers of the Spanish Armada are said to have been confined, and an impressive display of family heirlooms. There is also a small restaurant with home baking.

In the trees north of Duart the roof of Torosay Castle can be seen from the ferry. Built in 1856, its grounds were laid out by Sir Robert Lorimer and the proprietor, W.M. Guthrie, in Italian style in 1899. The statue walk, lined with azaleas, has 19 figures by Antonio Bonazza (1698-1763), originally found near Padua. There is a wild water garden, surrounded by rhododendrons, and a Japanese garden with a small wooden bridge over a quiet pool. Rare shrubs include eucryphia, embothrium and crinodendron. In the summer a miniature railway carries passengers between Craignure and the Castle through masses of rhododendrons.

As the ferry approaches Craignure a rather unattractive holiday development can be seen above the shore on the south side of the bay. On the north side the long, white buildings of the Isle of Mull Hotel have been carefully sited among the pine woods of Java Point to blend with the scenery and give its guests magnificent views down the Sound of Mull to Oban and Beinn Cruachan. The hotel was built by the Highlands and Islands Development Board (HIDB) to provide tourist accommodation and to stimulate the local economy. Although it provided some employment, few of its supplies were purchased on the island and, because local tenants could not be found, the profits did not remain on the island. Nevertheless it provides an excellent service with courteous and considerate staff.

Craignure is not the most picturesque village on Mull and sees very little of the winter sun but, being the focal point of the island as the port of arrival and departure, it does offer some first-class services. Bus tours leave for Tobermory, Iona and Staffa. There is a restaurant near the pier, a garage with a taxi service, a shop, a nine-hole golf course at Scallastle and an inn, which provided the only haven for travellers before the car ferry commenced in 1964 and which has been there for almost 200 years. Before the new pier was built for the car ferry, MacBraynes' steamers anchored in the bay and passengers had to descend through a side door into a small boat tied alongside, occasionally having to time their leaps as the boat heaved in the swell. Having successfully negotiated the transfer, they had to disembark at the old pier and carry their luggage up slimy stone steps. On a wet day the windows of the bus to Iona were often misted over as the sodden passengers steamed in the heat. It could be a hazardous journey. In order to transport a car to Craignure the vehicle had to be slung on to the deck by a derrick from Oban pier and slung off again at Salen, MacBraynes accepting no liability for damage!

There are several walks round Craignure which might be of interest to visitors. One, round the shore of the 'Minister's Point' south of the village, gives a superb view of Morvern and the Sound of Mull. Another, which follows the track up to the TV mast, starts at the road end almost opposite the south gate of Torosay. It climbs up through the oak woods to the open hillside where herds of red deer can often be seen in the Coire nan Dearc. The third, of course, is through Torosay gardens to the castle.

The church of Torosay parish stands on a green south of the inn. Built in 1783, it was thoroughly renovated in 1828 and again in 1832 after being struck by lightning. Craignure at that time was a quieter village as the main route to Oban lay through Achnacraig and Grass Point.

Leaving the village, the A849 to Tobermory, which is a double track road as far as Salen, passes the entrance to the Isle of Mull Hotel and Java Point. When the Isle of Soay was evacuated in 1953, many of the islanders were settled in Java. The 'Queen' of the Soay people lived at the point till recently. Her family and some of the original Soay folk are still there.

There is a splendid row of cypresses near the road north of Scallastle and just beyond Garmony road-end Strathclyde Regional Council has laid out a new football/rugby pitch. Mull has a remarkably good rugby team drawn from the most remote corners of the island. The road to Fishnish and the Lochaline ferry branches off just north of Garmony and, west of the junction, at Bailemeanach, there is a small nature park with a caravan and camp site. Unlike so many of these enterprises, this one is run by Muileachs (islanders). In Fishnish Bay the road passes the site of the fairs, where, three times a year, cattle and sheep used to be auctioned to the drovers. The green land, where these events occurred, is barely discernible from the road but it can be seen beside the cottage.

Salen

As the road winds round the coast, it passes the shelves of a raised beach covered in hazel and oak scrub before arriving at Pennygown chapel. This is an excellent place to stop, with parking space on the old road and an uninterrupted view across the Sound of Mull to the terraced hills of Morvern and north to Ben Hiant and Ardnamurchan. The grounds of the twelfth-century chapel are well kept and can be entered by the old stone stile set in the wall. Inside the chapel, sheltered from the storms which sweep down the Sound, the broken shaft of

an ancient Celtic cross has survived for more than six centuries
and the carvings of a virgin and child, a galley and a griffin
stand out clearly on the schist. Outside the chapel, two old slabs
are thought to mark the grave of one of the MacLean chiefs
and his lady, who, suspected of involvement with the 'black
arts', were denied burial within the walls. Other MacLeans and
MacPhails are buried in the graveyard.

Beyond Pennygown, on the south side of the road, Glenforsa
stretches towards Beinn Talaidh. In the early nineteenth
century 34 families lived in this glen before it was turned into a
single sheep farm and let to an Oban banker, Mr Campbell
Paterson, who, within a few years, had a stock of 20,000 sheep.
Beinn Talaidh was reserved for the wedders, castrated male
sheep kept mainly for their wool and traditionally sold for
killing when three years old. This type of mutton is rarely seen
now but no other meat can rival a gigot of three-year-old
wedder off the high hills.

When Colonel Gardyne bought Glenforsa, the estate was
divided into four 'tenements', the proprietor keeping one of
them in his own hands so that he could pursue his interest in
deer stalking. A witness from Salen complained to the Napier
Commission in 1883 that Gardyne 'would have game and
everything rather than any person in Scotland'. The Colonel
had taken part of the crofters' grazing on Callachally hill to
form a small deer forest, which he stocked with fallow deer in
1868. These timid creatures can still be seen in the woods. The
family also constructed a hydro-electric scheme and provided
electricity to the shepherds in the glen by supplying them with
cases of batteries which could be brought to Callachally for
recharging.

Shortly after the last War the estate was taken over by the
Department of Agriculture and once again run as a single
sheep farm, stretching from Pennygown to Ishriff in
Glenmore. Under the management of Angus MacGillivray it
became one of the most efficient farms on the island in the
1960s. By that time the stock of deer had increased to such a
level that other livestock could not thrive, so contractors were
employed to cull the herds. This was not very popular with
neighbouring landowners but it helped to restore the balance
in the glen. In the Gardynes' time the south-eastern end had

been fenced and cleared of sheep to encourage the deer – a policy which was obviously too successful. The old Rhoail forest fence can still be seen high in the corries.

The estate has been divided into two holdings leased to local men – the former manager's son and a shepherd from Ulva. This initiative was prompted by a controversial HIDB report in 1965 which recommended the creation of family farms on state-owned land in Mull.

It is a magnificent glen, and the ridge walk from Beinn Bhearnach to Beinn Chreagach Mhor is one of the most varied on the island. Watching the sun rise over Morvern from the top of Beinn Bhearnach, with a mantle of glistening, silver webs suspended in the heather, is an unforgettable experience. Winter, however, can be quite severe in the glen. In the winter of 1964/65 we lost scores of sheep when a sudden, prolonged snowstorm drove them into the burnsides and covered them before we could reach the hill. We had to search the white wreaths for the small, grey holes formed on the surface by the heat of the buried animals. In that winter I remember walking daily from Rhoail over the frozen shoulder of Beinn Talaidh to herd the Ishriff sheep, crouching for a few minutes behind a rock at lunchtime, fingers fumbling with the bread paper round the 'pieces' and too numb to whistle at the dogs.

Today there is a forestry road through the glen from Torness which makes a splendid walk for visitors keen to explore the glen.

Just after the road crosses the Forsa river, the entrance to Glenforsa Hotel and the airstrip turns off to the north among the trees. In 1966 the Royal Engineers, as a military exercise, arrived on the beach in a fleet of landing craft and built the airstrip, clearing a conifer plantation and filling in a deep burn. They were able to use the layer of gravel beneath the grass which had been laid down long before the last Ice Age. Until 1979 Loganair provided a regular service from the airstrip to Glasgow and it is still used by private aircraft. Near the runway Glenforsa Hotel, which has been run by the same family for more than twenty years, offers comfortable accommodation in an attractive pine building.

The first village on the road to Tobermory is Salen, where there is a fork for the western side of the island. Established in

1808 by Lachlan MacQuarrie of Ulva, Salen originally had 16 crofts, a blacksmith, a weaver, a tailor, a carpenter and a shoemaker. By 1883 half of the crofts had disappeared and the remaining holdings had been deprived of their hill pasture by Gardyne's deer forest. The village no longer depends on agriculture, relying instead on the tourist trade. It provides sheltered anchorage for yachts and pleasure craft.

North of Salen the road crosses a bridge over the Aros river. In a flat field on the left, just before the bridge, the Mull and Morvern Agricultural Show is held every summer. From all over the island stocksmen and their families converge on Salen for the day to exhibit their livestock, criticise or defend the judging, catch up on the gossip or meet their friends. The day before the show the sheep are washed (occasionally in the family bathroom), trimmed, combed and dried; horns are filed, faces are oiled and brows are clipped in the hope of winning the champion's rosette. The cattle are subjected to the same ritual. Any visitor who wishes to capture the atmosphere of the island community should not miss Salen Show.

The field in which it is held is Dal na Sasunnach (The Field of the Southerner). Apparently an Englishman had settled in Ulva as a shepherd to the famous piper MacArthur. Secretly he copied and practised MacArthur's technique on the pipes until one day, when the master had assembled a great company to hear his own rendering of an unusual and complex pibroch, the Englishman appeared and played the tune with skill and panache. MacArthur was furious and his sons chased the foreigner to Aros, where he was killed on Dal na Sasunnach – a warning, perhaps, to other settlers who might be tempted to beat the Muileachs at their own game and flaunt their superiority!

On the point north of the showground are the ruins of Aros Castle. In 1308 this fortification was in the hands of the MacDougalls but, when 'Lame John' MacDougall took the English side in the Scottish Wars of Independence, Robert the Bruce granted the lands to Angus Og MacDonald. The great string of castles in the Sound of Mull, including Duart, Ardtornish, Aros and Mingary were of vital importance to the seafaring dynasty of the Lords of the Isles and the Council of the Isles met in Aros in 1496. With its ten-foot thick walls and

Felling spruce in Fishnish forest, Mull.

location on a steep rock, it would have been virtually impregnable before siege guns demolished the fortifications. In the early eighteenth century there was a plan to establish a Highland University at Aros but this was abandoned when Prince Charles Edward Stuart landed in 1745. The history of the island might have been very different had the proposal been implemented.

At the bridge the road forks left for Glen Bellart and Dervaig but the main route to Tobermory crosses the bridge and climbs north through a narrow cutting. All roads north of Salen are single-track with passing places. It is quite incredible that, with the vast improvements in ferry services since 1964, the road to Tobermory should remain in virtually the same state as it was in the days of horse carriages. North of the bridge on the left are the main offices of the Forestry Commission on Mull. The mature forests on the hillsides behind the offices were planted before the last war after the Commission bought Lettermore farm in 1930. The major acquisition of land on Mull, however occurred in the 1950s. In 1952, when the Commission held only 6,700 acres on Mull, it employed about 60 people; now, with improved technology, 20 staff look after 15,700 acres.

It is possible to walk through the woods on the east side of Loch Frisa to the Dervaig road.

Unfortunately the loch is scarcely visible through the trees from the eastern track, which ends before the edge of the forest, leaving hikers to scramble through the branches towards the fence. The walk on the western side of the loch is much more satisfactory, giving clear views of Loch Frisa and the Sound of Mull, but, as it passes through Tenga farm, it is advisable to consult the farmer before proceeding, in case he intends to gather sheep on the hill. There are brown trout, salmon and even sea trout in the loch and boats can be hired from Lettermore farm to fish on the four miles of dark water.

At the summit above Aros the A848 gives a splendid view of Ardnamurchan and, far below, the shipping lanes of the Sound of Mull. On the shore below Ardnacross there are the ruins of a broch and, on the steep hill above the road, two standing stones.

Tobermory

As the road climbs the hill behind Ardnacross there are several spectacular views of Ben Hiant and the hills of Morvern. These disappear as the road descends to Tobermory. At Aros Park the Forestry Commission has laid out a car park with picnic tables and several short walks through woods of pine, cypress and rhododendrons. Aros estate once contained more than 16,000 acres and stretched to the Aros river at Salen. The grounds contain a loch edged with water lilies and fed at the north end by a waterfall which pours over the cliffs surrounding the garden. Beneath the fall there is a ruin, which once housed the turbine of a private hydro-electric scheme built to supply Aros House with electric light. The picnic tables at the north end of the loch are located on the site of the mansion house, which was demolished in 1962. Only the walled garden remains to remind us of the multitude of servants once employed there.

On the west side of the main road Linndhu House has been converted to a hotel, which offers fishing and deer stalking. Beyond it, on the same side of the road, there is a group of

Tobermory.

craft workshops built by the HIDB. The premises are let to a silversmith, a potter and a printer, all of them producing goods of exceptional quality. A visit to the complex is well worth while, particularly as it is possible to see the craftsmen at work.

Tobermory is renowned for three things – the Spanish Galleon, a malt whisky and a Womble of Wimbledon Common bearing the same name. It was, however, founded as a fishing village in 1788 by the British Fisheries Society which feued the land from the Duke of Argyll. The main settlement prior to this initiative was a farming community of about 100 people, using what the enlightened landowning class regarded as primitive and unsuitable agricultural techniques. The upper part of the town, in the vicinity of the present Argyll Terrace, was laid out by the society in small plots with houses, gardens and some grazing ground for the cattle. Settlers were offered a loan of £10 towards the cost of a house. The fishing, however, because of its distance from the best fishing grounds and the lack of skill in the settlers, was not a success. The people, nevertheless, were secure as long as their holdings remained in the hands of the Society.

In 1843 the Society sold its lands to David Nairne of

Drumkelbo, Forfarshire, who, at the same time, purchased Aros estate. Immediately the rent of the 120 settlers was increased from between 3s. and 7s. to £1 per acre. Many decided to leave. Nairne's factor also tried to deprive the people of their pasture land but they courageously ignored his instructions and put their cattle on the grazing as usual. Nairne sold the estate after two years and, for a brief period, the settlers had a proprietor who recognised their right to the land and reduced their rents by 20%.

The famine of 1847, however, brought great hardship, as people evicted from neighbouring estates poured into the town. In the first year 96 such refugees settled in Tobermory, in 1849 five families evicted from Ulva arrived in the town and, in 1850, another 13 families followed from the same island. The population increased to 1,750. Between 1846 and 1852 more than 630 summonses of removal were issued to the crofters in the vicinity by the Sheriff Court, many of them for multiple tenancies. 100 of these were obtained by David Nairne.

As the famine subsided, the fishing improved and the Crimean War revived one of the traditional sources of employment for young Highlanders. The new proprietor of Aros from 1856, Farquhar Campbell, like Nairne, tried to deprive the crofters of their grazing round Loch nam Mial behind Linndhu, taking the case to the House of Lords but losing it. The settlers celebrated by marching on to the land, turning a few sods with their spades and sowing some seeds. The supreme court had at last guaranteed their security and the Crofters' Act of 1886 extended this privilege to crofters throughout the Highlands.

The distillery, which can still be seen at the foot of the brae, was built by John Sinclair in 1822, a remarkable local entrepreneur who issued his own bank notes and founded Lochaline village in Morvern. But the distillery closed in 1837, possibly due to the serious crop failure in the West Highlands that year. It reopened in 1878, remaining in production till the Inter-War depression. It opened once again in 1972 but survived for only three years. On that occasion many of the farms, which had been feeding draff (used grain) to their cattle, were left to find an alternative fodder with little warning. The copper stills remain in the building, waiting for the revival of the Scotch whisky industry.

The remains of the Spanish ship scattered on the sands of Tobermory Bay have attracted more attention than any other wreck in the Highlands. The legend of its treasure has absorbed many explorers, including Kings of Scotland and England and Commander 'Buster' Crabbe, who disappeared beneath the Soviet ship *Ordzhonikidze*. The source of the legend was the 7th Earl of Argyll, who, as Admiral of the Western Isles, just happened to have the salvage rights. Apparently, while in Spain, he had been given information by a Lieutenant Pereira which indicated that the wreck was that of the *Admiral of Florence* with '30 million of money' aboard. Unfortunately for Argyll the story not only reached salvage experts but also came to the attention of King James VI and I, who immediately had him declared a rebel so that the rights would revert to the Crown. Charles I, James's son, unable to exploit the privilege, generously sold them back to the 8th Earl! Charles II tried to retrieve them through the courts but they found in favour of Argyll. Charles had him beheaded in 1660. There was a public outcry over the execution and, in an attempt to placate the Scottish nobility, the rights were returned to Argyll's successor. The 9th Earl employed a James Mauld of Melgund to dive for the treasure. Mauld, diving in an inverted bell with only trapped air for an oxygen supply, managed to recover two brass cannon by holding his breath and making quick trips from the bell to fix ropes on the barrels. In 1695 the Earl granted the rights to the Honourable Goodwynn Wharton of Westminster for £600 to retrieve 'such Shipps, Goods, Chattels, Merchandise, Wares, Gunns, Armour, Treasure, Gold, Silver, Jewells and other things'. Wharton recovered some ship's timbers but no treasure. Various cannon, however, and other artefacts were lifted from the sand over the centuries but the '30 million of money' eluded the treasure hunters. The reason for this has only just been discovered. The Tobermory galleon was not a Spanish treasureship after all but a Ragusan carrack, the *San Juan de Sicilia*, hired as a troop carrier to join the Armada. It had a crew of 60 seamen and carried almost 300 soldiers. Putting in to Tobermory in November 1588 for repairs to its sails and rigging, it was engulfed in an explosion while the crew was taking off the powder to dry. It caught fire and sank, creating a legend which ensnared numerous explorers till modern historical research in the Spanish archives revealed the truth.

In 1874 Farquhar Campbell sold Aros estate to Alexander Allan of the Allan Shipping Line. The new owner was a keen supporter of the Temperance movement and built a Temperance Institute in 1882 to lure the working classes away from the hostelries. Aros Hall had a billiard room, a lending library and a reading room in which the citizens could keep up with the latest news, a facility which some of the local lairds may have resented when, in the following year, the crofters' agitation in Skye spread across the Highlands and the Highland Land League was formed. The movement received the full support of the local newspaper, the *Oban Times*, which, under its radical editor, Duncan Cameron, reported the debates and activities of every Land League branch in the West Highlands. The success of the organised political protest against the landlords was partly due to Cameron's reporting of events and, when the British Government responded to the crisis by sending a Royal Commission to the Highlands, the *Oban Times* followed its progress through every township. Ironically the Royal Commission met in Aros Hall in August 1883 to hear the complaints of the crofters and cottars of the north end of Mull. A written statement from 65 merchants, crofters, tenants, mariners and tradesmen was submitted referring to Allan as 'a most kindly, liberal and dutiful landlord'. Other crofters, however, appeared before the Commissioners, accusing Allan of depriving them of their grazing and of improving his own estate while neglecting the crofts. Allan naturally denied this. He was a powerful figure in Tobermory, having been elected the first Provost when the town became a Burgh in 1875 and remaining in that position till 1927. Allan's Aros Hall, just south of the Gallery, is still used for public functions. The position of Provost disappeared with local government reorganisation in 1975, the last person to hold the position being Bobby MacLeod, the Scottish dance band leader and owner of the Mishnish Hotel.

There is a superb walk north of Tobermory towards the lighthouse, passing the Western Isles Hotel. Built by F.W.

Caldwell of Mishnish in 1883 to cater for wealthy Victorian visitors, the hotel stands in a prominent position above the pier. Passing the gates, a path follows the coastline, initially through woodlands and then over open ground with remarkable views of Ardnamurchan. Beyond the lighthouse, which was built in 1857, and enclosed in a crescent of precipitous terraces, the inlet known as Bloody Bay faces Ben Hiant. Here John, the fourth and last Lord of the Isles, described as 'a meek, modest man . . . more fit to be a churchman than to command so many irregular tribes of people', fought a sea battle with his belligerent 'natural' son, Angus Og. Young Angus despised his father for allowing King James III to deprive the family of the Earldom of Ross and, in this great naval engagement involving hundreds of galleys, he defeated him. It is said that the blue water of the bay turned red with blood after the battle. North of the lighthouse, above the cliffs, are the ruins of Rairaig from which nine families were removed to form Erray Farm. The eight tenants of Ardmore on the point above Bloody Bay suffered the same fate. Erray, which is on the edge of the golf course, was, in the last century, let to Mr McKill of Tobermory Distillery, who offended the citizens by erecting gates and notices prohibiting dogs and generally trying to deny them access to the land. Fortunately visitors today can walk freely along the shore.

Tobermory provides one of the most sheltered anchorages on the west coast and, as part of the West Highland Week, the Tobermory Regatta brings yachts from all over Scotland. The town not only offers a golf course but also contains an excellent museum, craft shops, a gallery and a bank, from which that remarkable character, Angus MacIntyre, used to direct the financial affairs of the whole island. The ceilidhs organised by Angus were always successful, with singers like Janet Tandy, fiddlers like Pibroch Mackenzie, accordion players like Calum MacLean and, most popular of all, his own recitations, which are now available in print in the town. The MacIntyre boys obviously inherited some of their father's talent – Lorn as an author, Kenny as a broadcaster, Angus as a professor of Mathematics and Eric as a lecturer in Librarianship.

Glengorm

The B8073 to Dervaig passes the road leading to Glengorm, which provides a most interesting diversion. Just north of the junction there is a thriving dairy farm run by Jeff Reid, who migrated to Mull from Somerset in 1983, bringing with him the basis of his 80 head dairy herd. Until he arrived, Sgriubruadh was a ruin and the fields and fences neglected. The house has been renovated, fences repaired and a byre, barn and milk house built. The farm supplies 90% of the island's fresh milk and makes the splendid Isle of Mull Cheddar Cheese. Some milk is also shipped to Coll and Tiree. Reid's success is encouraging and proves that agricultural decline can be reversed. His enterprise, hard work and stalwart family have transformed Sgriubruadh. As 18 families were cleared from the holding in 1847 to make a farm for a Mrs Petrie of Mull Hotel, it is good to see young people working the land again.

The narrow road winds through heather knolls and green mosses towards the summit above Glengorm, where a path leads up to the radio masts on Meall an Inbhire. From this point there is a spectacular view of the northern coast of Mull and Ardnamurchan.

Near the coast Glengorm Castle overlooks Port Chill Bhraonain. Built by the notorious James Forsyth in 1860, it stands on ground previously held by five crofting families. When Forsyth bought the estate in 1850, 27 tenants were dispossessed in his programme of rationalisation, and another 44 were removed over the next few years. It is said that, when he asked an old woman to think of a name for his new castle, she suggested 'Glengorm' (the Blue Glen). Delighted with the sound of it and not understanding Gaelic, he adopted the title, not realising that the islanders knew that the 'blue' referred to the smoke from the burning roof timbers of the houses of evicted tenants.

The walled garden of Glengorm is thought to have been filled with Irish soil brought over as ballast in trading ships. It is certainly black and very fertile. Just over 20 years ago a small market garden was started here to supply fresh vegetables to the whole island. The enterprise was successful and is still in operation. West of the castle there is a group of standing stones

A signpost near Dervaig.

and two ancient forts, Dun Ara and An Sean Dun. The former can be reached by parking near the home farm and following the estate track to the hay sheds where a path leads north past the standing stones. Dun Ara, held by the MacKinnons in the fifteenth century, controlled the sea between Mull and Mingarry Castle in Ardnamurchan.

Dervaig

Returning to the B8073 below Sgriubruadh, the road to Dervaig winds up a steep hill to Mishnish Lochs. The fishing here is owned by the Tobermory Angling Association and permits can be obtained from Brown's shop in the town. There is a camp site in the grounds of the old Poor House. In a hollow west of the summit there is an artificial loch called Loch an Torr, which contains rainbow and brown trout. Permits for the fishing here can be obtained from the Tackle Shop in Tobermory.

As the road climbs up again from Loch an Torr, it passes the grounds of Achnadrish, where mature larch, spruce and beech trees hang over the verges and provide shelter for the gardens. From the pass above Dervaig there is a splendid view of the Isle of Coll, Loch Cuan and the flat land of Glen Bellart Moss. In the graveyard below the summit one of the stones marks the grave of James Forsyth, the proprietor of Glengorm. Born in Jamaica in 1801, he left his mark in Dervaig as well as in the 'blue glen'. In 1857 he deprived the 27 crofters in Dervaig of grazing for their cattle and horses on the Torr and at Monabeg. By 1883 only 13 of them remained. Seven men left the village to fight with the 79th Regiment in the Crimea and three of them reached India with the 92nd to help quell the Indian Mutiny. In 1883 the villagers possessed 14 war medals, a star and 21 clasps as evidence of their heroism.

Dervaig was founded as a 'planned village' in 1799 by MacLean of Coll, containing 26 houses with gardens and common grazing. In spite of Forsyth's interference, it has survived and now contains a post office, a shop and an hotel. Among the trees at the crossroads the tall, round tower of the parish church has deceived visitors into assuming that it is of Celtic origin. In fact, it was built in 1905. Nevertheless it is most picturesque, particularly when seen as a reflection in the dark water of the Bellart from the south side of the old bridge.

The Mull Little Theatre, claiming to be the smallest theatre in the world, is on the road to Salen. It was founded by two professionals, Barrie and Marianne Hesketh, who had fled from the pressures of southern city life to settle in Mull and run Druimard as a guest house. It was their involvement with a local amateur drama group which rekindled their enthusiasm for theatre but the idea of converting their barn to an auditorium was entirely their own. It was an immediate success, attracting audiences from all over the island with its varied repertoire. It even embarked on tours of Scotland, assisted by the Scottish Arts Council. Tragically, however, Marianne contracted cancer and, having fought the affliction with remarkable courage, was finally forced to abandon her work. Barrie moved away after she died but the company has survived to stage performances through the summer and tour in the winter.

Beyond the theatre, there is a collection of banal 'A' frame chalets, which contrast rather sharply with the soft lines of the landscape. The road to Salen continues through Glen Bellart with a wide moss on the west side and gentle, heather slopes on the east. A building, which I remember as a ruin, has been converted to a country house hotel.

North of Dervaig a track leads to Quinish Point. On the shoreline, near Dun Leatham, there is a fossil tree embedded in the basalt. It is much easier to reach than the one at Burg and is in a better state of preservation. From Quinish it is possible to arrange sea fishing and trips to the Treshnish Islands and Staffa, where the colonies of seabirds and the plateaux of wild flowers, being rarely disturbed, flourish in their isolation.

The B8073 crosses the bridge and, about half a mile beyond it, forks for Torloisk. At the junction there is an extraordinarily tasteless wooden statue in the shape of a 'Highland' warrior pointing to the Old Byre at Torr a Chlachain. The Old Byre contains a good restaurant, which offers home baking, a craft shop and a tableau/video presentation of Highland history, which has won two national awards. Returning to the junction, the main road passes Penmore Mill, which still has its water wheel and which was still grinding corn in 1849. In the late eighteenth and early nineteenth centuries such mills prospered as the small tenants were bound by their leases to have their grain ground in mills controlled by the lairds – a system referred to as 'multure'. Old hand mills or 'querns' were banned and sometimes actually destroyed by the factors so that the landlords could estimate the amount of corn grown on their estates and fix the rents accordingly. Progressive proprietors abolished multures at the end of the eighteenth century and discovered that few tenants returned to the old handmills. In remote areas, however, the system continued into the Victorian age. At the end of the eighteenth century there were eight corn mills in this parish, three of which were 'black' mills with their wheels placed horizontally in a lade running through the house under the floor. These disappeared as the small tenants lost their land and had to rely on imported meal bought with earnings from kelp, seasonal employment on the mainland or labour on the larger farms.

Beyond the mill a narrow road leads north to Croig and the old pier, where cattle used to land from Coll and Tiree before being driven across Mull to Grass Point. A small packet service, carrying mail and passengers, started here as early as 1801. The pier is used now by a local lobster fisherman, whose creels decorate the head of the jetty. Between the black rocks and headlands there is a magnificent view of Ardnamurchan Point. During the 1960s, several artists and craftsmen settled in this area, building or renovating houses on the point, where there is a wide, white beach within walking distance of the pier. Near the main road, the shell of Penmore House stands in the trees. Built by the MacNab family, who still own the burial island in the harbour, it was destroyed by a fire in 1948 in which the proprietress, a Mrs Dudgeon, was killed.

As the B8073 descends to Calgary another road turns off to Calliach Point. The small farms along this route were, like many other holdings on the island, owned by the State and administered as tenant farms by the Department of Agriculture and Fisheries for Scotland (DAFS). They were well-run family holdings and could be held up as examples of successful State ownership. Since 1980 most of the 1,000 units of this kind in Scotland have been sold to the sitting tenants. On one of the farms Thomas Campbell, the author of 'Lord Ullin's Daughter' and later Rector of Glasgow University, tutored the children of the MacLean family; Campbell became Poet Laureate and was buried in Westminster Abbey in 1844.

Calgary Bay, surrounded by steep, terraced hillsides, is sheltered from every wind but the mild westerly and, with its broad, white sands, is the most popular beach on Mull. Calgary House is set in the trees above the bay. In 1870 this estate was purchased by John Munro Mackenzie, who, as factor for James Matheson of Lewis from 1848 to 1854, had been responsible for more than 2,000 evictions. Mackenzie's diary has survived and it is possible to follow every detail of these removals from the issue of the writs to the departure of the people on the emigrant ships. The clearing of the Calgary townships, however, ocurred before Mackenzie's time in 1822. The ruins of two of the four townships can still be seen in the bracken above the old pier. It is often assumed that the town of Calgary in Canada was named by the people who left the bay in 1822; in fact it was christened much later by a Colonel MacLeod, who had visited Calgary House.

As the road climbs up from the bay, there is a superb view of the island of Coll. It is worth stopping briefly in one of the passing places to enjoy the scenery. The terraced hills tower above the road on the east side and the sea breaks over the black lava beds far below. This narrow carriageway, which clings to the precipitous hillside, was built in 1849 by starving people who were forced to work in order to obtain a supply of meal for their families – one of the many 'destitution roads' in the Highlands.

At Ensay a road branches off to Treshnish and the most impressive coastline on the island. At Treshnish itself there is a woodland walk, open to the public between April and October, with a great variety of azaleas and rhododendrons. This is an ancient settlement – a charter of 1390 by Donald, Lord of the Isles, granted the lands of Treshnish, Calgary and the islands to Lachlan MacLean. It is now owned by Lady Jean Rankin, at one time a lady-in-waiting to the Queen Mother. Beyond Treshnish farm there is a road to Haunn, where a group of deserted houses has been fancifully converted to holiday homes. Beyond the holiday houses an old track leads down to the coast, where fulmars glide beneath the cliffs, wheeling round tall stacks, and the swell breaks white over the rocks. In the summer, the sun sets over the Isle of Coll, casting dark shadows over the Treshnish Islands and the hills of Mull.

The most northerly of the Treshnish Islands is Carn a' Burgh Mor, where the ruins of one of the most important castles on the west coast stand above a steep rock face. From this fortress the Lords of the Isles could control the high seas between Ireland and the Hebrides. In 1343 it was granted to 'John de Yle' by King David II along with the castle on the smaller island of Carn a' Burgh Beg. The Lords of the Isles, in turn, placed the twin fortifications in the hands of the MacLeans of Duart. One MacLean of Duart, finding himself heir to the Lochbuie estate, imprisoned the Lochbuie chief on Carn a' Burgh Mor, sending an old woman, MacPhee, to keep him company on the lonely, windswept island and thinking that, even if Lochbuie's solitude led him to lie with her, she was too old to conceive. He was mistaken. The stalwart old lady conceived and bore Lochbuie an heir, a rival to Duart. The enraged MacLean, seeing his inheritance threatened, sent a doctor to kill the child. The old lady, however, had given birth to twins and handed only her daughter to the doctor, who returned to Duart to report that the child was dead. The son, Murachadh Gearr (Dumpy Murdoch) survived to become a protégé of the Earl of Antrim and return to Lochbuie to claim the estate. Carn a' Burgh was last garrisoned during the Civil Wars in 1649.

No-one lives on the Treshnish Islands now. A crofter from Iona sends cattle to the larger islands, some of the bullocks growing so wild and so heavy that they cannot be taken off. Other than that, the land is left to the seals, puffins and eider ducks.

The path along the shore south of Haunn, carved out of a steep rock face, leads to a wide, fertile plateau below Beinn Diull, where, surprisingly, there are no signs of habitation. Beyond this arable ground, there is an easy walk round to the deserted township of Crakaig. Like Bourblaig on Ardnamurchan and Auliston in Morvern, this village is well preserved and provides another poignant reminder of the departed Gaels. There are several caves in the cliffs along the shore, one of which was used to conceal an illicit still. Much of the bere (barley) grown on the rigs round the old townships was used to make whisky; indeed the sale of illicit spirits provided many families with the cash to pay their rent until the Government, determined to stamp out the trade, made the landlords legally responsible for stills discovered on their land. This change in the law in the 1820s could not have come at a more unfortunate time for the Highlanders, who were already suffering from collapsing kelp and cattle markets and contraction of other sources of income such as military service and work on the Caledonian Canal. Some of them, particularly those who lived in remote townships, chose to risk discovery by the 'gaugers' and continued to make whisky in secret caves and crevices. The last family to produce aqua vitae in this area apparently avoided detection by conveying their produce to Ireland.

Treshnish Point near Haunn, with the Treshnish Islands.

Kilninian

From Ensay the main road climbs to the moss near Reudle. Before it descends to Burg there is an amazing view of the island of Staffa and the steep headland of Ardmeanach. Beneath the summit, south-west of Burg at Dun Aisgean, one of the best-preserved Iron Age forts on Mull is within easy reach of the road.

The parish church of Kilninian was built ten years after the Jacobite Rising of 1745 and repaired by the Duke of Argyll in 1775, the seating being made of pine from a shipwreck. A century beforehand the parish had been in the care of John Beaton, the last of the Beatons of Pennycross to practise medicine in the Gaelic tradition. Beaton was deprived of his position after the Revolution of 1690 for supporting the MacLeans and the Episcopal cause against Argyll and turned up in Ireland as 'a poor sojourning clergyman'. A Gaelic scholar, historian, physician and minister, this remarkable islander was responsible for the survival of many Gaelic medical manuscripts. He returned to Mull and died at Torrelock in 1710.

In the grounds of the church there are several eighteenth century gravestones of the MacLeans of Torloisk and a modern monument to the eighteenth MacLean of Ardgour. The medieval slabs have been moved into the building to protect them from the weather. The kirk session very sensibly produces a leaflet on the history of the church, which is left for visitors just inside the door – a practice which ought to be adopted by every parish as a service to strangers.

At the next junction Torloisk House can be seen through the trees north of the road. In 1542 Torloisk was one of the numerous properties granted to Hector MacLean of Duart. The MacLeans of Torloisk, however, seem to have remained there, for, when Hector's son, Lachlan Mor, visited the estate, he seduced one of Torloisk's daughters and left her with child. When her time came, she gave birth to a boy on a bed of straw in the kitchen. Ailean na Sop (Alan of the Straws) was a few years old when his mother married another MacLean, who resented the boy's presence as a constant reminder of her encounter with Lachlan Mor. He tormented and abused Ailean until his mother decided to send him to Ulva to be brought up by the MacQuarrie chief. Eventually Ailean left the island to join a Danish pirate ship and become one of the most notorious raiders in the Western Isles. When he returned to Torloisk, he found that his mother had died in his absence and that his step-father was installed as the chief. The new Torloisk, anxious to get rid of his unwelcome guest, suggested to Ailean that he should dispose of old MacQuarrie and take over Ulva. Initially Ailean agreed but, when he landed on Ulva, the old chief greeted him so kindly that, comparing this generosity with his step-father's cruelty, he returned to Torloisk and killed the latter. Ailean na Sop became MacLean of Torloisk and was buried on Iona in 1551, where his grave can still be seen.

In the 1640s Hector MacLean, who had become a successful businessman and a burgess in Glasgow, bought the Torloisk titles. When David Leslie invaded Mull in 1647, he left Hector to hold Carn a' Burgh for the Estates of Parliament. Torloisk had to garrison the remote island fortress at his own expense and was besieged there a year later by MacLean of Duart. Eventually Parliament granted him a garrison of four officers, a drummer and 30 soldiers – the last company to be stationed on the island. For his trouble poor Torloisk was fined £4,000 Scots for his allegiance to Parliament when the King returned to the throne.

In the nineteenth century the estate became the property of the Marquis of Northampton, one of the Compton family. During the potato famine Earl Compton obtained no less than 60 summonses of removal. Five families (34 people) left for Australia and the parish lost more than 18% of its population. In 1849 there were 260 crofters and 216 cottars in Kilninian parish with a population of almost 4,000. Now there are 11 crofters.

Below Torloisk on the Allt a Mhuilinn (Mill Burn) there is the ruin of an overshot water mill, remarkably well preserved. The great millstones are still there and the bearings for the drive shaft. Inside the building, there is a small threshing mill, which may have been driven off the main shaft in recent years, and also signs of a small hydro-electric scheme.

On the eastern side of Ballygown Bay the remains of a broch, Dun na Gall (Fort of the Strangers), can be seen clearly from the road. Very little is known of the people who built these remarkable towers on the coast of the Highlands and Islands. Even their enemies remain unidentified. The tall, round towers are normally sited near fertile ground on the shore and it is thought that they stored their precious grain within the walls to protect it from marauders.

As the road climbs up to the shoulder of the Bruach Mhor, it crosses a bridge over the Allt an Eas Fors, where a magnificent waterfall cascades over the cliffs to a deep pool below.

Ulva

Beyond Lagganulva a road turns south to Ulva Ferry. Tours to Staffa, fishing trips and the regular ferry to the island of Ulva leave from the pier on the north side of the sound. The ferry house is on the island so the ferry has to be summoned by sliding a board to reveal a large, red panel, which can be seen from the other side.

When Johnson and Boswell visited Ulva in October 1773, the

island was still in the hands of the MacQuarries. The old chief entertained the visitors in what is now the factor's house. A few years later the island was sold to MacDonald of Boisdale – the first time for centuries that it had not been owned by a MacQuarrie. It became a centre of kelp manufacturing, producing an average of 256 tons between 1817 and 1828, 4% of all the kelp in the Highlands. Even when kelp prices collapsed in the 1820s, the islanders continued to send 100 tons annually to Liverpool. It was a laborious process. The seaweed had to be cut on the ebb tide, hauled above high water mark, dried over peat fires in shallow pits and constantly raked. Only the ash was of value, as a chemical in the manufacture of soap and glass. During the French War regular supplies of a cheaper substance, called barilla, were curtailed and the demand for kelp soared. The people of Ulva and their landlord prospered. At the end of the war, however, prices began to fall as barilla once again became available and, as new chemical processes were developed and duties on salt removed, they finally collapsed.

In 1837 there were 116 families (604 people) on the island, including shoemakers, carpenters and tailors. Disaster struck in 1847, when the potato crop failed and kelp became virtually unsaleable. The new proprietor, Francis William Clark, a solicitor from Stirling, decided that the only solution to the appalling destitution lay in a radical reduction in the number of tenants and conversion of part of their grazing to a sheep farm. Through a systematic process of removal he reduced the population from 500 to 150 in 4 years. Seventy-three families were evicted from their homes. Some of them went to Tobermory, some to the Lowlands and six families sailed for Australia with the Highlands and Islands Emigration Society. Ulva is littered with the deserted townships from which these people were removed.

The volcanic terraces, which give the island its distinctive shape, are edged with columnar basalt, like that of Staffa, and floored with fertile plateaux. On the south side, the most dramatic columns, shaped like battlements, are known as 'The Castles' and, near them, in the face of the cliff, there is an immense cave in which the islanders are said to have concealed their cattle when Clark tried to impound them for arrears of rent. On a terrace above Caisteal the ruins of Ormaig mill, with its millstones still intact, stands among the bracken and, further west at Cille Mhic Eoghainn (Kilvickewen), a cross, surrounded by a low, stone wall, marks the burial place of the MacQuarries.

Ulva is perhaps best known for its part in Thomas Campbell's poem, 'Lord Ullin's Daughter':

> A chieftain to the Highlands bound,
> Cried, 'Boatman do not tarry!
> And I'll give thee a silver pound
> To row us o'er the ferry!'
>
> 'Now who be ye, would cross Lochgyle
> This dark and stormy water?'
> 'O, I'm the chief of Ulva's isle,
> And this Lord Ullin's daughter.'

The story ends with the young laird and his lover, fleeing from the wrath of Lord Ullin, meeting their death together in the waters of Lochgyle – presumably Loch na Keal. A melodramatic tale and one which was often chanted in Scottish primary schools.

In 1864 Colonel Gardyne of Glenforsa brought his guest, David Livingstone, the African explorer, to Ulva to see the place where his grandfather lived between 1780 and 1792. David was born in Blantyre in 1813 after the family left Ulva for the south. When Gardyne and Livingstone landed, there were 61 people living on the island and two schools still open. In 1971 there were 23 people and only green mounds marked the site of the schools.

The small island of Gometra is joined to the western end of Ulva by a bridge. In 1837, 26 families (168 people) lived on Gometra and one family on the tiny island of Little Colonsay. When the famine struck ten years later, the island was in the hands of the Misses MacDonald, who employed some of the men in building the causeway. Only four summonses of removal were obtained by these ladies during the crisis – rather a different approach than that of F.W. Clark. In spite of the restraint shown by the MacDonalds, the population had fallen to 23 by 1861.

On the north side of Ulva the roofless houses of 'Starvation Terrace' stand as a stark reminder of Clark's policies. When he cleared part of the island for a sheep farm, some of the victims moved to this area. As the others departed, the Clarks remained, living comfortably in the handsome Georgian mansion built by MacDonald of Staffa about 1790. Parts of the older house, the seat of the MacQuarries, are still used as farm buildings and traces of the old walled garden can still be seen. The MacDonald mansion, however, was destroyed by fire in 1953.

Gruline

Returning to the mainland, the road to Salen passes through Killiechronan estate. The boundaries can be recognised by the signs warning in a distinctly alien manner, 'No Camping for 5 Miles'. However, there is a camping place on the shore near the sandy estuary of the River Ba. The B8073 joins the Salen to Fionnphort road at Gruline. On this estate the mausoleum of Major-General Lachlan MacQuarrie stands in a clearing in the trees beyond what was the home farm. Born in Ulva in 1761, he joined the army and eventually became Governor General of New South Wales between 1810 and 1820. His contribution to the development of the territory was quite remarkable. He started the Colonial Bank and, after a meeting with the Aborigines, opened a school for their children in 1815. His attempts to 'civilise' the indigenous people may be criticised as an assault on their culture but he saw the school as a means of improving their prospects. He established orphanages in Sydney for the 'great number of helpless, illegitimate children' in the city and his determination to rehabilitate and integrate released convicts earned him lasting respect. On Mull he bought Gruline, Salen, Beinn Talaidh and Ishriff and, in 1817, Killiechronan, which he named 'Jarvisfield' after his first wife, Miss Jarvis. MacQuarrie died in 1824, leaving the estate to his son.

East of Gruline, accessible from Knock, lies Loch Ba. Permission to fish on the loch, which offers three miles of excellent sport, can be obtained from Killiechronan estate

The Mull Rally, held every October.

office. There is a right of way on the west side of the glen which forks at Knockantivore, one track leading to a cairn on the summit of Creag Mhic Fhionnlaidh and down to Ardvergnish and the main track following the loch to the head of Glen Cannel where it joins the old drove road over Mam Bhradhedail. Glen Cannel was traditionally the seat of the MacGillivrays until they lost their lands to the Beatons.

At the head of the glen Beinn Chaisgidle is all that remains of a vast volcanic centre, which erupted about 60 million years ago, laying lava beds over 1,800 metres thick. The felsite ring, which crosses the head of Glen Cannel and stretches round Glenforsa to appear again halfway down Loch Ba, may have been formed by gas explosions at the time of the eruptions. The walk up Allt a Choire Bhain to Mam Bhradhedail gives a superb view of the steep scree slopes of Beinn Talaidh and provides access to an easy ridge walk westward to Cruach Choireadail above Glenmore. The soft sedges along the ridge attract herds of deer in the summer and the peat banks round the small lochans are used as rubbing places by the stags.

The mansion house behind Knock farm is the residence of Lord Masserene, who owns most of the land between Loch na

Keal and Glenmore. As a motor racing enthusiast he won the Le Mans Grand Prix in 1937 but as a landowner he opposed the establishment of the Mull Rally in 1969, one of the most successful events on the island. Beyond Knock, the road travels along Loch na Keal with the terraced slopes of Ben More and a raised beach on the left and a shoreline coloured with yellow irises on the right. There are few beaches here but numerous places to stop for a picnic before the Gribun Rocks. South of Derryguaig, the road is carved out of a steep cliff face and needs to be negotiated with great care.

Gribun and Inch Kenneth

Off the shore, beyond the inevitable fish cages, is the small but fertile island of Inch Kenneth. Dean Munro in 1549 described it as 'a fair Ile, fertile and fruitfull, inhabit and manurit, full of cunnings (rabbits) about the shores of it, with a paroch kirk', which at that time, belonged to the Prioress of Iona. The small chapel, the walls of which are still standing, was dedicated to Saint Kenneth, the Abbot of Achabo in Ireland, who was one of Columba's acolytes and who died in 600 AD. When Doctor Johnson visited the island in 1773, he was entertained by Sir Allan MacLean and his two daughters in 'a habitation raised not very far above the ground, but furnished with unexpected neatness and convenience'. The learned doctor found it remarkable that the cottage was floored and 'well lighted'. In the evening Sir Allan told him of his experiences in the American War, while one of the ladies played a harpsichord and Mr Boswell danced a reel with the other. Sadly the cottage was already a ruin when Sir Walter Scott visited the island in 1810 and the next laird, Colonel Robert MacDonald, had to build a new mansion in 1837. In mid-century the island came into the possession of the Clarks of Ulva, who held it till about 1900. The house, however, was destroyed by a fire, apparently started by the shepherd, who had despatched his family across the sound well in advance of the conflagration. The house which exists today and which incorporates part of MacDonald's building can be seen clearly from the road. The flat roof, giving the building a distinctly Art Deco appearance, was included in the design to provide a source of fresh water as the water on the island is excessively alkaline.

In 1933 Sir Harold Boulton, the musician, purchased Inch Kenneth but died just over a year later. When Lord Redesdale (or Freeman-Mitford) bought the estate, he could not have foreseen the tragedies that lay ahead. One of his daughters, Diana Mitford, married Sir Oswald Mosley, who had been one of the leading Labour politicians in 1930 but who had turned to Fascism in his frustration with Ramsay MacDonald's failure to deal with mass unemployment. Another daughter, Unity Valkyrie, travelled to a Nazi summer festival in 1935, addressed the crowd and declared herself to be a 'woman Fascist'. She visited Hitler's mountain chalet at Berchtesgaden frequently and was in Germany when war was declared. Five days later she shot herself and was taken to hospital in Munich with a serious head wound. When she was well enough to travel, she was sent back to England in a special ambulance train arranged by Hitler, reaching London in January 1940. Lady Redesdale tried to take her to Inch Kenneth to recuperate but, because of Unity's connection with the Fascists and because the island was in a restricted area, she was not allowed to return till 1944. It was an unnecessary and callous decision for she was afflicted with severe amnesia and almost an invalid. She did return to Inch Kenneth after the war and died in Oban on 24th May 1948. The island no longer belongs to the Mitfords but is owned by a Mr Barlow.

Beyond Gribun the road climbs up to the pass on the shoulder of Beinn an Lochan. Completed in 1849 as part of the famine relief scheme, it affords some spectacular views of the Treshnish Islands and Loch na Keal. Balmeanach Farm, formerly one of the state-owned holdings on the island, lies in a green, sheltered hollow beneath the road. Behind the farm the terraced mass of Ardmeanach towers over the hostile shoreline of the Wilderness. Set in the precipitous headland, MacKinnon's Cave has drawn visitors to the area since it was described in detail by Doctor Johnson.

There is a legend telling of twelve men who entered the cave with a piper to establish its depth, hoping that the sound of the pipes could be followed by a party on the headland above. The explorers apparently were attacked by a Bean Sith, a faery woman, and slain. The piper's dog is said to have appeared from a cave at Tiroran, bereft of its hair! By a strange coincidence, exactly the same story is told of a cave on the island of Lismore, stretching from Bailegrundle and Creaganaich to Salen. Any one wishing to emulate the intrepid clansmen should remember to approach the cave on the ebb tide and to carry a torch.

The peninsula of Ardmeanach has been in the hands of the National Trust for some time and its remarkable columnar basalt cliffs and fertile terraces provide a sanctuary for numerous seabirds and wild goats. On the shore just north of Allt Airidh nan Chaisteal the fossil of a tall, coniferous tree is embedded in the lava which overwhelmed it millions of years ago. The best way to reach the tree is through Tiroran past the farm of Burg, where leaflets containing information on the area can be obtained.

Kilfinichen

The road between Gribun and Kilfinichen descends by Gleann Seilisdeir through plantations of mature spruce and larch. At Kilfinichen church, which was built in 1804, a road turns sharply westward to Tiroran. The original church, dedicated to Saint Finichen, Abbot of Iona in the tenth century, was about half a mile east of the junction. The road beyond Tiroran deteriorates to a Land-Rover track, so visitors wishing to reach Burg or MacCulloch's tree should leave their cars beside the road. For those interested in archaeology, there is an impressive Iron Age fort at Dun Bhuirg overlooking Loch Scridain and the Ross of Mull.

Returning to Kilfinichen, the main road passes a Post Office and Kilfinichen House and follows the shore below Ben More to Kinloch. Just before the junction with the A849 there is a ford across Loch Beg to Kinloch, which can be crossed at low spring tides, but anyone who attempts it should beware – even the sheep, which come down to the shore to eat seaweed, can be caught by the incoming tide. On the north side of the road Ardvergnish farm house lies at the foot of Ben More, a magnificent hill, the only 'Munro' on Mull, from the summit of which it is possible to see Jura, Skye and even the hills of Ireland.

Glenmore

Turning east at the junction towards Craignure, the new road allows a rapid journey through the desolate hillsides of Glenmore. It passes through scenery in which the volcanic origins of the island are clearly apparent. Massive black rocks seem to burst through the thin mantle of earth and dark cliffs tower above the narrow valley.

As the road ascends towards the summit, the old route can be seen on the north side beside the fence which divides Beinn Buie estate from the lands of Lord Masserene. At the top of the hill there is a splendid view of the 'three lochs' and the pass to Loch Buie. On a ridge south of the road there used to be a colony of white mountain hares, which was almost impossible to find in the snow but which was all too obvious for the rest of the winter. I hope it has survived. At the eastern end of Loch Sguabain there is a man-made island which was apparently the home of a Maclaine of Lochbuie known as Eoghann a Chinn Bhig, Ewen of the Little Head. As the sole heir to Lochbuie estate his insatiable appetite for land led to a battle between his father, the chief, and himself at the head of this glen. Ewen was beheaded by one of his father's men in the battle and his headless corpse, its feet still in the stirrups, was dragged from the field by his horse. In spite of their enmity, old Maclaine was devastated when he heard of his son's death. For many years people in Lochbuie claimed to see a headless rider passing in the night, and the rattle of Ewen's harness was said to predict a calamity for the family. It was after this battle that MacLean of Duart, who had assisted Lochbuie, descended on his castle, captured the chief and had him imprisoned on Carn a Burgh.

As the road bends round towards Beinn Bhearnach, following a sharp bend in the River Lussa, there is a ruin called Torness. This marks the meeting of three estates – Glenforsa

Shearing the Ardura sheep near Kinlochspelve.

on the Beinn Talaidh side, Torosay on Beinn Bhearnach and Lochbuie to the south-east. Below Torness, there is a spectacular salmon pool, where the dark water swirls in a long, narrow channel in the steep rocks. Anyone who is keen to get an impression of the heartland of Mull should stop here to examine the scenery and walk down to the pool on the Lussa. Beyond Torness, the road crosses a cattle grid and enters a forestry plantation, where, once again, the Forestry Commission has succeeded in obscuring the view for a few miles. Emerging from the trees and crossing another cattle grid, the road descends to a junction where there is a monument to Dugald MacPhail, the composer of 'An t'Eilean Muileach', who died in 1887. Few exiles from Mull can remain unmoved when they hear the haunting melody of 'The Isle of Mull'. About half a mile above the monument there is a pool in the river known as 'The Pedlar's Pool', where, on the bank, an iron cross marks the grave of John Jones who died here in April 1891. Apparently the pedlar had contracted smallpox while nursing a family who were suffering from the disease. No-one else in the community would assist the victims so John had courageously stepped in. He died alone and unattended under the oak trees on the banks of the Lussa.

Lochbuie

The road to Lochbuie turns south at MacPhail's monument, leading to the finest and least frequented beaches on Mull. The first farm on the left as the road climbs up through the scrub oak woodlands is Ardura. At a time when sheep farming is in retreat, it is refreshing to see the flocks returning to the hills of Ardura. The new proprietor has built up a stock of 450 ewes and a herd of goats, which can often be seen by the roadside. The road descends again to the shores of Loch Spelve, a sheltered stretch of water almost cut off from the open sea. Golden Sea Produce have a large salmon farm here, producing about 600 tons annually and employing six people. The firm has recently established a second farm on the far side of the loch at Dalnaha, giving work to another couple of men.

At the west end of the loch the settlement of Kinlochspelve lies on a narrow neck of land between Loch Uisg and Loch Spelve. The old church, designed by Thomas Telford, the architect of the Menai and Conway bridges, and completed in 1828, is just beside the road. In 1841 there was a population of 453 in this small parish; by 1902 it had fallen to just over 200, of whom only 83 were communicants. By 1949, after the Second World War, the congregation had fallen to 19 so, three years later, the parish was united with that of Torosay. In 1975 the church was closed and seven years later it was sold.

West of the church the dark water of Loch Uisg can be seen through the trees. Lying on a geological fault running from Craignure to Lochbuie, it is one of the deepest inland lochs in the area. Tench, catfish, gudgeon and black bass were introduced to the loch and seemed to thrive. The road runs along the edge of the loch, passing under tall pines and larches and through a mass of rhododendrons. At the first gate lodge on the left there is a track, which deteriorates as it proceeds but which eventually leads to Laggan beach, a great expanse of grey sand facing south-west.

As the main road swings round into Lochbuie, it emerges from the trees on to open ground and, passing several croft houses, it reaches the shore, where there is a place to camp. Standing in a small valley and sheltered on the north by the steep hills of Ben Buie and Beinn nan Gobhar and on the south by Laggan Deer Forest, it is exposed only to the south-

Moy Castle, Lochbuie.

west. Unfortunately that is the direction of the prevailing wind, so visitors should listen to the weather forecast. Along the shore, south of the end of the road, stands the little church of Saint Kilda. Apparently it was built when Maclaine of Lochbuie had a serious disagreement with the minister of Kinlochspelve over the cleric's habit of herding his ducks on to Loch Uisg and spoiling the fishing. Incorporated in the wall of the building there is a stone carved with an ancient Celtic cross, which was unearthed when the foundations were laid. In spite of the sea air, the interior of Saint Kilda's is warm, dry and extraordinarily tranquil on a stormy day.

Further along the shore towards Laggan the fifteenth-century Maclaine stronghold of Moy Castle stands above a strip of sand which was cleared of rocks to allow access from the sea. When Doctor Johnson visited Lochbuie in 1773, he met the chief of the clan and described him as 'a true Highland laird, rough and haughty and tenacious of his dignity; who, hearing my name, inquired whether I was one of the Johnston's of Glencoe or of Ardnamurchan'. He added that 'Lochbuy has, like other insular Chieftains, quitted the castle that sheltered his ancestors and lives near it in a mansion not very spacious or splendid'. Maclaine had vacated the castle in 1752 to live in the new mansion but this was also abandoned in favour of another house in 1793, which is incorporated in the present building north of the castle.

The Maclaines of Lochbuie, like the MacLeans of Duart, were once a powerful family, holding lands in Lochaber, Morvern, Glencoe and Jura in the fifteenth century. Most of the lands were lost by 1707, only Lochbuie remaining in Maclaine hands. The last Maclaine to hold the estate toured Britain and America before the First World War singing in concerts in Gaelic and English. Young Kenneth won a Military Cross at Ypres but, unable to maintain regular mortgage payments after the war, was forced to sell the lands which had been held by the Maclaines for at least four centuries. It is now owned by John Corbett, who runs it as a farming and sporting estate.

On the shore, under the steep hills of Laggan, there is an old chapel called Cailbeal Mheamhair (Chapel of Remembrance) which fell into disuse in 1701 but was restored in 1864, becoming a mausoleum for the Maclaines. It contains a medieval font carved from Carsaig stone. The hills behind are part of Laggan Deer Forest, cleared of sheep in 1888 and developed with new blood from Black Mount, Ashridge and Vanol Deer Parks. It is a wild and beautiful peninsula, rarely disturbed by visitors.

Where the road ends in Lochbuie, there is a farm on the side of Ben Buie owned by George Sassoon, the son of one of the finest British war poets, Siegfried Sassoon.

Before leaving Lochbuie, it is worth crossing the flat ground north of Lochbuie House to see the circle of standing stones. It is the only ring of stones on Mull and is best approached from the bridge near the crofts. Returning to Kinlochspelve church, a road leads down the west side of the loch to Croggan. The old pier, where MacBraynes' steamers used to call to collect cattle and sheep, is set in the narrow stretch of water which connects Loch Spelve with the sea. The road ends just beyond the pier but there is a track leading to a quiet beach near Porterfield with a splendid view of Kerrera and the hills of Lorn.

Achnacraig

The A849 leaves the MacPhail monument and passes Ardchoil farm and, on the left, the old Beinn Bhearnach sheep fank. Just after it turns north at the forestry plantation, an old track leads over the hill to the settlement of Gualachuolish. Near these ruins are the remains of the fourteenth-century chapel of Saint John. When Doctor Garnett visited this area in 1798 there were 20 or 30 'miserable huts', being, in his view, 'extremely poor indeed, being little, if at all better than the cabins of the South Sea Islanders or the wigwams of the American Indians'; with wicker doors and narrow windows, the buildings which he described were indeed extremely primitive. No-one lives there now. Lichen covers the walls and sheep shelter in the doorways.

At Lochdonhead, a road turns south, following the old drovers' way to Grasspoint. Before sheep replaced cattle as the major source of income on Mull, the ferry from Grasspoint provided transport to Kerrera for the great herds of black cattle which converged on Lochdon from all over the island and from Tiree, Coll and Iona. Around 2,000 cast cows and stirks were shipped across the Sound every year from Grasspoint. The old pier is used occasionally by lobster boats and pleasure trips from Oban. On a fine day it is an excellent place for a picnic with beautiful views back to the 'cool, high bens' of Mull and across the Sound to Beinn Cruachan and Loch Linnhe. It is usually a peaceful place with the silence broken only by the cries of seabirds or the cough of a seal.

Lochdonhead is a crofting township with cottages scattered round the crescent of a sheltered bay. The Church at the junction was built in 1852 for the Free Church congregation. When the Free Church was formed in 1843, the people of Lochdon became adherents of the new faith. Their landlord,

The old pier at Grasspoint.

Campbell of Possil, refused to grant them a site for a church, so they met in a tent in a gravel pit near the bridge. When the famine occurred, Campbell provided work for them, building the road to Ardchoirk, but also evicted those whom he considered to be helplessly impoverished. So straitened were the villagers that, when Campbell's son offered them a site, they could not raise the money for their church. The new proprietor and his sister generously contributed to the fund and the church was built. A hundred years ago there were 22 crofts and 69 people in the community, including two teachers, a blacksmith and a mason. Now there are seven crofters in the two parishes of Torosay and Pennygown and the population of Torosay parish has fallen from 1,616 in 1841 to 583 in 1981. Several new houses have been built recently, however, and the village benefits from the increase in tourist traffic.

CHAPTER 4

The Ross of Mull and Iona

Pennyghael

West of the junction at Kinloch, the long peninsula that stretches towards Iona is known as the Ross of Mull. Beyond Kinloch, where the road crosses the River Leidle by an old, humpbacked bridge, the hamlet of Pennyghael stretches along the shore. A road turns south at Kinloch Lodge for Carsaig, giving remarkable views of Colonsay and Jura as it descends towards the sea on the other side. Passing Inniemore Lodge, which has been run as a painting school by Julia Wroughton since 1966, the road ends at the old pier. From here there is a path leading east to Lochbuie and a track, heading west, follows the shore below the arable land. Enclosed in a great amphitheatre facing the sea, Carsaig is remarkably sheltered from the cold north winds and contains some of the most fertile land in Argyll, enriched by the ancient chalk sediments laid down before the lava sheets. The flat lava beds on the shore below the western headland contain a rich variety of fossils. The walk along this shore is one of the most dramatic on the Ross, passing beneath towering cliffs and steep terraces. Wild goats, which sometimes can be smelt before they can be seen, graze along the narrow ledges.

There is a cave under the cliffs called the Nun's Cave. Ancient crosses are carved on its walls, some of them said to be from the sixth century and, among the modern graffiti, the date 1633. The cave is thought to have provided shelter for the nuns of Iona, fleeing from the presbyterian fanatics of the Reformation. There is a quarry nearby from which the stones were hewn to build Iona Abbey and which was used again for the same purpose in 1974. Carsaig Arches, at Malcolm's Point, are extraordinary phenomena and well worth the long walk from Carsaig. These huge arches, carved by the waves before the departing ice allowed the land to rise from the sea, are set in narrow 'dykes' from which the surrounding rock has been eroded. The successive layers of lava are clearly visible in the stacks.

Above the cliffs, the soft grasses, washed with salt spray from the winter storms, provide unusually rich grazing and a mass of small wild flowers in the spring. In a southerly gale the wind seems to lift above the cliffs, leaving a sheltered strip along the edge. Binnein Ghorrie or Gorrie's Leap is the name given to one of the headlands beyond the Arches. John Gorrie apparently was a clansman of Maclaine of Lochbuie who inadvertently allowed some deer to pass him during a tinchel, or deer drive, for the chief. The infuriated laird had him castrated. When he recovered from the barbaric punishment, Gorrie kidnapped Lochbuie's son and carried him to the cliff. When the chief and his followers approached, Gorrie threatened to jump with the child unless Lochbuie subjected himself to the same form of mutilation. The chief pretended to have his men conduct the operation but Gorrie was able to discover the deception by asking Lochbuie where he felt the pain. He knew from his own experience that the seat of the agony was not in the wound and, when the chief replied incorrectly, Gorrie jumped with the heir.

Returning to Pennyghael, the main road passes the old Free Church, north of which a cairn and cross commemorate the 'Mull Physicians', the Beatons of Pennycross. This remarkable family of medical practitioners, who came originally from France with the name 'de Bethune', had branches throughout the Highlands and Islands. They became physicians to the Lords of the Isles and later to the Kings of Scotland, appearing on the Crown payrolls of every monarch from Robert I to Charles I. On the cross appear the initials GMB above the date 1582, while below the date are the letters DMB, probably standing for Gille-Coluim (Malcolm) MacBeatha and Domhall MacBeatha. Malcolm was personal physician to Lachlan MacLean of Duart in 1593 and was probably the Doctor Beaton, 'the famous physician from Mull', who was sitting on the upper deck of the Spanish ship in Tobermory when the explosion occurred in 1588, surviving 'by admirable providence'. The lands of Pennycross seem to have been reserved for these physicians, the first writ recording the grant of Pennycross to Malcolm's father 'together with the supreme and principall office of surgeon'. The last of the family to receive the classical medical training was John Beaton, who is buried on Iona and whose grave slab reads: 'Here lies John Beaton, physician to the family of the MacLeans, who died on 19 November 1657, aged 63. Donald Beaton made me 1674'. The Beatons remained in Pennycross till 1732. Medical science in their time was somewhat primitive. Cures for epilepsy included eating ravens' eggs or wolf's flesh or drinking warm water flavoured with spiders or dogs' excrement! The Beatons' techniques, however, were as advanced as any in Europe and their fund of knowledge extensive, with Gaelic copies of the latest European theses on their shelves. They were renowned for their skill in 'cutting stones' (lithotomy) and for their knowledge of herbal cures. Their herb garden at Pennycross was still visible in the nineteenth century.

The road passes several sheep farms and, as it approaches the crofting community round Bunessan, the Treshnish Islands and Staffa appear behind the steep headland of Burg. Just past Ormsaig, there is a cairn on the south side of the road built as a memorial to Mary MacDonald who, in the early nineteenth century, composed the Gaelic hymn translated as 'Child in the Manger'. Its melody was used in recent years by Cat Stevens in the song 'Morning has broken'. North of the road the peninsula of Ardtun stretches towards the islands. The crofts scattered over the headland are the remains of a settlement established by the Duke of Argyll in 1800 as part of his scheme to encourage small tenants.

When the potato crop failed and the prices for black cattle collapsed, Argyll responded by offering assisted passages to Canada and by providing meal in return for work on roads, drainage schemes and piers.

By March 1847 the estate had the names of 778 individuals from the Ross (30% of the population) intending to leave for Canada. It is not clear how many left the area that year but half of those who did cross the ocean died of fever in Canada. As the famine continued, another 260 sailed on the *Charlotte* and *Barlow* in 1849 and at least 140 more over the next two years – another 23% of the population. Had the departure of the emigrants led to improvement in the condition of those who remained, the removals could be defended, but the vacant land was rarely given to the landless and was normally added to the larger farms.

On the point of Ardtun the lava beds contain the fossil outlines of hazel and oak leaves which fell over 50 million years ago. These beds were first described by the Duke of Argyll in a learned journal in 1851 and have suffered from the perpetual attention of geologists and souvenir hunters since then.

West of Bunessan Primary School, where the local Agricultural Show is held every August, a road leads south to Scoor. No visitor to the Ross should miss this area. Passing the Glebe croft and a long row of sloe bushes, the road forks near Loch Assapol. The farm road to the right leads to Saorphin, where, just behind the farm house, there are the remains of yet another deserted settlement. One of the larger buildings is said to have been a school. Thirteen families (64 people) lived here in 1841. By 1861 only 29 people remained. Now there is only one family on the farm. Behind the house there is a path leading to Uisken, which passes one of the many standing stones in the area, and, on the shore, two remote but beautiful bays.

The road on the east side of the loch passes the old manse, which has been converted from a croft house to a guest house. At the far end of the loch the ruins of the ancient parish church of Kilvickeon stand in the arable land beside the Cnoc Mor. According to legend, the stones for the chapel were passed from hand to hand in a human chain from the shore to the building site. The white sands of the magnificent beaches below the graveyard contain so much phosphate and calcium that, in the 1960s, local crofters were able to obtain the Government fertiliser subsidy when it was applied to the fields. One of the bays is called Port Bheathain. Here the MacPhees of Colonsay, attempting a raid on Shiaba, were defeated by MacLean of Duart, many of them losing their fingers when the MacLeans hacked at their hands as they tried to climb aboard the galleys.

At the end of the road Scoor farmhouse (and the surrounding arable fields) is all that remains of a substantial sheep farm which stretched from Loch Assapol almost to the Carsaig Arches. It was sold to the Forestry Commission about twenty years ago and the hill pasture has been planted. By following a track north of the house past the old sheep fank it is possible to reach Shiaba. Standing on a headland overlooking the sea and the distant hills of Jura, the empty doorways and roofless walls of this deserted township are more evocative of the sorrow of the departed inhabitants than any other ruins in Mull. In 1847 the nine families, containing more than a hundred people, were issued with notices of removal. They were not in arrears, they had received no aid from the estate during the previous winter and they were in no sense a burden on the parish. Some of the people were moved to the holdings of those who had emigrated earlier that year. Others chose to emigrate and the fate of those who sailed to Canada is, unfortunately, all too clear.

One of the emigrants, Archie MacGillivray, who settled in King, Upper Canada, wrote to his nephew, John MacLean in Shiaba. 'I am sorry to say that a great number of them [the emigrants] suffered after arrival at Toronto . . . on the first night 13 – on the second 8 – were seized with cholera; in all 48 were sent to hospital'. The condition of the islanders stirred the compassion of the people of Hamilton, who raised £150 to send them to Fergus, 45 miles away. They travelled in wagons and one of the drivers reported that three of his passengers died on the way, 'their bodies thrown into holes by the wayside'. Those who survived the ordeal settled in the Fergus district.

There are some older houses above the cliffs east of the main settlement. Standing in a row above the Eas Dubh, they are gradually disappearing in a sea of conifers. It is extraordinary that so much is done to preserve the historic buildings of the rich and powerful while these humble memorials to the ordinary people are left to decay or to be swallowed in forests. Shiaba is a beautiful place and, when the summer sun rises over Carsaig arches, catching the hills of Jura in its first light or when the moon, rising over the sea, casts shadows in the ruins, it is almost unsurpassable.

Bunessan village faces north into Loch na Lathaich. In the middle of the bay there is a small island called Eilean Ban, where, according to legend, a Celtic hero called Fraoch was killed. Apparently the young man, who lived at Suidhe west of Bunessan, fell in love with Main, the daughter of Mev, who lived at Larach Tigh Meidhe near Ardfenaig. Mev was not happy about the relationship and set out to destroy her daughter's suitor. Falling ill, she asked him to gather some healing berries from the island, knowing that the tree was guarded by a sea monster. In spite of the danger, Fraoch reached the island and managed to collect some berries without disturbing the creature. Disappointed, Mev sent him back to get the tree. On his second visit he was caught by the monster and slain. Versions of this Celtic tale appear in other districts, one referring to an island in Loch Awe.

In the middle of the village, beside the hotel, a road climbs up the hill past the Baptist Church towards the sands of Ardalanish and Uisken. At the top of the hill it passes the shell of a former smithy, said to have been the first house in the district with gables. South of the bleak moss below Knocknafenaig a side road turns west to Ardalanish farm, where there is a wide, sandy beach below the fields. The main road continues to Uisken, which has been a fishing station for centuries and is still used as a base for salmon and lobster fishing.

Returning to Bunessan, the main road to Fionnphort leads west past the village hall and the pier. The landscape alters quite dramatically here as the underlying rock structure changes from schist to granite. The first indication of this is the remarkable drystone granite wall at Tirghoil. It is almost tall enough to conceal a huge standing stone in one of the fields. Apparently these stones used to form a line within sight of each other along the Ross but some were torn up and the largest, 'An Caitcheannach Mor', was split up by the local quarrymen in 1864. The pink granite of the Ross has been extracted commercially on several occasions and in several locations. The nearest one to Tirghoil is in a bay north of Ardfenaig known as Camas Tuath and provided stone for the lighthouses of Skerryvore and Ardnamurchan in the 1840s.

Ardfenaig was the home of the infamous 'Factor Mor', John Campbell, who was responsible for numerous evictions on the Ross of Mull and whose death in 1872 was celebrated by bonfires in the exile settlements in Canada. Twenty years ago young children in Bunessan were still hurried to their beds by the cry, 'Quick! Up to bed! The Factor Mor is coming!' Whether the man deserves to be remembered as an ogre is debatable but he set out to intimidate the small tenants and must have known that his acts of oppression would be recalled by their descendants. He despised them and told his master, the Duke, that a stern approach was necessary to force them to work: '. . . nothing but harshness and dread I find will do, they are so naturally slothful and indolent . . .'.

The first settlement after Ardfenaig is Criech, where a road turns north past the old schoolhouse to Kintra, where in 1785 the Duke of Argyll established the first fishing village on Mull. It was not a success, and now most of the houses are holiday homes and the old pier is rarely used.

The main road passes Loch Poit na h-I, where, it is said, the monks of Iona used to fish for trout. Just beyond Achaban, formerly the Free Church manse, travellers can catch their first glimpse of Iona, the squat tower of the Abbey scarcely visible against the hill of Dun I. The car ferry leaves from Fionnphort, where there is a restaurant, a shop and a copious car park. The latter is a vital facility as only residents of Iona are permitted to take their vehicles on to the island. From Fionnphort a narrow road leads south to Fidden farm and the island of Erraid. Strictly speaking, Erraid is not an island, as the narrow strait, which divides it from the Fidden shore, is left dry on the ebb of spring tides and it is possible to wade across below Knockvologan at neaps. The row of dressed granite houses on Erraid was built for the workers who constructed Skerryvore and Dhuheartach lighthouses between 1867 and 1872 and to accommodate the keepers and their families. The engineer for Skerryvore was R.L. Stevenson's father and the author apparently stayed in one of the old cottages behind the row of houses. In *Kidnapped* David Balfour is shipwrecked on the island, remaining there for some days before discovering that it is a tidal island. Recently the houses have been taken over by some families connected with the Findhorn community who are making full use of the fertile walled gardens. There is excellent sea fishing round the reefs and one of the best piers on the west coast. Seals and otters can be seen in the Sound.

North of Fionnphort a track leads to the old granite quarry. From here and from Torr Mor, south-east of Loch Poit na h-I, granite was exported to Glasgow, London and America. The Albert Memorial in London contains Mull granite and the massive blocks of circular stone supporting Blackfriars Bridge were quarried at Torr Mor. The Catchean quarry was opened in 1868, in a short time doubling the population of the surrounding settlement, the men working in the quarry for 75p to £1 per week. Unfortunately the stone was not suitable for kerbstones or 'setts' and the quarry, therefore, unable to benefit from the extensive municipal improvements at the end of the century, had to close.

Fionnphort itself is an attractive village, surrounded by huge outcrops of pink granite and dark, heather knolls.

Iona

So many books have been written about Iona that further comment seems almost superfluous. Yet, because the island and its community have had such an effect on my life and that of many others, I cannot resist the temptation to offer my own perspective and reminiscences, hoping that they will be of interest.

When I first saw the island from the deck of the *King George V*, the most elegant of MacBraynes' fleet, I was struck by the brilliant white sands, set between green machair banks and the clear, turquoise sea. The ship anchored in the Sound and the passengers were taken ashore in the smaller, red boats. When we landed, tractors with trailers, a taxi and an old, green lorry arrived to carry luggage to the different places of accommodation. There was no car ferry in 1959 and, when the steamer left and the tractors departed to the crofts, the road was almost deserted. It is the peace that I remember and the sense of being enveloped in a different tide of history, less violent perhaps than the storms which swept across Europe and the rest of Scotland but equally implacable and somehow more significant. It is not the ancient Celtic crosses nor the medieval ruins which create the extraordinary atmosphere of antiquity but it is the landscape itself, which seems to resonate still to the primeval forces that created the island. The rocks, formed deep in the earth's core more than 700 million years ago, seem to be still rising from the crust, caught for a moment in our era in a state of suspended activity and waiting only for our

The *King George V* leaves Oban, September 1974.

extinction to continue their transformation.

Doctor Johnson said of the island, 'That man is little to be envied whose patriotism would not gain force upon the plain of Marathon or whose piety would not grow warmer among the ruins of Iona'. Yet it is not the Abbey nor the Nunnery which make Iona such a remarkable place but the colours, contours and context of the island itself and, most of all, its community. After all, there were people there when the fiery Irish prince, Columba, landed in 563 AD with his twelve companions to establish a Christian enclave, and the islanders remained when the Benedictine cathedral lay in ruins after the Reformation. Their story has yet to be told.

Columba was born at Gartan in Donegal in 521 AD, the descendant of the Irish king, Neil of the Nine Hostages. A scholar and a warrior priest, he founded the religious centres of Kells and Durraw in Ireland, only to become involved in a bloody conflict with the King when he broke one of the sacred rules of the Irish church by copying an invaluable manuscript without permission. Thousands were killed in the battle of Cuil-Dremhne and he was forced to leave his native country, sailing from Donegal with his companions in a skin and hazel currach to land in a bay at the south end of Iona, still called 'Port na Curaich'. Here they buried the boat and set off for the uninhabited part of the island, building their cells round Tor Abb, west of the present abbey. From this small settlement Christian missionaries were eventually despatched to the rest of Scotland and parts of England. Iona became the centre of Christianity in Scotland and a respected seat of learning. A vast library of intricately illustrated and illuminated manuscripts, such as the Book of Kells in Dublin, was gradually compiled as the monks laboriously copied existing texts or created their own.

For two centuries this remote settlement influenced the development of Christianity in Scotland and Ireland. In the eighth century, however, the Viking longships, with their tall, carved prows and striped sails, swept down the west coast. The Norse raiders descended on Iona three times between 795 and 806 AD, carrying off corn, cattle and women from the farming settlements and silver chalices, gold caskets and illuminated manuscripts in jewelled binding from the monastery. On the last occasion 68 monks were slaughtered on the sands of Martyrs' Bay. Fortunately many of the manuscripts were concealed from the raiders and sent to Ireland.

By this time the monks had been forced to abandon many of their Celtic traditions. Until the Synod of Whitby in 664 the Columban settlement had cherished its independence, having scant regard for the authority of Rome and refusing to practise celibacy. At that convention, however, a critic of the Celtic autonomy had asked their spokesman, 'Even if your fathers were true saints, surely a small company on a corner of a remote island is not to be preferred to the Universal Church of Christ?' The Columbans had lost the argument but, returning to their remote sanctuary, retained some of their old ways until 717 when King Nectan of Scotland banished any clergy refusing to conform to the edicts of Rome. By 767 AD Iona had capitulated. Yet signs of the old church lingered on in its title of 'Cenn na Cele De' – Chief of the Culdees. With increasing Norman influence affecting the rest of Scotland and a Papal Bull of 1188 bringing Scotland firmly under Roman control, Iona's traditions were doomed. Although there was a brief revival of Celtic art and sculpture under the Lords of the Isles, Iona became a centre for the Benedictine order. When the elegant cathedral was built on the instructions of Reanald, son

Iona Abbey in 1811.

of Somerled, in 1203, it was for the Black Friars. Within 200
years, however, it was in a serious state of decay and had to be
restored. This fifteenth-century renovation forms the core of
the present abbey and many of its sculptured details are
associated with the mason, Donald O'Brolchan. When the
Lordship of the Isles collapsed a few decades after the
renovation and the last Abbot, John MacKinnon, died in 1499,
the vacant position being absorbed into the Bishopric of the
Isles, the remaining shreds of its independence disappeared.
Its lands on Mull, the rents of which had formed the bulk of its
income, were given to MacLean of Duart.

By 1561 Iona was seen to be so close to the central authority
of Rome that religious fanatics destroyed the abbey and any
signs of 'idolatrie'. 360 Celtic crosses were broken or cast into
the sea. In 1567, when John Carswell of Carnasserie became
Superintendent of the Isles and therefore Abbot of Iona, he set
out to plant his diocese with ministers of the 'true religion'. By
1573 reformed services were being conducted on Iona by his
representative, Fingan MacMullen. In 1609 nine of the most
powerful Hebridean chiefs met in Iona to submit to the
authority of the reformed church. The Statutes of Iona, to
which they agreed, bound them to pay the salaries of approved
ministers, repair the churches and enforce religious discipline

on their estates. Subsequent legislation also contained a frontal assault on Gaelic culture. The eldest sons of the chiefs and tacksmen had to be educated in English in the Lowlands. The bards were threatened with confinement in the stocks and banishment, if they persisted with their craft. The 'unChristian language' of the islands had to be suppressed. Iona, which had been the centre of the Celtic church, thus lent its name to a series of statutes which set out to destroy Celtic traditions. From 1609 the significance of the island diminished and only the ruins of the cathedral remained as a testament to its former status.

Columba is said to have written:

> In Iona of my heart, Iona of my love,
> Instead of monks' voices will be heard the lowing of cattle,
> But, before the world ends,
> Iona shall be as it was.

In 1938 the parish minister of Govan, the Rev. George MacLeod who, like Columba, had been a soldier and had himself been awarded a Military Cross in the First World War, revived the Celtic tradition of worker priests, gathering a small group of ministers, divinity students and unemployed artisans to rebuild the cathedral. His experience among the unemployed in Govan had convinced him that the Church should be involved in every aspect of society – spiritual, social and political – and that ministers should sample the fatigue of physical labour. 'Work is worship' became one of the principle themes of the Iona Community. Members had to spend some time each summer working with the craftsmen on the restoration and, after their initiation of a summer on Iona, had to work in industrial parishes or the mission fields. This concept attracted a group of dedicated pioneers. MacLeod, personally assuming responsibility for fund-raising, succeeded in raising money from the most unlikely sources, including a wealthy shipping magnate. Building continued through the Second World War, the roof of the refectory being constructed of timber washed ashore on Mull. By 1959, the refectory, the chapter house and the workmen's quarters had been completed. Most of the men were from Mull or Iona and

Dr George MacLeod outside the Abbey on Iona.

therefore were native Gaelic speakers. One was a piper,
another a Gaelic singer and composer and another an
accordion player. They were part of the island community.
The rebuilding is almost complete now and these remarkable
characters have departed, but the work of the community
continues among the poor and disadvantaged and MacLeod's
commitment to peace and justice is being carried forward into
the new century.

The abbey is open to the public and, just off the cloisters,
there is a bookshop which also sells cards and souvenirs. The
foundations of the Columban settlement and the pathway to
the graveyard – the Street of the Dead – have been exposed by
archaeologists and a collection of medieval burial slabs have
been housed in the Michael Chapel. In the centre of the
cloisters there is a bronze statue by Jacob Lipschitz, copies of
which were placed in the Owenite community at New

Sacristy doorway, Iona Abbey.

Harmony, Indiana, and another at La Rochelle in France. Entitled 'The Descent of the Spirit', it depicts a descending dove, holding in its beak, in the shape of an inverted heart, the gathered corners of the universe, in which the figure of Mary is enclosed. The inscription reads, 'I, a Jew faithful to the Faith of my Fathers, have made this Virgin for goodwill among men, that the Spirit may reign'. Lipschitz had fled from four countries to escape persecution. The abbey is still used for daily services and every visitor, even unshakeable atheists, should try to attend one of them. On a summer evening, when the setting sun casts a thin beam of amber light through the shadows of the nave from the western door to the chancel, setting the plain, silver cross ablaze and the cadences of ancient Celtic hymns echo round the medieval pillars, it is not difficult to imagine the Columban monks, weary after a day's toil, their bald heads shaven from ear to ear, burnt with the sun, singing their thanksgiving in the same manner.

Outside the west door there are two ornate Celtic crosses and a small chapel, in which two stone cists are concealed beneath the floor. South of the abbey Saint Oran's chapel stands in the ancient burial ground called the Reilig Oran, which is said to contain the graves of 48 Kings of Scotland, including Kenneth MacAlpin and MacBeth, four Kings of Ireland and eight Kings of Norway. The chapel, now completely restored, was probably built in the eleventh century, although the arched doorway, distinctly Norman in character, was obviously added later. A legend connected with the construction of the original chapel is designed to show the superstitious nature of the early Church. Apparently, every time the walls of the chapel were completed, they collapsed and the community decided that a human sacrifice was the only way to placate the evil spirit which impeded the work. Oran volunteered and was buried alive. After three days Columba, anxious to see the face of his friend for the last time, had some of the earth removed. Oran, having survived the ordeal, smiled and commenced to recount his experience, claiming that he had been to hell and found it to be nothing like the frightful place portrayed by the Church. Shocked by his blasphemy and concerned for the authority of the Church. Columba ordered the monks to cover Oran's face with earth and fill in the grave again. The story bears the stamp of a Reformation zealot, attempting to discredit the Celtic church.

The new MacLeod Centre is carefully concealed in the hills west of the abbey. When it was decided to build the new centre for youth, the community ran a competition to find the best design. The result is a singularly unimpressive piece of architecture, its redeeming feature being the light and space within.

The Nunnery is located in the village, well away from the monastery, following the Columban belief that women caused conflict. Columba is said to have banished the women to Eilean Nam Ban on the Fionnphort side of the Sound, declaring that '. . . where there is a woman there is mischief'. Like the abbey, the Nunnery was a Benedictine foundation, built by Ranald of the Isles, and most of it has survived remarkably well. Within the walls, the gardens are kept in good order by the National Trust – a transformation from the 1920s, when the building was used as a shelter for cattle and one visitor, searching for the tomb of the last Prioress, had to remove layers of cattle dung to expose the effigy. Agnes or Anna MacLean died in 1543 and the tomb, decorated with unusual symbols such as a comb and a mirror, has been restored.

The village, at the head of the pier, contains two exceedingly well stocked shops, a post office, a hotel and a restaurant, which offers home-baked bread and the finest view in North Argyll. When Thomas Pennant visited Iona in 1772, the village consisted of 'about fifty houses, mostly very mean, thatched with straw of bear (barley) pulled up by the roots and bound tight on the roof with ropes made of heath'. He was not describing the present village as it was in 1772 but a much more scattered settlement of croft and cottar houses with a population of 250. A few years later the Duke of Argyll decided to reorganise the farms on the island, an initiative which laid the foundations of the present village. The middle of the island, known as the West End, was laid out in 30 crofts and the village reserved for non-agricultural tenants. New houses, without gables but with thatched hip roofs, were built between 1802 and 1804. The island, apart from the Church land and the crofts which have been purchased by the tenants, is now held on behalf of the nation by the National Trust, having been sold by the Duke in 1980.

The east side of Iona contains the places of historical interest and the tourist facilities but, away from the crowds, on the west side and at the far ends of the island visitors will discover the real character and extraordinary beauty of Icolumkill. It is only a mile to the west side, where the wide beach faces the Atlantic swell and, on the horizon, the island of Tiree. There are two routes to the west, which join again halfway across. One leads south from the shops past the war memorial and the old Free Church towards Sligneach. Across the croft land south of Sligneach there is a superb beach, sheltered from the prevailing wind, and, some distance beyond it, the old marble quarry. Believed to have been worked intermittently since medieval times, it was last reopened in 1906 by a Swedish company, which exported much of the elegant white and green marble to the continent but, although it was subsequently taken over by the London-based Iona Marbles Ltd., it was forced to close in 1914. Some of the machinery, including a gas engine and a cutting frame, still lies rusting in the quarry and small pieces of marble are scattered round the site. At the extreme south end of the island it is possible to find polished pebbles of clear, green serpentine in Columba's Bay or Port na Curaich. It is said that these small stones will protect travellers who carry them from drowning. For rock-climbing enthusiasts there are some splendid climbs along the shore with sheer drops into the sea.

The road west of Sligneach climbs up to the junction, where it is joined by the second route from the village. The latter leaves from the Nunnery, passing the library, which was opened in 1904 and where the islanders used to gather in the winter to see films shown by the travelling cinema.

After the junction, the road leads to the machair, a wide expanse of soft, green sward, dusted with the sand from the shore and clinging precariously to its sandy bed. At one time the machair was cultivated and the long ridges can be seen clearly in a winter's evening running towards the sea. In summer the ridges are sprinkled with the small yellow flowers of birds' foot trefoil and the banks hung with wild thyme. In 1886 a golf course was constructed here and enthusiasts still use the greens. In the rocks at the south end of the machair there is a submarine cave with a small outlet in its roof, through which, at a certain height of tide and in a swell, the sea is driven with such force that a tall jet of water shoots into the air high above the rocks. In the right conditions it is an amazing sight. North of the machair there are several beautiful bays with headlands where the gulls nest among the thrift and seals swirl in the surf.

From the village the road to the north end passes the parish church and manse, designed by Thomas Telford and completed in 1828. Just beyond the church, there is a tall, narrow building, which used to contain a printing press. The Iona Press, founded by William Muir, the retired manager of the Torr Mor granite quarry, and John MacCormick, the eldest son of the quarry foreman, survived till the 1920s, producing books of rhymes, proverbs and prayers with hand-painted illustrations. *Blessing of the Ship* is said to have sold 400 copies. MacCormick's son became a lawyer and a founder member of the Scottish National Party in 1928. His grand-nephew, Iain MacCormick, displaced Michael Noble as M.P. for Argyll and Ian's brother, Neil, is Regius Professor of Public Law in Edinburgh University. The building has been converted recently into a bookshop, containing a fascinating collection of new and second-hand publications.

At the north end, below Dun I, the only real hill on Iona, there is another stretch of machair and some white beaches among the dunes. Visitors who choose to remain on the island for a few days should try to climb Dun I at sunset or at dawn. When the sun rises over Mull and the whole island beneath the summit is hidden in a mist stained red with the first light, that is the time to stand by the cairn on Dun I.

From Iona tours to Staffa can be arranged with local boatmen; indeed, it is possible to book a day trip to Iona and Staffa from Oban with lunch at Martyrs' Bay restaurant. Most people associate Staffa with Fingal's Cave and Mendelssohn's overture but there is more to the island than the caves. Eider duck nest there in the spring and puffins flit across the cliffs. The land above the rocks provides grazing for cattle from Iona and a nesting place for a multitude of seabirds. The geological structure of the island is certainly remarkable with tall columns of black basalt supporting a cushion of conglomerate. When Queen Victoria visited Fingal's Cave in 1847 she described it vividly in her journal:

> . . . the effect was splendid, like a great entrance into a vaulted hall; it looked almost awful as we entered and the barge heaved up and down on the swell of the sea. It is very high, but not longer than 227 feet and narrower than I expected, being only 40 feet wide. The sea is immensely deep in the cave. The rocks, under water, were all colours – pink, blue and green – which had a most beautiful and varied effect.

A mid-nineteenth-century view of Staffa.

The Queen did not land but the Prince Consort spent three quarters of an hour on the island, examining the other extraordinary rock formations. The Clamshell, in which the columns are curved like the ribs of a ship, is 130 feet deep and the Buchaille forms a strange, twisted stack offshore. The landing places have all been improved since Victoria's visit and it is possible to land on most occasions.

Few people leave Iona without regret. It is an island which seems to infect visitors with an irresistible urge to return. It seduces the romantic, impresses the prosaic and captures the contemplative. I can never leave it without looking back and remembering the lines of an emigrant lament, written by Donald Morrison, about another island:

> O's laidir na bannan 'tha'm tharruing a null
> Gu Eilean Beag Donn Mhicleoid;
> Gu'n stiuiruin gun solus do d'chala mo long
> Nuair ruigeas mi ceann mo lo.

> O strong are the cords that are drawing me over
> To the little brown island of MacLeod;
> I would steer my boat in the dark to your harbour
> When my end is drawing nigh.

CHAPTER 5

Lochgilphead, South and West Lorn

Auchindrain

The A83 from Inveraray to Lochgilphead follows the shore of Loch Fyne to Dalchenna, then climbs slowly through mature conifer plantations to Kilian. Beside Douglas Water the ruin of a spinning mill, which was built in 1776 and had a workforce large enough to warrant its own school at Bridge of Douglas, stands in the trees. On the headland below the mill lies the old settlement of Kenmore, the birthplace of the poet Evan MacColl. He published 'The Mountain Minstrel' in 1836 and, two years later, 'Clarsach Nam Beann'. It is astonishing that Evan managed to produce any verse in Gaelic, for, in his schooldays, a boy caught speaking a word of his native tongue could be forced to 'mount the back of some one of his sturdier schoolmates and then, moving in a circuit round the master, tawse in hand, get his hips soundly thrashed . . .'. Another punishment forced the offender to wear the skull of a dead horse round his neck. Nevertheless, according to Hugh Miller, 'in point, glitter and polish, he is the Moore of Highland song'. MacColl's family emigrated to Canada in 1831 and, eight years later, he moved to Liverpool to work as a Customs clerk, following his parents across the Atlantic in 1850.

As the road descends towards Furnace there is a collection of low, thatched buildings forming Auchindrain Folk Museum. Inspired by two eminent Scottish historians, Marion Campbell of Kilberry and the late Eric Cregeen, and using the old township as the basis of reconstruction, a team of enthusiasts set out to create a simulation of Highland life as it was in the eighteenth and nineteenth centuries. Old implements have been collected and located to show how they were used. Buildings have been restored and furnished to reproduce the atmosphere of the original interiors. The visitor centre provides a profusion of information, a comprehensive selection of books on the Highlands and a tearoom. Unfortunately the museum is not open in the winter and, even in the summer, access is limited to the hours between 10 a.m. and 5 p.m.

Opposite Auchindrain there is a public footpath over the hill to Loch Awe, following the old drove road across Leacann Muir to Braevallich. According to local tradition, the last wolf in Argyll was killed near the Leacann burn by a woman returning from Loch Awe, who, having been attacked by the animal, stabbed it with her spindle before she died. This route was used by caravans of pack horses in the eighteenth century, carrying huge bags of charcoal from the woods of Loch Awe to the iron works at Furnace. Another much longer track leads past Brenchoille along the side of Beinn Laoigh to Kilneuair chapel near Ford, passing close to the old copper mine on Creag an Iubhar.

Furnace

The village of Furnace, as the name suggests, developed round the iron works, which were established there in 1754 by Duddon of Furness. An integrated plant using English ore, it contained a blast furnace, a forge and a casting bay but, unlike the company at Taynuilt, it did not survive and closed in 1813. The blast furnace, which once produced about 700 tons of pig iron annually, has remained relatively intact and can be found just behind the village. The huge granite quarry beyond it exploits an isolated plug of granite forming the headland of Dun Leacain. In the 1870s 100 men were employed here on three great faces bearing the romantic names of Colorado, Bulgaria and Klondyke. The heavy work affected the health of the quarrymen and many of them died prematurely to be buried in Killevin cemetery. At that time much of the granite was shipped to the Clyde to pave the cobbled streets of Glasgow. Today only a dozen men are employed in the quarry and the stone is used mainly for road metal.

From Furnace the road follows the shore towards Minard. Near the old quarry pier at Crarae there is a fish farm and visitor centre, offering diving, boat hire, fishing, seafood and refreshments. Beyond this lies the small settlement of Cumlodden, named after Cumloden in Dumfriesshire by John

Tait, who owned the estate of Crarae between 1799 and 1825. South of Cumlodden, on the west side of the road, is the finest woodland garden in this part of Argyll. Crarae Glen Garden is said by one expert to resemble a Himalayan ravine and, with its magnificent collection of conifers, rhododendrons and maples, it is difficult to believe that it is located in Argyll. In the early summer there is an astonishing variety of colours with delicate, pale azaleas and scarlet rhododendrons beneath tall, green pines and emerald acers. In the autumn the display is equally amazing, as the leaves of the trees change colour, with golden Himalayan birches and scarlet Japanese maples among the evergreen conifers. There are twenty species of eucalyptus and the largest collection of acers in the country. An elegant silver fir (abies grandis), planted in 1908, is now more than 100 feet high with a girth of 13 feet. There are beautiful magnolias, a wine-red disanthus cercidifolius and a bronze cornus kousa. There are also some extremely rare shrubs such as a detonsum from a Chinese island and an azalea nipponicum – both said to be the only examples in Europe. The whole garden is well laid out with paths, seats and bridges, from which visitors can obtain exceptional views of the river as it flows between banks ablaze with colour in the deep shade of tall conifers.

The road south passes through the village of Minard, a small settlement on the shore of Loch Fyne, and climbs away from the waterside through conifer plantations to a plateau below Creag Fheargach. In the woods below the road the nineteenth-century castle of Minard stands on a headland above Minard Bay. Just north of the castle, in Brainport Bay, there is an extraordinary formation of mounds and rock thought to be a prehistoric astronomical observatory and, among the trees nearby, a sheet of rock from which quern (handmill) stones have clearly been quarried.

As the road descends to sea level again, it skirts Loch Gair, one of the safest and most picturesque anchorages in Loch Fyne. Almost surrounded by deciduous woodlands, it is exposed only to the east. Asknish House, a Georgian mansion at the north end of the loch, was built by one of the Campbells shortly after 1745, when the previous owners of the estate were dispossessed for their Jacobite sympathies in the Rising. When he constructed his new mansion, however, Campbell decided not to remove the unusual seventeenth-century sundial and it can still be seen in the garden. Standing almost nine feet high and dated 1695, this strange, slender obelisk was erected in memory of the original owner, Duncan Campbell of Achnabreck, and his wife, Henrietta Lindsay.

Lochgilphead

South-west of Port Ann, the estate of Castleton and Silvercraigs lies on a headland between the road and the sea. In 1862 William Smith of Silvercraig Lodge formed the Castleton and Silvercraig Mining Company and started to mine zinc and copper on the estate. Traces of his operations can still be found behind Lingerton Lodge, although the company folded in 1865. A second attempt to extract the minerals was made in 1911, when, after gold deposits were discovered on the far side of the loch, the Shirvan Mining Company sank a 90-foot shaft near Smith's excavations. The seam proved to be fruitless and was abandoned in 1912. No-one struck gold (or copper), except the local contractor, John Carmichael, who had been handsomely paid for sinking the shaft.

Lochgilphead is the administrative centre of Argyll, containing the headquarters of Argyll and Bute District Council and the district offices of Strathclyde Regional Council. Until 1975 the administration of local government was the responsibility of Argyll County Council with various burgh councils organising services in the larger towns. Under the Local Government (Scotland) Act of 1973 Argyll and Bute became a District of Strathclyde Region, by far the largest of Scotland's nine regions, containing almost half the nation's population and based in Glasgow. The District Council offices are in Kilmory Castle on the north side of the road just beyond Castleton. This nineteenth-century Gothic mansion was built by Sir John Orde, an eccentric and rather unpopular laird, who, having provoked the wrath of the Lochgilphead people when his carriage ran over a child, built a causeway across the loch to avoid the village. Eventually he was forced to breach the embankment to give the Lochgilphead boatmen access to the sea but the remains of the structure can still be seen at low tide and the curious building known as the Clock Tower, which stands on the roadside near Kilmory gates, was the gate lodge at the end of the causeway. Orde's unorthodox approach to farming led him to import cattle from India and cross them with Highland and Ayrshire stock. Apparently they thrived in Argyll and their humps were regarded as a great delicacy.

Until recently Lochgilphead was a market town with regular sheep and cattle sales but, with improved access to Stirling and the south, the market declined and finally closed. It was still a 'small village' when Queen Victoria landed there in 1847 but, after her Highland tour, the London travel agents promoted trips following the 'Royal Route' and, by 1858, 44,000 passengers were passing through the nearby Crinan Canal every year. Lochgilphead began to grow, the population reaching 1,670 by 1861. It is now a major tourist centre with hotels, shops and an excellent sports centre near the secondary school. It also contains a hospital and Argyll's main centre for the treatment of psychiatric and psychological disorders. Alcoholism is a major but carefully concealed problem in many Highland communities and the tragic consequences of the traditional reverence of the 'dram' have to be dealt with by the staff of the Argyll and Bute hospital. The whispered statement 'He's in Lochgilphead' usually means that a person is receiving treatment for alcohol abuse. Fortunately the town has other assets which are more obvious to visitors. It is close to the Crinan Canal and an area of Argyll that is littered with prehistoric remains.

The proposal to join Loch Gilp and Loch Crinan by a canal was first considered in the late eighteenth century when James Watt surveyed the ground in 1771, but the Crinan Canal Act was not passed till 1793 after the British government declared war on France. At that time, before the age of steamships, vessels sailing from the Clyde to the Western Isles had to tack round the Mull of Kintyre, a tedious and sometimes treacherous passage. A direct route promised to facilitate the movement of goods between Glasgow and the west and also increase the speed with which the Navy could respond to emergencies on the west coast. The canal was opened in 1801 but had to be virtually rebuilt 16 years later to Thomas

The Crinan Canal.

Telford's specifications. These repairs were so costly that the Government had to provide the additional £18,000 and eventually had to take over the canal completely. In spite of its difficulties, the waterway survived and is used regularly today by fishing boats and pleasure craft. The A816 west of Lochgilphead gives a splendid view of the long section between Ardrishaig and the Cairnbaan locks. As the canal is slightly above the level of the road, it often seems as if the yachts are sailing through the fields.

At Cairnbaan a road forks west to cross the canal and follow its embankment to Crinan. This is a beautiful drive with views across the canal to the great moss of Moine Mhor. The first settlement on this side of the water is Bellanoch, which curves round a calm, wide basin in the canal. The old inn at Bellanoch was the scene of an extraordinary affray during the Great Famine in 1848, when, in one of the very few examples of resistance to eviction in Argyll, nearly 200 people marched on the inn to attack the police and release five of their comrades who had been arrested.

Beyond Bellanoch the road becomes very narrow as it approaches Crinan. The old harbour south of the Crinan Basin is most attractive and can be reached by turning off the main road just before it climbs over the hill to Crinan. Sheltered from the south-west by the steep, wooded headland of Ardnoe Point, it is an excellent place for a picnic. In the trees beside the road a tall, brick chimney stands above the ruins of what was once a 'vinegar' factory. Built about 1824, it was designed to extract acid from oak and birch wood for preserving herring and bacon. Beyond it there is a car park and a jetty with a multitude of moorings for pleasure craft.

The road down to Crinan Basin passes a small boatyard, which repairs yachts, fishing boats and even some ferries. There is a superb view across the loch to Duntrune Castle and westward to the islands of Jura and Scarba. In the deep water of the canal basin yachts and fishing boats gather to wait for access to the locks. The pier on the far side was built as a berth for larger ships to collect passengers bound for Oban and the Western Isles who had travelled from Ardrishaig by canal boat. The basin, surrounded by whitewashed buildings and green lawns, is a most picturesque setting for the western entrance to the canal. On a summer day, with the sound of halyards snapping against the masts, and the lapping of waves against the hulls, it is quite idyllic.

Returning to Bellanoch, it is possible to reach the A816 to Oban by crossing Islandadd Bridge and following the straight road across the Moine Mhor. Standing on a promontory in the west is Duntrune Castle, a Campbell stronghold until 1792 when the laird, having lost money in the Ayr Bank failure, sold it to Neill Malcolm of Poltalloch. It has remained in Malcolm hands since the purchase and is still the principal residence of the family. Its foundations were laid in the thirteenth century but most of the present building, with its tower and crowstepped gables, was constructed in the sixteenth century. Besieged but not overwhelmed by Colkitto MacDonald in 1644, it has survived to become a comfortable home. The majestic stags on the gateposts originally adorned the gates of Poltalloch House, which was the family seat until the Malcolms moved to Duntrune after the Second World War. West of the castle a track leads to Ardifuir, once the refuge of Sir Ian MacGregor who prepared the British Steel Corporation and the National Coal Board for privatisation. Beyond the house, near the old sheep fank, there are the remains of a galleried 'dun' or fort with an intramural staircase. Constructed between the last few centuries BC and the first century AD, it was excavated in 1904, yielding a wide range of artefacts, including a bronze ring, a polished stone axe and a stone mould. The remains of another Iron Age fort can be seen in the heather on the shoulder of the hill. To the south the point shelters one of the most beautiful bays in the district.

On the northern edge of the Moine Mhor the sinister shell of Poltalloch House stands in the trees above a wide meadow. Built in 1849 for Neill Malcolm of Poltalloch, this immense mansion was the centre of a vast estate which stretched 'as far as 40 miles in one continuous line'. Designed by William Burn in neo-Jacobean style with trefoiled gables flanked by elegant pinnacles, it contained 15 bed and dressing rooms, 6 bathrooms, a pipe organ and a balcony for a piper. Even as a shell, it is a splendid piece of architecture. Trees grow inside the walls now and debris covers the mosaic floors, which were once brushed by the hems of Victorian dresses. Nevertheless, it is still worth a visit, if only to gain an impression of the power of the landed gentry in the nineteenth century. The roof was removed in 1960 after the Malcolms moved to Duntrune. Beside the mansion the family built their own Episcopal chapel just outside the gates. The Church of Saint Columba, as it is called, is open to the public and has several Celtic crosses in its grounds, including the slender Cross of Argyll, which was carved in 1355 and which, like the others, was transferred to the chapel from other parts of the estate.

On the eastern edge of the Moine Mhor a solitary mound of rock rises from the moss. When the Scots landed in Argyll in the sixth century, bringing their language, religion and Celtic traditions, they chose this rock as the centre of their kingdom, which they called Dalriada after their lands in Ireland. King Fergus, landing with his brothers Loarn and Angus, built his fort on the summit of the rock and set out to establish his authority over the Pictish inhabitants. The Scots eventually ruled virtually unchallenged in Argyll until the eighth century, when, according to the Annals of Ulster, 'Aengus, son of Fergus, king of Picts, laid waste the territory of Dalriata and seized Dun At and burned Creic and bound in chains the two sons of Selbach'. This is thought to have taken place in 736. However, the Annals also refer to an earlier siege of Dun At in 683 but few details of that conflict have survived. In spite of the invasion, the Scots remained in the area and, mingling with the Picts, provided the first King of Scots and Picts, Ardrigh Albainn, Kenneth son of Alpin.

The foundations of Dunadd can still be seen on top of the rock and, near the summit, three symbols are cut in the stone – the outline of a boar, the clear shape of a foot and a circular bowl. The boar, although the emblem of the royal line of Scots, is actually of Pictish origin, but the foot was probably used as part of the Dalriadan coronation ceremony, the new king having to place his foot in the imprint. It is said that Fergus brought with him the carved marble Stone of Destiny, the 'Lia Faill', on which the kings of Ireland were crowned. It was eventually taken to Dunstaffnage, near Oban, and then to Scone, where it was appropriated by Edward I and taken to England. However, the sandstone block, which rested in Westminster Abbey, bore no resemblance to the stone described in the chronicles.

In the area round Dunadd there are numerous prehistoric stones, many of them bearing the distinctive 'cup and ring' markings of British petroglyphs. Most of the carvings are thought to be more than 5,500 years old. There is a splendid collection at Achnabreck near Lochgilphead, first described in 1864 by Sir James Simpson, Queen Victoria's Scottish physician and the first surgeon to use chloroform as an anaesthetic. There is another collection near Cairnbaan, but the most accessible are the slabs at Kilmichael Glassary. In this quiet village there is also an ancient graveyard and a small church, completed in 1827 but almost entirely rebuilt in 1873.

The Neolithic people who settled on the edges of the Moine Mhor about 5,000 years ago were farmers with primitive tools and domesticated animals. They were able to weave cloth and make pottery vessels. They cleared the woodlands with their stone axes and grubbed corn seed into the ground with digging sticks. When their relatives died, they were buried in stone cists formed by great slabs of rock and held in place by piles of stones. Examples of these burial chambers can be seen at Nether Largie on the east side of the road from Slockavullin to the A816. The site is well laid out and placards containing a wealth of information have been provided beside the remains. The most remarkable of these Neolithic sites is at Temple Wood, on the west side of the road, where a ring of 22 short standing stones is set in a vast mound of small stones. Shaded by oak and rowan trees, the clearing is coloured with a mass of bluebells in the spring. Just to the north-east of this circle there is an older ring, originally made of timber, which is thought to be the earliest in Scotland and which has been marked out by short concrete pillars. All these sites are supplied with information placards, which help to place the remains in context and bring them to life by describing the people who built them.

Kilmartin

Kilmartin is a small village on the road north to Oban. In the churchyard, opposite the first row of houses, there is a rare collection of medieval burial slabs and crosses, including a ninth-century standing cross. A covered mausoleum, dedicated to Neil Campbell who was Bishop of the Isles from 1580 to 1608 and minister of Kilmartin, shelters more than a score of medieval slabs decorated with Celtic designs. Unlike the sites at Largie, these interesting examples of the school of sculptors which flourished in Argyll in the fifteenth century, are not supplied with explanatory placards. The church itself is not of great antiquity, being completed in 1835 just before the Disruption. Behind the hotel, however, there are the remains of a sixteenth-century castle with shot holes in the walls and iron grilles in the windows. It was built by John Carswell, who, like Neil Campbell, was minister of Kilmartin and 'superintendent' of the Isles, a euphemism in the Reformed Presbyterian Church for Bishop.

Carswell, the representative of the Reformed Church in Argyll, zealously embarked on a campaign to revive religious worship in the west and to plant a loyal minister in every parish. He is particularly remembered for his 'Foirm na n-Urrnuidheadh', a Gaelic translation of the Book of Common Order published in 1567, and he is often presented as a champion of Gaelic. Yet he despised Gaelic traditions, condemning contemporary Gaelic composers and authors, accusing them of preferring the 'vain, hurtful, lying earthly stories' about Celtic heroes to the 'faithful words of God and the perfect way of truth'. The Reformed Church was, in some respects, pedestrian, sterile and repressive. To give Carswell credit, however, he ensured that every parish in Lorn, Mid-Argyll and Cowal had a minister before he died in 1572 and that his recruits were supplied with a stipend. Carswell also built Carnasserie Castle on the site of an older fortress just north of Kilmartin.

This building is exceptionally well preserved and liberally supplied with information panels explaining its origins. Standing above a raised beach overlooking Kilmartin Burn, it and its predecessor were clearly built to control the northern access to the Great Moss and the fertile lands around it. It is possible to climb from the kitchen to the fourth floor by a stone stairway to obtain a marvellous view of the valley. The carvings and interior architecture possess a refinement and grace which suggest a French influence and, although the castle was built before 1572, the gateway to the courtyard is dated 1685. In that year Carnasserie was sacked by the Royalist MacLaine of Torloisk after its owner, Duncan Campbell, had foolishly joined the Duke of Argyll in the Monmouth Rising. In spite of the devastation, most of the building has survived and can be reached easily by a firm track from the car park below.

Ford and Loch Awe

Directly opposite the castle the B840 leading to Ford and Loch Awe leaves the Oban road and heads east. The quiet village of Ford lies at the southern end of the largest inland loch in Argyll, in which there is a profusion of 'crannogs' or artificial islands constructed by early lake-dwellers. At one time it was assumed that these sanctuaries were of prehistoric origin but more recent documentary research has revealed that some of them were still in use in the sixteenth and seventeenth centuries, and modern radiocarbon dating places the Loch Awe crannogs no earlier than 370 BC. Yet it seems likely that they were used in the Iron Age and perhaps as early as the late Bronze Age. The extraordinary correlation on Loch Tay between the crannogs and the ancient land divisions on the shore suggests that the islets were used for habitation or storage while crops were grown on the neighbouring patches of land. This pattern is not so pronounced on Loch Awe but, when there is arable land with no offshore crannog, there is often a 'dun' nearby, suggesting that the settlers chose to build either a 'dun' or a crannog, if they found a convenient gravel bank in the loch. There are several theories about their structure but generally the crannogs seem to have consisted of a mound of stones surrounded by wooden piles on which a platform was constructed to hold a circular, thatched building. An exact description of a Highland crannog is impossible to obtain but modern marine archaeology is gradually revealing the secrets of the lake-dwelling communities.

Until the glaciers carved a gorge through the Pass of Brander, the water of Loch Awe escaped to the sea through the Eurach Gorge at Ford and indeed it is not difficult to imagine such a phenomenon, for it would not take a great deal of excavation to allow the water to flow westward again.

At one time three estates met at Ford – Poltalloch, Ederline and Auchinellan. Poltalloch extended north to Braevallich on the east side of Loch Awe and included Glennan. Ederline, which lies on the east side of the small loch by that name, was always more modest in extent. It first appears in the Scottish charters in 1346, when David II refers to 'Gilbert of Glacestr of the lands of Edyrling' and others. Yet it is a Campbell holding in later charters and it remained in their hands till 1871, when it was purchased by Henry Bruce of Elgin as a sporting estate. Bruce built a mansion with its own golf course, sawmill and pier but, sadly, this was demolished and replaced by the new house on Loch Ederline in 1964. Some members of the Bruce family were buried on the small island in the loch.

Because of its tranquillity and attractive setting in the woodlands, Ford tends to attract an unusually large number of what are termed 'white settlers' – of the 59 houses in the last census, only seven had native heads of household. Nevertheless it still has the appearance of a Highland village and visitors are welcomed with traditional Celtic courtesy. The hotel, which is the focal point of the community, was built in 1864 as Auchinellan Inn to cater for fishermen and passengers from the steamers and has retained much of its Victorian character. It provides an excellent base for exploration of the loch side.

An alternative route south to Lochgilphead leaves the main road near Loch Ederline and, skirting the reed-bound banks of an arm of the loch, climbs up past Stronesker farm. On a flat piece of ground before Ederline road end stood the mill of Goc um Go, where Sir Alexander MacDonald or MacDonnell, the great Irish warrior who fought for Montrose and the King in the Civil War, was defeated in single-handed combat by a man called Zachary Mor MacCallum. It may have been this defeat which encouraged him to leave Argyll before the Marquis of Argyll and General Leslie took their revenge on the Royalist forces by slaughtering 300 MacDonald men and their allies after they had surrendered at Dunaverty Castle in Kintyre. The mill, however, has disappeared and there is nothing to mark the site of this event. There are several farm gates on this road but visitors who are prepared to tolerate this slight inconvenience will discover that it leads through some of the finest scenery in the district. At one point it follows the shore of a beautiful hill loch called Loch Leathan, which attracts a profusion of wild fowl and migrant birds and which is an ideal place for a picnic.

The B840 turns east at Ford to follow the eastern shore of Loch Awe to Cladich, where it joins the Oban to Inveraray road. About a mile from the village, where the old drove road leaves the loch, the ruins of Kilneuair church lie in the trees. Dedicated to Saint Columba, the 'Chapel of the Yews' was formerly the main church of the district, with a market at its gates. A stone is built into the wall containing the 'Devil's Hand Print', a shallow impression, now barely discernible, of a foot with five toes, three of them having nails. The print is said to have been left in the stone by Satan himself when he came to fetch a tailor who was sewing in the chapel – no doubt on the eve of the Sabbath and slightly after midnight! The old building is remarkably intact with aumbries, piscina and a font, carefully reassembled from fragments. The Cross of Argyll, which is now in the grounds of the Malcolms' chapel at Poltalloch, originally stood at Kilneuair.

Beyond Kilneuair the ancient castle of Finchairn stands on a headland above Loch Awe. Originally 'Fianna charn' – the Grave of the Fingalians – the name comes from a large, plundered cairn in the steading of the farm across the road. One of the oldest charters relating to Argyll, dated August 1204, refers to the granting of 'Fincharne' and Glennan to Gillascop MacGillchrist by Alexander II. By 1309, however, it was in the hands of John MacDougall of Lorn, who, trying to excuse his treaty with Robert the Bruce, explained nervously to the newly-crowned Edward II, to whom he had sworn allegiance. 'I have three castles to keep as well as a loch twenty-four miles long'. A few months later the MacDougalls were defeated in the Pass of Brander at the north end of the loch and Bruce gave their lands to the Campbells. It is said that Finchairn was burned when one of the lairds, exercising his traditional right to bed the bride of any tenant on her wedding night, provoked the groom into such a fury that he set fire to the castle, destroying it completely.

North of Finchairn the road follows the lochside through woodlands containing a stand of elegant cypress trees to Braevallich. Here there is an extensive trout farm and a nursery with a remarkable variety of azaleas and rhododendrons, grown mainly for the wholesale market. At Durran, near Braevallich, there is a public footpath over the hills to Auchindrain on Loch Fyne and, about two miles beyond Durran, the hamlet of Eredine, with its own school and pier, stands in the shadows of the immense Eredine Forest. At the beginning of this century the hill pasture of Braevallich farm was converted to a deer forest and then sold to the Forestry Commission in 1934. Most of the plantation, therefore, consists of mature conifers.

At Portinisherrich – the 'Port of the Foals' – the small island of Innis Searraiche can be reached by a submerged causeway. Set in a glade among the trees and sheltered by tall trees, rhododendrons and a drystone enclosure, lie the ruins of an ancient chapel. Sitting among the stones in peace and solitude, it is easy to see why people are so fascinated and captivated by islands. Suspended in a capsule scented with pine resin, coloured with green shadows and flashing lake water and echoing with bird song, an unwary visitor can become so

Innis Chonnel Castle, the battlements.

bewitched by the experience that the cold bite of dusk and the faint light of the evening star penetrate the consciousness with a shock.

Just north of the little island cemetery the sombre battlements of Innis Chonnel Castle can be seen through the trees. Thought to have been built by the founder of the Campbells of Loch Awe, it was held, like Finchairn, by John MacDougall of Lorn in 1308. It was, however, given to Sir Colin Campbell by Robert the Bruce in 1315 and became the centre of Campbell power in Argyll till they moved to Inveraray at the end of the fifteenth century. After their departure they appointed various 'captains' to keep the castle, using it regularly as a prison, and it was not abandoned till 1704. Donald Dhu MacDonald, the son of Angus of Islay and the Earl of Argyll's sister, was imprisoned here as a child in 1484, having been carried off from Islay by the Earl of Atholl. As a descendant of the last Lord of the Isles, the Scottish Parliament regarded the boy as a threat and he was held in Innis Chonnel till he was rescued, at the age of 19, by MacIan of Glencoe. After his escape in 1501 he declared himself Lord of the Isles and headed the last great rebellion of the island chiefs against the Scottish Crown, but he was defeated and imprisoned in Edinburgh in 1506. Escaping from the capital 37 years later, Donald Dhu raised another vast army in the Isles and, forming an alliance with Henry VIII, took his men to Ireland to help the English sovereign quell a rebellion there. Fortunately for his fellow Celts, he died before he could accomplish anything. After their failure to hold him in either Innis Chonnel or Edinburgh, his demise must have been a great relief to the Scottish Government.

The castle has survived remarkably well since the eighteenth century, perhaps because of its island location. The dungeon, in which the Campbells incarcerated their enemies, can still be seen under the drawing room and the ramparts can be reached by a stairway on the north wall. In the 'pleasure ground' tall Spanish chestnuts provide shelter in the winter and shade in the summer.

Portsonachan, as the name suggests, was a port of call not only for the steamers, which linked the lochside villages with the railway at Loch Awe station, but also, long before the age of steam, for the ferry from Taychreggan on the western shore. The two settlements were linked in this way as early as the fifteenth century, when the ferry rights were granted to the Portsonachan innkeeper on condition that he carried the Duke of Argyll and his retainers free of charge. In the late eighteenth century the inn, unlike so many in the West Highlands, provided comfortable accommodation and good meals.

Portsonachan is becoming a major centre for tourists, with a proliferation of self-catering accommodation and services such as pony-trekking, boating and fishing. Sonachan House, which was enlarged by the Malcolms after they bought the estate in

Portsonachan and Glenstrae.

1850, stands in colourful, sheltered gardens and contains self-catering flats of an exceptionally high standard.

An island in Loch Awe, not far from Cladich, contains the ruins of a chapel. In 1257 the teinds of the 'Church of Saint Findoca on Inchaelt' were given to the Augustinian Canons of Inchaffray, who held the chapel till the Reformation. It eventually became the parish church. In 1615 Sir Duncan Campbell of Glenorchy put fallow deer and 'cunnyngis' or rabbits on the island, thus introducing an alien species which spread with alarming rapidity throughout the district. In 1736 a new church was built at Cladich, much of the stone apparently being taken from Innishail. The old burial ground on the island still contains burial slabs of great antiquity, some of them bearing the Celtic swirls and elegant symmetry of the pre-Reformation renaissance.

Fraoch Eilean, another wooded island near Innishail, contains a thirteenth century castle, which was converted to a dwelling house in the seventeenth century. Because of its isolation, this has remained virtually intact. It is first referred to in a document of 1267, when Alexander III granted custody of the castle to a Gillechrist MacNachdan. The seventeenth-century re-occupation and reconstruction of the property was carried out by the Campbells of Inverawe but unfortunately nothing is known of its history in the late Middle Ages. The island itself gets its name from Fraoch, son of King Fidhach of Connaught, who, pursuing cattle thieves to Scotland, met Gealcheann, the daughter of a local chief, and was immediately bewitched by her beauty. Determined to terminate the relationship, the girl's mother lured Fraoch to his death by sending him to gather rowan berries on the island, which was guarded by a monster. Almost exactly the same tale is told of an island in the bay of Bunessan on the Isle of Mull.

West Loch Awe

The road on the western side of Loch Awe provides a slow, but interesting, drive through woodland scenery to meet the main A85 at Taynuilt or the Lochgilphead to Oban road at Kilmelford. North of Ford there are numerous forest walks in Inverliever Forest. This was one of the first plantations acquired by the State in the twentieth century. Purchased from the Malcolms of Poltalloch in 1907, the ground not already afforested was immediately prepared for planting by the Office of Woods and, in 1908, the hillside was covered with young spruce, larch and pine. At that time forest development was a labour-intensive activity and the estate workforce gradually increased. In 1908 there were 55 people on Inverliever estate, 43 of whom were associated with farming operations; by 1952 there were 285 people, 232 of whom were involved in forestry work. This expansion, however, was not to last. As forestry operations became mechanised and the forests matured, the demand for labour contracted. In 1957 there were 200 full-time forest workers in the entire Loch Awe district; by 1987 there were 40 and many of the houses, built to house the workers, had been sold as holiday homes. In the meantime, the Office of Woods had been replaced by the Forestry Commission, formed in 1919 to replenish the woodlands devastated by World War I and to reduce Britain's dependence on imported timber. Although it provided extensive employment in remote parts of the Highlands, its priorities did not include regeneration of the local economies. The fact that little permanent benefit has accrued from the expansion of forestry on the lochside is, therefore, not surprising. Nevertheless, it has provided visitors with some attractive walks through the plantations.

At Torran Mor there is a massive standing stone, on which crosses have been carved on both sides – to claim the primitive relic for Christianity no doubt – and, at Dun Toiseach, the 'Fortress of the Chief', stands an Iron Age fort. There is, in fact, a remarkable line of these forts in the hills west of Ford, suggesting that the narrow neck of land between Loch Awe and Loch Craignish was of strategic importance. At the foot of Creag Beathach near Dun Toiseach a hoard of bronze tools and weapons was found in 1888 and additional artefacts in 1958.

Passing Inverliever Lodge, formerly the hub of the great estate and now an outdoor centre, the road climbs away from the loch into the forest. Inverliever Nurseries, which specialise in heathers and which exhibited at the Glasgow Garden Festival in 1988, are near the shore below the road. At Arinechan there is a forest walk leading round Duin Chorraich through an area replanted after the hurricane of 1968. Although most of the trees are young, there are some old Western Red Cedar in the plantation and there is an excellent view of the loch from the top. At Kilmaha, a little further on, the Forestry Commission has provided a viewpoint with a picnic bench. From here a track leads down to the shore, where the ancient chapel of Saint Mochoe lies almost hidden in the bushes. Although very badly damaged in 1968, when the storm uprooted the surrounding trees, the site still contains some extraordinary rock carvings, possibly dating from the pre-Columban period. Certainly the strange figures display the abstraction of Pictish art. Beyond Kilmaha there is another forest walk at Cruachan, which passes through a stand of tall spruce, larch and Douglas Fir nearly eighty years old.

Dalavich is the first village encountered travelling north on this side of the loch. It was mainly a forestry village but now contains a multitude of self-catering cabins in a well-planned holiday complex overlooking the loch. South of Dalavich the old pier and pier house of New York mark the centre of operations of the York Building Company in the eighteenth century. Like the settlement by the same name at Strontian, it was established by the company to facilitate its exploitation of the natural woodlands of the lochside. The Dalavich operations were part of a plan to strip the woodlands of the north to satisfy demand in England, a sensible financial proposal, for, by 1770, England was so short of naval timber that a Government report claimed that 'there is not a sufficient quantity of timber in England to be purchased at any price'. The forests of the Highlands provided the solution, with bark for tanning, branches for charcoal and trunks for commercial timber.

The Forestry Commission has laid out a trail through the remaining oakwoods, west of Dalavich, in which pied flycatchers and numerous other woodland birds thrive in the open woodland. Near the beginning the remains of two charcoal-burners' or colliers' hearths can be seen. Here the colliers stacked the branches, carefully filling every space with twigs, covered the wooden dome with turf and burnt it slowly for up to a week with the minimum amount of air. The finished charcoal was taken by boat and pack pony to the Bonawe iron furnace at Taynuilt.

West of Dalavich there is a magnificent drive over the hill to Kilmelford, which, for a short distance, follows the shore of Loch Avich until it climbs up to the remote shepherd's house of Lagalochan. This high plateau contains real West Highland scenery, with bare, terraced hillsides and damp, sedge-covered hollows and, at the west end, a truly spectacular view of Loch Melfort.

North of Dalavich the main road crosses the Abhain Fionain at Inverinan, where, in the woods above, there is a dramatic waterfall with a deep, still pool at the foot of the chasm. This can be reached by a walk laid out by the Forestry Commission, details of which can be obtained from the office at Dalavich. Indeed leaflets on all the local walks are available there. From Inverinan the road climbs up again through the plantation, eventually arriving at Kilchrenan, the largest settlement on the west side of the loch. In the grounds of the church there are several medieval burial slabs carved during the Celtic renaissance in the Iona and Loch Awe 'schools' in the fifteenth and sixteenth centuries. Built into the east end of the church is the gravestone of Cailean Mor, Sir Colin Campbell of Lochawe, the founder of the Argyll dynasty, who was killed in 1294 on the old road between Loch Avich and Loch Scammadale. In the hills west of Kilchrenan there are numerous walks around Loch Nant, which, since 1963, has been dammed to produce hydro-electricity for the national grid. The track on the southern side of this hill loch, thought to be an old droving route for cattle bound for Taychreggan, leads to the remote sheep farm of Musdale at the head of Glen Feochan. On a hill above the loch there is a cairn called Carn MhicDhonnaichaidh, where Campbell of Inverawe was killed by an arrow from his nephew's bow. Apparently the boy had a claim to his title and the laird had invited him to dinner at Inverawe, hiding a knife under the tablecloth to dispose of him at the end of the meal. During the evening the deer hounds in the dining hall started to fight over the bones and, in the fracas, the cloth was pulled aside, revealing the knife and the laird's intention. The boy fled from the hall and crossed the river with Inverawe in pursuit. As his uncle gained on him above Nant, the boy turned and shot him. Inverawe was buried where he lay and a cairn erected by the grave.

Craignish and Ardfern

North of Carnassarie Castle the A816 climbs into the terraced hills between Loch Awe and Loch Craignish to descend through the Bealach Mor (the Big Pass) to the fertile lands of Barbreck, enriched by a narrow band of limestone in the hillside. These lands at one time belonged to John MacDougall of Lorn but apparently his widow, having sought protection from the 'Knight of Lochow' at Innischonnel Castle and having married again, lost her second husband. However 'she found it not convenient to ly alone and, though her age advanced, yet her youthful inclination did not abate', and she ran off with a youth called Iver Campbell, following the hill route through Glen Domhain to her lands in Craignish. As they passed through a wood, unable to contain her passion till they reached their destination, she bundled the youth into the long grass to satisfy her craving. Some months later, finding with child', she pleaded with the Knight of Lochow, who was Iver's master, to let her marry him. The Knight agreed on the condition that she made over her lands to him and, on 11th November 1361, Craignish became Campbell property.

Near the foot of the pass a cairn and standing stone are said to mark the grave of King Olaf of Norway, slain by the Scottish King in single-handed combat on the banks of the river at Druim Righ. There were several Olafs and this was not, as some guides suggest, Olaf Tryggvason who terrorised the entire west coast of Britain at the end of the tenth century, for, having been defeated in a sea battle in the Baltic, he threw himself into the sea and drowned. Nor can it have been Olaf the Saint in the eleventh century, who was such a keen evangelist that he marched through his country with armed men converting people with fire and sword, for he was killed in the battle of Stikklestadt in 1030. Olaf III did not visit the west so it can only have been the Swedish-born Olaf Traetilia (Tree Feller) in 640 or the obscure Olaf Gierstada, who died in 840 three years before Kenneth McAlpin became the first king of Scotland. The identity of the slain warrior is still a mystery.

On the north side of the river a road turns west along the shore of the loch past Ardfern towards Craignish Point. Ardfern has become a major yachting and tourist centre, and it is not surprising that the area attracts visitors, for the peninsula west of Ardfern is largely unspoiled and Loch Craignish, with its small, rocky islands, is a sheltered and attractive anchorage. One of the islands, Eilean Righ, was formerly the home of Sir Lionel Johnstone, tutor to the last Emperor of China and recently featured in a major film.

West of Ardfern the road follows the shore down to a sheltered bay, where there is a fishing station and the shell of an ancient chapel, its lancet windows still intact and its walls sheltering a collection of medieval grave slabs. Dedicated to Saint Maelrubha, it is thought to have given its name to the parish of Kilmore (Kilmaelrubha), now known as Craignish. Opposite the chapel, in the grounds of Craignish Castle, the massive walls of an Iron Age fort called Dun Mhulig rise from the roadside, its long gallery and several lintels still in place. Craignish Castle, behind it, was a plain rectangular tower block

A cave west of Craignish, showing the extraordinary folding of the ancient rocks.

until it was extended in 1837 in neo-Elizabethan style to the design of William Burn. The core of the building is said to date from the twelfth century but the modern outline gives only a faint impression of antiquity. From 1860 to 1954 it was in the hands of the Gascoigne family, who generously built the small school in Ardfern in 1861.

At Craignish Point there is a car park and picnic site near the old pier. At one time the small, black cattle from Jura, Islay and Colonsay were landed here; in 1842, 1,000 head of cattle and 3,000 sheep were still passing through the ferry gates. The ferry continued to operate long after the demise of the droving trade. South of the pier the notorious Dorus Mor sea lane lies between Craignish Point and the island of Garbh Reisa. Here, in 1820, Bell's *Comet*, the first seagoing steamship in the world, was wrecked as its captain tried to reach Crinan in a storm. Even in the summer fierce squalls can sweep up the Sound, whipping the crests off the waves, but, on a fine day, when the islands lie in a blue haze, a short walk round the Point leads to some magnificent coastal scenery. North of Ardfern a rough road climbs over the hill past Soroba to Lunga and Craobh Haven. Craobh Haven is a modern holiday village, built round a marina, with a shop, laundrette, chandlery, craft shop, self-catering houses and an hotel. In trying to recreate a Highland village, mixing traditional materials with modern styles, the architects have produced the most incongruous settlement in Argyll. The twenty-first century Baronial style of some of the buildings is quite incompatible with the surrounding scenery. Nevertheless, the complex has created employment. It also seems to provide exactly the kind of services, facilities and environment which some visitors want.

Craobh Haven can be reached, of course, by the main A816. North of the marina the road follows the shore, providing a spectacular view of the islands of Shuna and Luing. On Arduaine Point, there is a garden containing one of the finest collections of rhododendrons in Scotland. Although it is advertised as a plantsman's rather than a tourist's garden, its magnolias, azaleas and water plants should not be missed. It is open from April to September but unfortunately closes on Thursdays and Fridays. The road descends to Loch Melfort and, passing the sheltered anchorages of Kames Bay and Loch na Cille, reaches Kilmelford village. In the nineteenth century two-thirds of this parish belonged to the Marquis of Breadalbane but, in 1838, part of it was feued to the owners of the Lorn Iron Furnace in Taynuilt to build a gunpowder works. Using charcoal from the sessile oakwoods and importing potassium nitrate and sulphur, the company continued to produce explosives till 1867, when an explosion brought their operations to an end! Some of their buildings, which included a cooperage and magazines, can still be seen at Melfort House. On the hill above, known as An Sithean, Mesolithic settlers made flint tools and weapons more than 5,000 years ago, and chipped stones can still be found at their quarry. West of Melfort House, the offices of which have been converted to a time-share holiday complex, a narrow road leads through natural woodlands to Degnish Point, where, from the top of

Craobh Haven.

Dun Crutagain, there is an unforgettable view over the islands of Luing and Seil to the hills of Mull and the wide sea lanes of the Firth of Lorn. It is some distance from Degnish to the summit of Dun Crutagain, which is 273 metres high, but well worth the effort.

It is a steep climb from Kilmelford to Blaran and the Braes of Lorn but the scenery changes with the ascent. Just above Kilmelford a path leads down to the old road and the dramatic ravine of the Pass of Melfort. Geologically this area is very different from Kilmartin and Craignish. The Lorn lava plateau lies on sediments of Old Red Sandstone, thought to be more than 800 million years old, the edges of which can be seen in Oban and on Kerrera. The plateau is crossed by basalt dykes, intruded from the volcanic centre on Mull into cracks in the sandstone, then worn down by the ice and the weather to produce the extraordinary landscape of Lorn. The rock formations are most obvious above Loch Tralaig in the Braes of Lorn and can be seen from the road at Blaran before it descends to Kilninver through the woods of Glen Gallain.

The old settlement of Kilninver lies on the shore below the main road and, behind it, the route to the 'Bridge over the Atlantic', which spans the sound between the island of Seil and the mainland. As it leaves Loch Feochan, this narrow road climbs through birch and hazel woods to the shoulder of Beinn Bhan. Just beyond the summit a track leads north through white iron gates to Barnacarry, a sheltered bay facing the island of Kerrera. Near the farm a massive, flat rock, once used as a source of millstones, still bears the marks of the quarriers, with some of the circles chiselled out and almost ready for lifting. On the west side of the bay the remains of a deserted township stand in a hollow overlooking Barnacarry burn.

The road to Seil continues past Loch Seil, a slender stretch of water below a steep face planted with conifers, and descends to Auchnasaul where it divides, a sharp turn to the right leading to Seil and a narrow branch to the left heading for Ardmaddy. Ardmaddy Castle contains an extraordinary mixture of architectural styles, the core of which is a late medieval tower house originally held by the MacDougalls of Rarey. The MacDougalls, however, lost the estate in 1648, when John MacDougall was imprisoned in Inveraray by the Marquis of Argyll, who appointed Campbell of Jura to be keeper of Ardmaddy. By 1728 it was in ruins but, when Colin Campbell of Carwhin, a partner in the slate quarries of Easdale, moved to the area, he rebuilt and added to the tower in 1737. Further additions were made in 1862. The building thus contains medieval, Georgian and Victorian styles of architecture.

The Slate Islands

The high, single arch of Clachan bridge, built by Thomas Telford in 1790, allows small sailing vessels to pass through the narrow sound but the fragile structure limits the weight of vehicles crossing to the island, an inconvenience to some of the residents. The old inn, now called Tigh an Truish – the House of Trousers – is said to have been the place where young Highland soldiers, forbidden to wear the kilt unless they were on duty, changed into trousers on their return from service. The vindictive legislation, which proscribed the kilt, was enacted after the 1745 Rebellion as a means of destroying the clan system. It also banned the use of the bagpipe, as being an instrument of war.

South of the village a narrow road turns west towards Ardfad Point and Ardincaple House, which was built in 1793 and was later the residence of Doctor Archibald Smith, a remarkable surgeon who spent many years in Peru during the turbulent years of the Wars of Independence. On Ardfad Point lie the ruins of Ardfad Castle, formerly a MacDougall stronghold, and a fort called Caisteal Ach a Huarach.

The main road continues due south to the crossroads, where, in the cemetery, the medieval chapel of Kilbrandon was located. Named after Brennan, an Irish missionary who arrived before Columba, it was abandoned before the Reformation and little of the original building has survived. East of the junction the settlement of Balvicar, which grew round the slate quarries in the nineteenth century, faces north across the Sound.

The road west at the junction leads to Easdale and to Ellanabeich, which contains hotels, shops and a large craft complex. The latter is a very successful enterprise, selling souvenirs of a Highland culture which exists only in the imagination of tourists and which most Gaels find rather offensive.

Like Balvicar, the village grew round the slate quarries, the remains of which can be seen all round the harbour and on the islands of Easdale, Luing and Belnahua. Quarrymen have extracted slate here since the sixteenth century to clad the roofs• of castles and manor houses and, later, the houses of Glasgow and Edinburgh. When Castle Stalker in Appin was rebuilt in 1631, Easdale slate was used on the roof. However, in November 1881 a great storm flooded the quarries and, although some of them were pumped dry again, Easdale Slate had been dealt a fatal blow. Facing increasing competition from the highly mechanised Welsh quarries and then foreign slate, they closed in 1914.

The island of Easdale, which can be reached by ferry from Ellanabeich, is only about 400 yards from the pier. In 1971 barely a score of people lived on Easdale and only the flooded quarries, the company offices and the workers' houses remained as a reminder of the hundreds who toiled in the deep pits and sat in the cold dressing sheds, with their legs stretched uncomfortably, splitting the slates. Today, however,

Easdale Island.

the island is experiencing a revival. Between 40 and 50 people now reside in the quarriers' houses and the nearest school on Seil has more than 50 pupils. There is a small seafood freezing and packing plant and plans have been drafted for some holiday houses. The present proprietor, until recently a director of Urch, Harris Stamp Company, has organised the issue of Easdale Island stamps, which can be purchased locally. There is a restaurant, a bar and a folk museum, which sells hand-painted stones. Easdale Island Shipping operates two cargo boats, one of which, the *Eilean Easdale* is skippered by a local man and delivers goods such as coal, hay and tar to remote islands and isolated townships. Although it is rather barren and marred by slate waste, Easdale is a fascinating island in a beautiful setting.

Luing

There were several other quarries in the neighbourhood – one at Glenalbyn, for example, on the mainland north of Seil run by J. and D. MacDougall of Oban from 1885 to 1894. The largest, next to Easdale and Ellenabeich, were on the island of Luing, south of Seil. The road to Luing leaves the crossroads near Kilbrandon chapel and leads south to Cuan ferry, passing the parish church of Kilbrandon and Kilchattan, built in 1864. The original plain glass windows of the Victorian church were replaced in 1938 by stained-glass panels designed by the artist Douglas Strachan. At Cuan there was an older place of worship known as the Covenanters' Church, which was built in 1837 but fell into disrepair, being no more than a shell by 1950; fortunately it was rescued and restored to operate as a tearoom and shop. The car ferry to Luing runs regularly across the Sound, but to avoid disappointment, visitors should check the times of sailing in the Oban Tourist Office.

Luing is an extraordinary island, with terraced hills and damp hollows in the north and fertile, open pasture and arable land in the south. Renowned in the farming community for a breed of cattle perfected by the Cadzow family, the name of the island is well known in Canadian and European livestock circles through the Luing Cattle Society. The island now carries a herd of about 400 head, providing employment for nine people. The Cadzows, however, were not the first farming pioneers on Luing. In the middle of the last century the Marquis of Breadalbane laid out an experimental dairy farm at Kilchattan, with slate drains, a long byre with slate troughs and fresh air grilles, and, underneath the byre, a slate cistern for slurry with a water wheel to spread the contents round the fields. A remarkable enterprise. Unfortunately the Marquis died before its success could be ascertained but the long byre can still be seen beside the road and the old slate stalls, still with their neck chains attached, have been laid flat to form a floor.

As at Easdale, the Breadalbanes helped to develop the slate industry on Luing, starting at Cullipool in the west in 1749. Although the quarries were bound to close eventually, it was an industrial dispute which precipitated their premature demise in 1908. In 1904 the men had taken strike action to obtain an

Luing cattle on their native island.

increase in wages and the company had agreed to pay 30 shillings a week but, once the men returned to work, it reduced the offer by 2 shillings, thus souring labour relations until the final strike in 1908. Slate was quarried intermittently and on a limited scale during the first half of the twentieth century but the work ceased completely in 1965.

Cullipool was the main slate centre on Luing and the settlement is surrounded with dramatic quarries and slate debris. Many of the old quarriers' houses at the north end of the village have been restored and there are several modern bungalows with remarkable views across the Firth of Lorn to the steep shoreline of Mull. At the south end of the village there is an art gallery run by a local artist who trained at the Royal Academy. The approach to Cullipool is unfortunately marred by a group of council houses, which must be among the least attractive buildings in Lorn and quite inconsistent with other council housing in the district, for Argyll has some of the finest local authority housing in Strathclyde.

From Cullipool it is possible to arrange a sea trip to the deserted island of Belnahua, where the ruins of the quarriers' cottages overlook the flooded quarries. Last century, when Easdale slate was still in great demand, more than 150 people lived on the barren rock. No fresh water was available and, although a well was sunk into the slate, water had to be carried in casks from Lunga.

At Achafolla, in the middle of Luing, the shell of a water mill lies just below the road. The iron water wheel is still intact, although the buckets have disintegrated, but, inside the building, all the gearing and four great granite millstones are still in place in their wooden frames. The mill is built into the side of the hill so that the tenants of the neighbouring farms could unload their grain on the same level as the millstones and collect the meal from chutes below. It should be preserved but no-one has taken any steps so far to ensure its survival.

South of Achafolla, the ruins of Kilchattan chapel stand precariously in the graveyard beside the road. First mentioned in the records in 1549 and dedicated to Saint Cathan, it was used till 1735, when a new church was built at North Cuan on Seil to serve both islands. Most of the gravestones and burial slabs are made of slate and the inscriptions therefore are very clear. On some of the slabs there is some early 'graffiti' depicting late medieval galleys, one with a wolf-head prow. In the wall outside the graveyard and on adjoining stones inside, there is an extraordinary text commemorating Alexander Campbell, a religious eccentric, who inscribed and decorated his own tombstones with flying angels before he died, insisting that no other corpse was to be laid in his grave. The full text of his instructions and the details of his faith, which cover four stones, provide a fascinating insight into the esoteric religious views of the 1820s.

West of the chapel a tarred road leads to the coast at Black Mill Bay, where there is further evidence of quarrying and the stark remains of an old pier. This bay, rather exposed to the prevailing wind, faces across the Sound of Luing to the steep slopes of Scarba and the sharp spine of Lunga. The island of Scarba was clearly formed by a great fold in the metamorphic rock, leaving a tilt of about 40 degrees in the strata, with high cliffs and stacks on the western side and a sheltered basin round Kilmory on the east. In 1764 the two farms on the island, Kilmory and Maol Bhuidhe, contained a population of 60 people. Now no-one lives there permanently and the island is left to the red deer, cattle, sheep and the great flocks of

Old Water Mill on Luing.

seabirds that nest in the cliffs. North of Scarba lies the long, low island of Lunga, which supported a dozen people in 1764 and is now, like its neighbour, uninhabited apart from the occasional influx of youngsters to the Adventure School.

Unlike the houses of Ellenabeich and Easdale, which were built largely by the quarrymen themselves, those of Toberonochy on the east side of Luing, were built by the slate company in 1805. The village is therefore slightly less haphazard than that at Cullipool but is also surrounded by slate waste. It is much more sheltered than the western settlements and faces across Shuna Sound. The island of Shuna, which is only about a mile from Toberonochy, is remarkably fertile, and supported nearly 70 people in 1841. In 1829 its proprietor left it to the City of Glasgow for charitable purposes and it remained in the hands of the city fathers till the end of the century. It is noticeably different from the 'slate islands', being heavily wooded and containing a band of blue limestone, which fertilises the soil and which was extracted commercially in the nineteenth century.

North of Toberonochy, just off the road leading to Leccamore farm, the ancient fortress of Dun Leccamore overlooks the burn flowing down to Ardnamir. Built about

2,000 years ago, its walls still stand up to two metres high with the dimensions of the small inner cells clearly marked in the masonry. In one of the doorways the recesses for the door-bar are still intact, the one for storing the bar while the door was open extending almost three metres into the wall. One of the door posts, thought to have been removed from an older burial chamber when the fort was built, bears the cup marks of the previous civilisation. The stone steps to the wallhead are built into the west wall. When the site was excavated in the nineteenth century, it yielded some stone implements, querns and a bronze pin. Dun Leccamore, which is quite accessible, is one of the two Iron Age forts on the island, the other being north of Ardnamir glen at Dun Ballycastle.

The island of Torsa can be reached at low spring tide from a point north of Ardnamir Bay. At the north end the ruin of Caisteal nan Con, the 'Castle of the Hounds', can still be seen from the sea. According to legend, this was the hunting lodge of the Lords of the Isles. However, the same explanation is put forward for the origin of Caisteal nan Con in Morvern and it was not built till the seventeenth century – long after the Lordship of the Isles had lapsed.

The Garvellachs

West of Lunga a group of islands known as The Garvellachs lie in the deep water of the Firth of Lorn. In 542 AD the Celtic missionary Brendan the Navigator founded a community on the southern island, Eileach an Naoimh, twenty years before Columba landed on Iona. Nothing remains of Brendan's chapel but the remains of other ninth-century buildings have survived. Near the remains of the small chapel there is an underground cell, said to have been for penance or meditation and, near the shore, a double beehive cell, part of which was restored in 1937. The old Gaelic name for the islands was Na h'In Ba – Isles of the Sea – and local enthusiasts believe that this was Hinba, Columba's sanctuary, and that his mother, Eithne, is buried above Port Columcille. The island obviously remained sacred for some time, for the remains of a later medieval church and associated enclosures suggest a substantial monastic settlement.

In the fourteenth century the significance of the islands lay in a castle guarding the sea lanes from the northern island of Dun Chonnuil. After the Wars of Independence, in 1343, King David granted all the southern Hebrides and the key island fortresses of Cairn na Burgh More off Mull and Dun Chonnuil to John, Lord of the Isles, as a means of securing his loyalty to the Scottish Crown. At the time Edward III was courting John to cause division in the Scottish ranks. John McDomhnaill, by balancing delicately between the two and by judicious marriage, built a vast Gaelic kingdom in the west, stretching from Kintyre to the Outer Hebrides, and Dun Chonnuil was part of his empire. The 'constabulary of the Castles of Dun Chonnuil and Dunkerd' was granted to Lachlan MacLean of Duart. It is said that MacLean held John of the Isles prisoner in Dun Chonnuil in 1365 until he consented to give his daughter in marriage to MacLean. Given John's position of power at the time, this seems rather unlikely. Nevertheless MacLean was certainly confirmed as 'constable' of Dun Chonnuil in 1390. Eventually, however, the islands, like so many other lands in Argyll, became part of the Campbell empire and suffered from this proprietorship in 1675, when Maclaine of Lochbuie landed with his warriors to kill or carry away 52 cows, 12 stirks and 120 sheep, leaving the islanders destitute. This raid was in retaliation for the devastation caused by Argyll's men on Maclaine's estate on Mull the previous year.

Now the islands are deserted, visited only by passing yachtsmen and tourists from Oban. Cruises round the islands run from the Esplanade in Oban, and longer visits can be arranged from Toberonochy on Luing. They are beautiful islands with an abundance of wild flowers, seabirds, seals and even a pair of eagles that nest regularly on the cliffs.

CHAPTER 6

South Appin and Lismore

Ardchattan

Crossing the distinctive cantilever bridge over the narrows of Loch Etive at Connel, the A828 leads north through Appin to Glencoe and Fort William. It is a slow route, particularly frustrating at Loch Creran, where the disused Connel railway bridge spans the neck of the loch, and motorists have to travel right round the shore only to pass the bridge again on the north side. Yet, in spite of the narrow road, the route passes through some magnificent scenery, with steep wooded slopes to the east and the shores of Loch Linnhe, backed by the dramatic coast of Morvern to the west.

Just north of the bridge a narrow road turns sharply eastward heading for Ardchattan and Bonawe. This provides an alternative, and much more attractive, route to Loch Creran. Winding along the shore of Loch Etive, it passes the parish church of Ardchattan before it reaches Ardchattan Priory and Gardens. Founded in 1230 by Duncan MacDougall of Lorn, the Priory was originally a settlement for Valliscaulian monks, an austere order founded in Val des Choux in Burgundy, the members of which wore white habits, hair shirts and ate neither meat nor gravy. Only three Valliscaulian houses existed outside France – Pluscarden in Moray, Beauly near Inverness and Ardchattan. The monks lived in complete isolation, only the Prior and the Procurator being allowed out of the Priory, but there is a tradition that one of the Priors managed to sneak a nun into the building, hiding her beneath the floor of the Oratory. Apparently he kept her there too long on one occasion and she suffocated. It is said that her bones are still there today.

In the choir of the chapel there is a Celtic cross dated 1500 originally erected by John O'Brolchan, possibly one of the O'Brolchans who built Iona Abbey in the fifteenth century. Duncan MacDougall, the son of Somerled, is buried here with his brother, Dougal, who died in 1502, and there is a slab commemorating Roderick, Bishop of the Isles and ambassador for the Council of the Isles to Henry VIII in 1545. At that time the religious order here seems to have been in decline, for, in 1518, a Duncan MacArthur was appointed to the position of Prior by James IV specifically to revive the religious life and to restore the buildings. Nearly 40 years later he was followed by John Campbell, whose descendants still live in the Priory today. They claim that the thirteenth-century dining room has been in use for 755 years.

The Priory Church was destroyed by fire in the seventeenth century, apparently by Covenanting soldiers in revenge for assistance given to Montrose and his Royalist forces in 1645. Nine years later the entire Priory and its contents were burned by Captain Mutlo, the 'Governor' of Dunstaffnage, after the laird of Ardchattan took part in Glencairn's rising against Cromwell. The laird's mother, Catherine MacDonnell of Antrim, was a cousin of Colkitto MacDonnell, Montrose's general, and Ardchattan was seen as a nest of 'malignants'. Fortunately the property was rebuilt and is now the second oldest inhabited house in Scotland.

The Gardens, which are open to the public from April to November, are sheltered by old lime, beech and plane trees, some of which were planted by John Campbell in the sixteenth century. The front garden, leading down to the loch, is bordered with shrubs, roses and herbaceous plants and the wild garden west of the house contains 40 different varieties of shrub roses. There is also a splendid Cornus Kousa, an Hoheria Lyallii and a Himalayan musk rose growing 40 feet up a yew tree.

The road forks at Inveresragan, the easterly route crossing the River Esragan to reach Bonawe. The yew trees of 'Easragain' were renowned for their strength as bows in medieval times, verses extolling their resilience still appearing in the sixteenth century:

> Bow from yew of Easragain
> Eagle feather from Loch Treig
> Yellow wax from Baile nan Gaillean
> And arrowhead from smith MacPheidirean.

Connel Airfield with the Isle of Mull behind.

This was the perfect combination for a Highland archer.

Passing Blarcreen, the road follows the shore through mature oakwoods for about three miles before it reaches Bonawe Quarries. Granite has been extracted here for more than a century, most of it being used as 'setts' to surface the cobbled streets of southern cities. The entrances to the Mersey Tunnel and the King George V Bridge in Glasgow were built with Bonawe granite. Nowadays a fleet of eight ships carries crushed granite all over Britain. Occasionally these vessels can be seen gliding through the quiet waters of Loch Etive after negotiating the Falls of Lora. The ferry, which used to carry workers from Taynuilt, was closed in 1979, but the slipway is still intact.

In spite of the quarry, the ruined buildings and the abandoned stores, the views of Loch Etive from the headland of Eilean Duirinnis make the slow drive from Connel worthwhile. Beyond the quarry a track leads up the west side of Loch Etive to Cadderlie, Barrs and eventually to Glen Etive. The hillside between Barrs and Gualachulain, with its stands of natural oak and Scots pine and its abundance of oceanic ferns, mosses and liverworts, has been designated as a Site of Special Scientific Interest. At the head of the loch the track through this area joins the road to Glencoe.

At Inveresragan the B845 climbs over the shoulder of Na Maolean to the head of Gleann Salach. From the summit there is a marvellous view of Taynuilt and the hills of Lorn. However, as the road descends into Barcaldine forest, the scenery changes from open hillside to enclosed conifer plantations with rare glimpses of the countryside. There are some very poor specimens of contorta pine near the road, an alien species which thrives initially but tends to wither as the roots spread into the wet, acid soil, and there is some ugly clear felling on the east side of the glen. Nevertheless there are some beautiful larch and mature spruce near Barcaldine and the view from the summit compensates for the uninteresting drive through Gleann Salach.

Benderloch

The A828 passes through North Connel and runs parallel with the disused railway track to Benderloch. On the foreshore just beyond North Connel there is an airfield used by private aircraft and the local gliding club. From April to October gliding courses, run by qualified instructors, are available for beginners and flights can be arranged at the airfield. On the east side of the road at this point the great moss of Achnacree, from which peat has been extracted commercially for fuel and for horticulture, stretches towards Ardchattan. On the northern edge of the moss, near Achnacreemore, there is an ancient chambered cairn, which was excavated in 1871.

Benderloch, the first village on the way north, is rather uninspiring but benefits from its location in an interesting and attractive district round Ardmucknish Bay. At the southern end of the village the remains of Dun Mac Sniachan, a Bronze Age vitrified fort, can still be traced in a field beside the road. According to local tradition, Deirdre and the sons of Uisneach settled here before moving to Glen Etive. Certainly one of the headlands, called Fionn Ard, suggests a connection with the Fingalians and the hill above Benderloch, Beinn Lora, is named after an early Celtic hero called Laoighre.

The headland west of Tralee holiday complex contains colourful natural woodlands which run down to the shore and some remarkable views of Lismore and the Firth of Lorn. Lochnell House, approached by an avenue lined with tall chestnut and oak trees, is a most impressive piece of architecture. The oldest part of the mansion, the south-west wing, was built in the seventeenth century by Alexander Campbell of Lochnell but this was substantially enlarged by early and late Georgian extensions, followed by radical restructuring after a fire in 1853. In the late Georgian reconstruction an ancient yew tree, which apparently could shelter 1,000 people, was taken from Bernera Island, off Lismore, to make the staircase. Columba is said to have predicted that the crime of felling the yew would be repaid 'only by water, blood and three fires'. As the tree fell, one workman was crushed and several were drowned towing the logs from Lismore in a storm and the house was subsequently damaged by fire on three occasions. With its parapets, circular and octagonal towers and its strange, but mysteriously compatible mixture of styles, it blends with its surroundings surprisingly well. South-west of the house Lady Margaret's Tower, built by Lady Campbell in 1754, still stands on the headland of Garbh Aird overlooking the oakwoods.

At the northern end of the peninsula the Black Castle of Barcaldine stands immediately beside the road leading to Eriska. Built in 1609 by Sir Duncan Campbell of Glenorchy, 'Duncan of the Seven Castles', who constructed a line of castles from Loch Tay to the west coast, including Finlarig, Kilchurn and Achallader, it lay roofless during the latter part of the nineteenth century until it was restored between 1897 and 1911. In the late seventeenth century it was held by Patrick Campbell, known to the family as Para Djarak, who married a daughter of the Jacobite Cameron of Locheil. She was renowned for her thrift and it is said that she was so mean to her staff that they had to steal food from the kitchen; apparently she discouraged the practice by killing and cooking one of their dogs, laying it on the table like a roast and, after they had stolen most of it, announcing that they had just eaten their pet. Her son, Colin Campbell of Glenure, became a factor for the Hanoverian Government and was shot in the famous 'Appin Murder'. Patrick and his lady eventually abandoned the austere halls of the castle for more comfortable accommodation

Barcaldine Castle.

at Innerergan House in Barcaldine village, leaving their old home to fall into disrepair. It was restored by one of their descendants, Sir Duncan Campbell of Bowers Gifford in Essex.

West of Barcaldine Castle a narrow road leads to South Shian, which has become the headquarters of Golden Sea Produce, a leading salmon farming company. South Shian lies in a quiet, sheltered bay, which, in spite of the fish farm traffic, is an ideal place for a picnic. Another road leaves the crossroads at Barcaldine Castle and heads west across the moor to the island of Eriska, where the Victorian mansion, built in 1884, has been converted to an exclusive hotel. In its grounds, which take in the whole island, there is a herd of Jersey cows to provide the guests with fresh milk and a large vegetable garden to supply the kitchens with fresh produce.

Barcaldine

The main road north leaves Benderloch and follows the disused railway track towards Barcaldine, passing Dalrannoch farm restaurant and craft shop. Dalrannoch was one of the leading dairy farms in North Argyll, winning a multitude of rosettes in local agricultural shows. Like many others, it has suffered from the quotas imposed on milk production but, long before their introduction, its proprietor diversified into tourist facilities, one of which was the restaurant.

Concealed in the conifer plantation north of Dalrannoch, the timber buildings of the Sea Life Centre can barely be seen from the road but it provides a service not to be missed. It is an excellent facility, especially for children and disabled people, with a collection of seals, octopus and an extraordinary array of other marine life. Intelligently landscaped, using existing trees and the shoreline of Loch Creran, it contains a restaurant and shop selling crafts and souvenirs.

Barcaldine is a scattered settlement surrounded by woodlands. The large modern building on the shore is the Alginate Works. Owned by an American company, Kelco of San Diego, a subsidiary of Merck & Co., it imports seaweed from Chile, Tasmania and Ireland to produce alginates for use as a gelling agent in such products as pet food, toothpaste, ice cream, jellies, cosmetic creams, welding fluxes and beer. The firm employs 100 people at Barcaldine but it also provides work in the Western Isles by purchasing seaweed from a workers' co-operative factory in Lewis and from crofters in North Uist. Kelco have a second factory in Girvan, Ayrshire, and their container lorries, operating between the two, are a familiar sight on the main road south.

Beyond the alginate factory there is a large, sheltered caravan and camping park and, on the bank of the river, a forest walk through Sutherland's Grove. An old, gnarled Douglas Fir spreads its limbs over the car park at the entrance to the grove, where the Abhainn Teith flows under a lichen-clad stone bridge.

North of Barcaldine the road passes beneath the disused railway bridge which spans Loch Creran. Unfortunately this has not been converted to a road bridge, so motorists must

Disused railway bridge, Loch Creran.

follow the shore to the head of the loch. This extended journey, however, has many compensations for those who have time to enjoy them. The loch is nearly always in sight and, with the steep hillsides of Glen Creran reflected in its sheltered waters, the scenery is magnificent. The oak woods of Glasdrum on the north side of the loch have been set aside as a National Nature Reserve but, because deer culling and forestry operations are frequently in progress in the area, it is advisable to contact the ranger (at Ledaig 363) before arranging a visit.

North of the bridge over the Creran a road turns suddenly east for Glen Creran, ending just beyond the pottery at Elleric, but there is a forestry track leading to the head of the glen and a footpath through to Ballachulish. The fences above these plantations are difficult to maintain and red deer from the open hill have moved into the forests, the stags growing antlers of extraordinary breadth of beam and the whole herd assuming the habits of woodland animals. They can often be seen from the tracks in winter, crashing through the trees.

The main road follows the shore westward to North Creagan. In the woods above, the remains of the ancient chapel of Cladh Chuirirlean can still be found on the shoulder of the hill. Funerals at the burial ground here, much to the

170

consternation of the parish ministers, used to include several pagan rituals. Birch and sycamore branches were strewn in the path of the funeral party and the bier on which the coffin was carried was ceremoniously smashed against a holly tree. The traditions of the old Celtic church, which retained a respect for nature and a spiritual relationship with it, were difficult to suppress.

Appin

For visitors with a little time to spare a diversion into the Appin peninsula is well worth the extra journey. Just west of the junction Glenleckan Knitwear at Inverfolla, which sells woollen sweaters and suits in traditional colours, is one of the few businesses of its kind to be run by a native of Argyll. The narrow road winds through sycamore, beech and chestnut woodlands, with the occasional glimpse of Loch Creran and the Isle of Eriska. Airds House, an elegant Georgian mansion built by Donald Campbell of Airds and extended by Robert MacFie of Langhouse in 1858, can be seen among the trees near Port Appin. Donald Campbell was factor for the Duke of Argyll and looked after his lands in Morvern. One of his descendants, John Campbell, reclaimed hundreds of acres in the district, much of which has returned sadly to its natural state. The house is still occupied and several of the buildings are let out as holiday flats.

One of Scotland's most successful silversmiths has a workshop in Port Appin. Basing her designs on 'art nouveau' styles and skilfully incorporating coloured glass, Pat Cheney has won international recognition for her brilliant work. The clean lines, delicate curves and translucent insets make it the most distinctive jewellery in Scotland. There is another craft shop in the village, from which bicycles can be hired to tour the area, a well-stocked community co-operative store and an excellent hotel overlooking the sea. Port Appin, being less than a mile from the island of Lismore, is the landing place for the passenger ferry and can be quite busy in midsummer. However, there is a large car park in which it is normally possible to find space.

Castle Stalker, Appin.

The landscape at the northern end of the Appin peninsula is quite different from that of the southern shore. With more bare rock, whins and open ground, it faces north across Loch Laich towards the high hills of Appin, sheltered from the prevailing wind. Dalnashean Gardens, which benefit from the shelter and contain a colourful variety of azaleas and rhododendrons, are open to the public between April and the end of July, although visits can be arranged at other times. The road follows the shore to meet the A828 again at Tynribbie.

The main road from North Creagan to Appin passes through the fertile Strath of Appin before it reaches Tynribbie, where, at Kinlochlaich, what claims to be Scotland's largest nursery garden centre is open in all seasons. It provides a remarkable range of trees, shrubs and plants, which are all properly hardened and therefore thrive reliably in nearly any conditions. Just before Kinlochlaich the roofless, ivy-clad shell of the old parish church of Portnacroish can be seen by the roadside. Built on or near the site of the older chapel of Annaid four years after the battle of Culloden, its walls contain a headstone, which originally stood on the battlefield, dedicated to the Stewarts of Appin who died for the Jacobite cause on the bleak moor near Inverness. The family not only remained loyal to the Prince but retained their traditional religion, building the small Episcopal church at Portnacroish in 1815.

Just beyond the church a track leads off the main road along the old railway track to the shore beside Castle Stalker, one of the most picturesque fortresses on the west coast. Eilean an Stalcaire – Island of the Hunter – was granted to Duncan Stewart of Appin in 1501 but the castle was not built till about 1540. Under the jurisdiction of James V it was constructed to 'suppress the Disorders in the Highlands' by Duncan's son. By the seventeenth century, however, it was in the hands of Donald Campbell of Airds, returning very briefly to the Stewarts when the Campbells were caught on the losing side in 1681. Garrisoned by Hanoverian troops after Culloden, it was roofless by 1841. Fortunately it has been restored and converted to a comfortable dwelling house. Built on a solitary rock in the middle of Loch Laich, the tall keep still seems to guard the sea lanes between Appin and Morvern, waiting for the tall prows and dipping oars of the swift galleys to appear in the Lynn of Lorn.

No account of Appin would be complete without a reference to the 'Appin Murder', the central theme of R.L. Stevenson's *Kidnapped*. After the rebellion of 1745, the estates of the leading Jacobites were taken over by the Crown and their rents collected by local factors. Colin Campbell of Glenure, in Glen Creran, was appointed to this position with responsibility for the estates of Stewart of Ardshiel in Appin and the Camerons of Lochiel in Lochaber, his mother's family. Glenure was accused of favouring Jacobite interests in the area and, threatened with dismissal, set out to prove his loyalty to the Crown. James Stewart – James of the Glen – who had taken the tenancy of the Ardshiel estate and who was suspected of diverting some of the rent due to the Crown to the Ardshiel family in France, was immediately deprived of his lands in Glen Duror and given an inferior holding at Acharn. Not content with this, Glenure proceeded to secure notices of removal against other tenants known to be sympathetic to the Jacobite cause. James, who had accepted his own loss with resignation, was furious – in spite of the fact that the evicted tenants were to be given other holdings. Unfortunately James let his feelings about Glenure be known and, when the factor was shot in the wood of Lettermore on May 14th 1752, he was arrested as a prime suspect. The outraged Campbell clan, determined to secure a conviction, marshalled more than 150 witnesses and brought all their powerful resources to bear on the trial. James was tried in Inveraray, in a court chaired by the Duke of Argyll, in front of a jury packed with Campbells and was, naturally, found guilty. He was hanged in Ballachulish, his corpse left to decay on the gibbet till the bones rattled in the wind as a warning to other Jacobites.

About a mile north of Castle Stalker, Appin House stands in the trees opposite the island of Shuna. Built by Robert Stewart of Appin in the early eighteenth century, it was enlarged by Hugh Seton of Touch after he bought the estate in the 1770s. The son of a wine merchant and a confirmed Jacobite, Seton held a senior position in the Indian service before returning to Scotland to become one of the great 'improvers'. He introduced crop rotation to his estate near Stirling and insisted that his tenants follow his example. In Appin he established the first postal service with a 'runner' three times a week to Bonawe and Inveraray and a service to Fort William and Oban. The house is still occupied, though altered significantly, and the present proprietors have built several self-catering apartments

Passenger ferry from Port Appin to Lismore.

in the garden overlooking Castle Stalker and the hills of Mull. Below Appin House, at the home farm, a retired forest ranger runs a small wildlife museum, containing stuffed animals, skulls, birds' eggs and antique rural implements. His daughter, who trained with Pat Cheney in Port Appin and Colin Campbell in Inverness, has returned to run a small jewellery business at the museum. Below the farm, at Lettershuna, there is a riding centre and a marine watersport centre, offering windsurfing, waterskiing and sea fishing.

Lismore

Lismore or Lios Mor (The Big Enclosure) is the most fertile island in Lorn, its rich redzina soil sweetened by bands of Dalriadan limestone. Tilted by movements of the earth's crust, carved by glaciers and eroded by the West Highland weather, the limestone assumes some dramatic shapes, particularly where it was washed by the seas of the Ice Age. Almost the entire coastline is a raised beach, with the cliffs, which were once at sea level, forming a shelf far from the shore. The island, which can be reached by car ferry from Oban or by passenger ferry from Port Appin, is still relatively quiet and unspoiled.

Lismore's early history is chiefly associated with Saint Moluag, who, having trained at Bangor, County Down, under Saint Comgall, came to Scotland in the sixth century to spread the Gospel to the inhabitants of the north. According to legend, Moluag and Columba were both keen to claim the green island as a missionary base and, as they raced towards its northern shore in their currachs, Moluag cut off his little finger, threw it ashore and claimed that, as he had touched it first, Lismore was his territory. As a similar story is told of the claiming of Ulster by two rivals – hence the red hand of Ulster – there may be some confusion between the two, arising from Moluag's country of origin. The saint apparently landed at Port Moluag and built his 'Lios Mor' on the west side of the island, possibly at Clachan. From this settlement he travelled as far as the east coast of Scotland, spreading Christianity among the Picts. He died in 592, leaving his staff or 'Bachull Mor' to the hereditary keepers, the Barons of Bachuil. Originally the family of Macanleigh, they eventually changed their name to Livingstone and held the lands of Bachuil for several centuries. Moluag's staff has survived, and is still in the hands of the hereditary keeper.

It was one of the Livingstones who saved the 'Appin Banner' at Culloden. Eight men from the island were killed or wounded in defence of the standard and, as the last one fell, young John Livingstone tore it from the shaft, wrapped it round his body and escaped from the field. Of the twelve Jacobite standards at Culloden, only this one returned to the West. The others were ceremoniously burned at the Mercat Cross in Edinburgh. Today, however, the black banner of Appin hangs with those of the enemy in Edinburgh Castle. Another member of the family is said to have cut down the remains of James of the Glen from the gibbet and buried them on Eilean na h-Iurach. He was known as Domhnull Mollach because one of his ancestors, Am Beathach Mollach (The Hairy Beast), fled from Lismore after committing murder to live wild in the woods of Appin. Eventually he was befriended by the Stewarts of Appin and given their protection. His real name was John Macanleigh but the 'Mollach' (Hairy) remained with him and was passed on to his descendants. When Domhnull cut down James of the Glen, his brother, Neil Macanleigh, fearful of the consequences, fled to the Isle of Ulva and is said to be the grandfather of the explorer David Livingstone.

The Vikings have left their mark on Lismore in place-names and the ruins of Castle Chaifen near Clachan. Apparently the sister of one of the Norwegian kings, a woman called Beothail, lived in the castle. She had left her lover behind in Norway, hoping that he would join her in Lismore but he died before the marriage could be arranged. Hearing of his death, she pleaded with her brother to be buried beside him when she died. When the time came, the king sailed to Lismore to collect her body. He washed it tenderly in the well of Saint Moluag and carried it back to Norway, only to discover that, because the body had been in an advanced state of decomposition, one of her fingers had been left behind in the well. Faithfully the king returned to Scotland, crossing the North Sea, sailing through the Minch and negotiating Ardnamurchan Point, to collect her finger for burial so that her remains might rest complete beside those of her lover in Norwegian soil. Since then the well has been known as Tobar Cnamh Beothail – Well of the Bones of Beothail. The tall ruins of Castle Chaifen, which stand on a point on the north-west coast, are not those of Beothail's residence, however, but are probably the remains of a castle built by the MacDougalls of Lorn before the dispersal of their lands by Robert the Bruce in the fourteenth century.

Even before the Vikings had departed from the west after the 'battle' of Largs in 1263, Lismore had become the seat of the Bishop of Argyll. The first Bishop, Harold, had his seat in

Muckairn but it was transferred to Lismore in 1236 and, a few years later, the cathedral was built. The remains of this building are incorporated in the parish church at Clachan, where the original sedilia, piscina and choir arch can still be seen. The Bishops seem to have lived in Achadun Castle on the south-west coast of the island. Standing on the summit of a limestone ridge, little of their castle remains, except part of the mural stair and some of the window stones which originally came from Carsaig on Mull. The castle is referred to in documents of 1304 and Bishop Loudon is known to have stayed there in 1452 but it probably fell into disrepair when Bishop David Hamilton moved to Saddell in South Argyll in 1508.

In 1814 Sir Walter Scott sailed past Lismore and, always keen to air his prejudices, recorded: 'We coasted the low, large and fertile island of Lismore, where a catholic bishop, Chisholm, has established a seminary of young men intended for priests and, what is a better thing, a valuable lime work'. Had he known that his descendants would build a small catholic chapel on to his house at Abbotsford, he might have concealed his disdain for the seminary. Founded in 1801 in the beautiful woodlands of Kilcheran, the institution only lasted till 1831 but the Georgian house, in which it was based, has survived.

One of the most unpopular ministers appointed to look after the spiritual welfare of the islanders was a John MacAulay, who was described as 'an obstinate, opinionative, dogmatic, domineering man; everyone else wrong and he alone right'. Prior to his arrival on Lismore in 1755, MacAulay had been in charge of a parish in Uist, where he incurred the wrath of his parishoners by trying to betray Prince Charles to the authorities in 1746. His grandson, inheriting some of his characteristics, became a renowned historian and peer of the realm.

Although Lismore does not seem to have suffered as seriously as other islands during the potato famine, it seems likely that about 400 people (30% of the population) left Lismore between 1841 and 1861. Some, no doubt, departed voluntarily to escape the unrelenting hardship but others were forced to leave. The south-east quarter of the island was in the hands of James Auchenleck Cheyne of Kilmaron and

A farm on Lismore.

Oxendean, Writer to the Signet. When he died in June 1853 the estate, including Lismore, was placed in the hands of Trustees. The Trustees, like those of several West Highland estates during these critical years, were legally bound to maximise profits on Cheyne's estates and therefore remove tenants who were seriously in arrears – on the west side at that time arrears amounted to 45% of the rent payable. The census books show that more than 80% of the households vanishing from Lismore between 1841 and 1861 had been on Cheyne's land.

In 1864 the north end of the island was sold to the Reverend James Fell of the Knells, Carlisle, a Church of England minister, who, in twenty years, spent almost £3,000 on improvements. Only £480 of this, however, was spent on the crofts – principally because he disapproved of the crofting system, maintaining that it encouraged idleness. Fell seems to have regarded himself as a fair, if not generous landlord, but, when the Crofters' Commission examined the estate in 1893, it reduced the rent of his 21 crofters by 28% and cancelled £300 of arrears.

At that time more than a dozen islanders were still employed in the lime quarries near Salen and five of the men in Port Ramsay owned smacks which carried the lime to Oban. When

179

the railway reached Oban, however, limestone came into Lorn in bulk and the lime quarries gradually declined. The old kilns can still be seen against a bank not far from the road.

On the eastern shore below Balure there is a broch with walls almost three metres thick. Known as Tirefour Castle, it has been described as 'one of the best preserved prehistoric monuments in the country'. The nameless people who built it 2,000 years ago were not the first inhabitants of these islands, for Mesolithic flints have been found on Shuna off the northern point of Lismore.

In recent years the island has established a reputation for its cross lambs and cattle but it is also well known on the Highland Games circuit for one of its athletes. Archie MacGillivray, one of the crofters, dominated the long-distance events on the west coast for two decades. His tall, fair-haired figure became a familiar sight on the starting lines. Sadly, he has had to abandon the hobby and none of the youngsters seems to be interested in maintaining the tradition.

The population, which was more than 1,000 in 1841, fell to 874 in 1861 and to 166 in 1971. Hundreds have left the island, taking their Gaelic traditions to America, Australia or New Zealand. Among the songs that stir the Gaels in these distant lands one of the most poignant is appropriately 'Leaving Lismore' or 'Fagail Liosmor', the chorus of which mentions all the lands surrounding the island.

CHAPTER 7

Ardgour, Morvern and Ardnamurchan

Ardgour

For those who have some time to spare or who cannot obtain a place on the Craignure Ferry there is an alternative route to Mull through some magnificent scenery. From Tyndrum the Fort William road crosses the desolate heights of Rannoch Moor and, passing beneath the steep scree slopes and black precipices of Glencoe, it emerges near the old slate quarries at Ballachulish. At this point a bridge spans the narrows of Loch Leven, where, until recently, motorists had to wait patiently for a ferry or take the long route round by Kinlochleven. The main road crosses the bridge and, passing through Onich, reaches Corran Ferry. This ferry, which can also be approached from Oban by the A828 through Appin, crosses the narrow channel between Ardgour and Bunree. The speed and strength of the tide can be quite dramatic, sometimes carrying the vessel well away from the jetties. The original ferry pier was built in 1815 by Thomas Telford, who was, at the time, supervising the construction of the Caledonian Canal linking Loch Linnhe with the North Sea.

The road to Lochaline (and the ferry to Mull) turns westward along the shore, passing the crofting township of Clovullin, where there is a shop and a petrol station. Motorists should bear in mind that petrol stations are few and infrequent on the peninsula and that, on the single-track roads, petrol consumption is inevitably increased.

Behind Clovullin the gables of Ardgour House can be seen in the trees. For many generations this was the home of the MacLeans of Ardgour. Of the many traditional landed families on the peninsula, Ardgour is the only one to have survived. In the great famine of 1847 Colonel MacLean was complimented by Government officials and the press for his generosity to his people. The following year, however, 150 people sailed from Fort William for New South Wales, most of them from

Corran Ferry.

Ardgour. MacLean claimed that they had not been evicted but had chosen to go. They left owing nothing to their landlord or anyone else in the district. Mainly young and single, they joined the thousands of other Gaels who were forced to leave the peninsula during those tragic years. The late Miss MacLean of Ardgour did all she could to prevent people leaving the area and devoted a great deal of her time to public service.

Those who are not in a hurry should consider taking the B8043 through Kingairloch, joining the Lochaline road again near Achagavel. It is a single-track road and, in some parts, very narrow – quite unsuitable for caravans. It winds up the hill to Lochan Doire a' Bhragaid, where there is some green, flat ground for camping, if you are prepared to risk being disturbed in the night by cattle tripping over the guys! As the road descends towards Camas Chil Mhalieu, there is a splendid view of Loch Linnhe with the island of Lismore in the distance. Beside the road there is a stand of mature pines and larches, the colours of which contrast with the thin, barren ground of the hillside where the soil has been torn away by the ancient ice-sheets, exposing the rock. Even the farming land of Chil Mhalieu (Kilmalieu) is very fragile, losing its organic matter and nutrients very quickly in the high rainfall. The road round the shore beyond Chil Mhalieu is extremely narrow with a sheer drop to the sea on one side and a steep, unstable rock-face on the other. Occasionally rocks become detached and tumble down the slope to crash into the sea or block the road. In spite of the hazards, this is a beautiful drive.

The small, quiet village of Kingairloch is right on the shore beside a wide, gravel beach. Originally this settlement was so isolated that it was linked with Lismore parish on the other side of the loch.

In recent years the Strutts of Kingairloch have replanted part of the estate to provide shelter on the lower ground. The main part of Kingairloch estate is off the main road in a wide valley below Beinn Mheadhon. The estate road descends through a conifer plantation to the shore and, where it emerges from the trees, there is a large salmon farm belonging to Marine Harvest and employing ten people. Beyond the fish farm there is an ancient chapel and a graveyard, in which there are headstones to the MacLeans of Loch Uisg and cairns built as memorials to the Strutts. Outside the graveyard there is a remarkable carved granite seat dedicated to George Strutt of Belper, Derbyshire, who bought the estate for the family in 1902. It has remained in their hands since then and is mainly a sporting estate.

The old mansion house of Kingairloch no longer exists in its original form as Arthur Strutt had part of it demolished to reduce it to more manageable proportions. Behind the 'big' house, north of the bridge, a path leads from the shepherd's house across the fields to the holiday homes at South Corrie. From there it is possible to walk to Glensanda by following the pony path, which winds up the steep side of Meall an Doire Dhuich to the ridge, or by taking the longer route round the coast.

Eilean Eisdeal, formerly Hugh Carmichael's *Eldesa,* dwarfed by the loading gear of Glensanda.

Glensanda

Glensanda used to be one of the quietest places on the peninsula, where hinds calved in the bracken and plovers nested on the shore. Now it is the site of the most ambitious civil engineering operation since the hydro-electric schemes carved their way through the hills of Argyll. Foster Yeoman Ltd. of Somerset are quarrying granite on a massive scale, their machines nodding like great dinosaurs on the horizon near Beinn Mheadhon as they scoop huge lumps of granite into the trucks. Two million tons of crushed rock every year are loaded for transport to America, Europe and the south-east of England, including some for the Channel Tunnel. The company intends to increase this output to 7.5 million tons by using what it described as the 'glory hole' method, in which a vertical shaft, 300 metres deep, is driven into the hill almost 2 km from the shore to meet a tunnel leading to the sea.

Local anti-nuclear campaigners are convinced that the tunnel will be used eventually to store vitreous nuclear waste, an accusation strenuously denied by Foster Yeoman. The company has invested £20 million in the project so far and intends to spend another £40 million to bring it to full capacity. It employs about 130 men at Glensanda, ferrying them to the camp from Appin and the Isle of Mull, and has built an airstrip beside the river. A flag now flutters in the breeze above the fifteenth-century castle, which has been partially restored.

It was here that Somerled, who was later to become Lord of the Isles, was recruited by the MacInnes clan to drive off a Norse raiding party. According to legend, Somerled was fishing for salmon in the Gear Abhainn, when the MacInnes men approached him and asked for his help. After consulting his father, Gillebride, in the cave where they lived, he agreed to assist them. Having established that the Norse raiding party outnumbered the local men, he devised a plan to deceive the enemy. He ordered the MacInnes people to slaughter some of their cattle. Astonished and, no doubt, beginning to doubt the wisdom of recruiting him, they reluctantly complied. He then asked them to march over one of the headlands in view of the Norsemen but, rather than mount an attack, to hurry back to him along the shore, concealed from their adversaries. When they returned, he told them to wear the skins of the cattle and repeat the performance. On the third occasion, they marched over the headland with the skins reversed, showing the pink flesh rather than the long, black hair. The Norsemen, convinced that they were about to be attacked by a superior force, withdrew. Apparently it was this event that led Somerled to take up arms in defence of the Gaels and, thereby, become Lord of the Isles.

In a summer dawn the hills above Glensanda are silent and still. Hinds stoop to drink in the crystal lochans and sometimes, when the sea lochs fill with mist and everything is obscured but the summits of the hills, a primeval tranquillity pervades the peninsula. As the sun rises over Lochaber, casting long shadows across the mist and gradually warming the night air, it could be another era . . . until the machines shatter the silence. In spite of the intrusion, it is still a pleasure to walk on these ridges. The deer are still there and the lochans are still alive with newts.

Rahoy and Loch Teacuis

The road north of Kingairloch climbs towards Loch Uisge through plantations of mature spruce and beech, some of their branches hanging decoratively over the road. The shores of Loch Uisge consist of red granite sand, which, at the western end, has built up into a long, soft bank. There are trout in the loch and the inevitable set of fish cages. Beyond it, the road passes through great peat mosses, which, in the summer, are white with the silk heads of bog cotton. One of the houses in this glen belongs to the fox hunter, who keeps a pack of hounds to control the fox population – an unusual, if not unique, method of hunting in the Highlands. As a shepherd I was never convinced by colleagues who claimed that their lamb crop had been devastated by foxes, perhaps because the most vociferous claimants were often the ones left to attend their lambing ewes as others were returning home for their breakfast. There is no doubt that the remains of lambs can be found round fox dens but they are often those of weak lambs which have died naturally. Foxes occasionally kill lambs but their predations are often exaggerated.

The Kingairloch road joins the A884 to Lochaline near Achagavel, a remote shepherd's cottage at the head of Gleann Dubh. When the bracken dies above the house and the sun is low on the horizon, the rigs, which grew barley for the 32 folk living in Achagavel 200 years ago, are clearly visible. Turning towards Lochaline, the road passes through Gleann Geal, a wide valley with a gentle slope on the east side – ideal sheep country. The farms of Beach and Altachonaich are on the far side of the river, which, with its dark pools and beds of red granite shingle, provides some of the best fishing in Morvern. Altachonaich at one time was part of Kingairloch estate and rented by the notorious Patrick Sellar, who was responsible for the Strathnaver clearances in Sutherland in 1814. Sellar bought the farm of Acharn, which can be seen in the trees near the Rahoy road junction, in 1838 and, evicting 44 families, had a flock of his Sutherland sheep driven south to stock his new property. Three years later he bought Clounlaid, on the west side of the glen, and Uladail, where another 100 people were removed from their holdings to provide pasture for his sheep.

At the deer farm, Rahoy.

When he purchased Ardtornish in 1844, he insisted that the crofters were removed before he became the legal owner of the estate. Sellar eventually owned more than 21,500 acres in Morvern.

Any visitor interested in Morvern's recent history should try to obtain a copy of Philip Gaskell's *Morvern Transformed*, which contains a list of deserted townships and photographs of the district taken in the nineteenth century. The history of many of the buildings seen from the road is presented in a concise and interesting appendix.

At Acharn, just south of the bridge, a road leads west towards Loch Teacuis and the deer farm of Rahoy. About a mile beyond the junction, this side road descends to Loch Arienas, where, above the granite sands, there are several good camping sites among the alders. The natural beauty of the area is somewhat marred by some clear felling of the forest. However, turning one's back on the felling, the sight of the high, terraced summits reflected in the dark water of the loch soon heals the affront. Even the salmon cages do not intrude on the beauty of Arienas.

The hills to the north-east, containing layers of ancient sediments such as siliceous limestone, Morvern Greensand and Lochaline Glass Sand, provide some of the most fertile grazing on the peninsula. This natural fertility also produces an extraordinary array of montane plants, including Mountain Avens, Globeflower. Holly Fern and the rare Arctic Sandwort. The woods at the water's edge on the north side of Loch Arienas mainly consist of Sessile Oak trees. Further down the glen, at Loch Teacuis, otters can be seen in the sea and pine martens have returned to the district.

The hills here used to be sheep pasture, owned by Mr A. Colville of Colville's Steel Works (now Ravenscraig). The grazing is quite exceptional. I remember the Kinlochteacuis lambs causing a stir at the ringside in Oban auction mart. The Rahoy part of the estate was acquired by the Highlands and Islands Development Board in 1977 and an experimental deer farm was established on the 'in-bye' land to assess the profitability and problems of intensive deer husbandry. The foundation stock was obtained partly from the keepers of sporting estates, who, for a bounty of £7.50, captured wild deer calves for Rahoy, and partly from another experimental farm in Kincardineshire. By 1978 there were 80 adult hinds and the same number of young beasts on the farm. Now it has a stock of 650 hinds and 50 stags. The success of Rahoy and Glensaugh in Kincardineshire has encouraged the establishment of other red deer farms throughout Britain – there are now 60 farms in Scotland and 250 in the UK. The demand for breeding stock has enhanced the market for young hinds and exceeded the expectations of the pioneers. Calves are now sold for an average of £110 and hinds at over £200. The gross profit margin per breeding hind amounts to about £45. All these farms, of course, are involved in the production of venison. Remarkably, most wild Highland venison – that is, meat from sporting estates – is normally exported to Europe. The catastrophe at Chernobyl caused a serious slump in demand for wild Scottish venison but it had little effect on the farmed variety, which now sells at about £3.00 per kilo. In the early stages the farmers encountered considerable consumer resistance to their product – a strange phenomenon as venison is unquestionably the healthiest red meat with scarcely any fat. Now, however, demand exceeds supply. It is possible to see the deer at the roadside near Rahoy but visits to the farm should be arranged through the Hill Farming Research Organisation, which now runs the operation.

The public road ends near Kinlochteacuis but there is a good path to Glencripesdale over the shoulder of Beinn Charmaig to meet the public road again at Laudale. The deciduous woodland beyond Glencripesdale is part of a National Nature Reserve, containing a rich variety of liverworts, lichens and mosses and almost 200 kinds of flowering plants and ferns, including the Atlantic hay-scented buckler fern and Wilson's filmy fern. In certain parts of the woods the air is scented with wild garlic and the shadows coloured with bluebells. Unfortunately the Reserve is fenced off and access has to be arranged through the Chief Warden.

Ardtornish

Returning to the A884 and turning east at Kinlochaline, a road leads to the north end of Loch Aline and Ardtornish. In the trees west of the river the tower of Kinlochaline Castle is just visible from the road. A fifteenth-century keep with a pit and vaulted cellar, it was partly restored in 1890. The key can be obtained from a neighbouring cottage and, as the building is remarkably well preserved, it is well worth a visit. Locally known as Casteal an Ime (Castle of Butter) because, according to legend, the labourers employed to build it were paid in butter, it was the seat of the MacInnes chiefs. In 1390 MacInnes and his five sons were murdered at Ardtornish Castle and their lands were given to MacLean of Duart. Like so many other fortifications in the area, it was burned by Colkitto MacDonald during the Civil War in 1644.

Just beyond the bridge the Victorian mansion of Ardtornish dominates the surrounding landscape. When this estate was purchased by Octavius Smith in 1845, there was no suitable residence for the new proprietor and he had to live in Achranich, where he entertained, nevertheless, distinguished guests such as Herbert Spencer, the philosopher. Smith, a wealthy London distiller, built Ardtornish Tower in 1856, a mansion with 35 rooms and a Romanesque clock tower which can still be seen behind the house. The rest of the original building, having developed dry rot, had to be demolished in

1884 and rebuilt to the design of Alexander Ross of Inverness. In the early twentieth century the novelist John Buchan was a regular guest at Ardtornish, the Tower featuring in his *Mister Standfast* and his experiences of deer stalking in *John MacNab*. The house is used now as flats for self-catering holidays. The gardens, containing 28 acres of shrubs and woodland walks, are open to the public from April to October. In the walled garden visitors can buy plants, shrubs and vegetables.

Beyond Ardtornish the road surface deteriorates but it is possible to reach the small boat repair yard, which has slipping and mooring facilities for eight vessels. It also produces its own design of fibreglass dinghy and has diversified into architectural mouldings and Morris Minor bonnets. Further south there is another fish farm, which is owned by Golden Sea Produce and employs six people to produce 400 tons of salmon a year. This company has started a hatchery at Ardtornish and provides work for twelve people in the Lochaline area – two more than the Forestry Commission, which has ten permanent staff.

Fish farming, which directly employs about 850 people in Scotland and is worth at least £100 million per year, is one of the fastest growing industries on the West Coast. This is particularly true of salmon production, which increased from 520 tonnes in 1979 to 15,000 tonnes in 1988 and is expected to yield 35,000 tonnes by 1991. Salmon farming in Morvern, Ardnamurchan, Mull and North Argyll is dominated by three major firms – Marine Harvest (a subsidiary of the giant Unilever), McConnel Salmon (part of Booker PLC) and Golden Sea Produce (a subsidiary of Norfisk). The operations of the three firms seem to be concentrated in different areas – McConnel in Ardnamurchan, Marine Harvest in Upper Loch Sunart, Loch Linnhe and Mull and Golden Sea in Lochaline and Appin. In Morvern these firms provide a total of 45 jobs – four times the staff of the Forestry Commission in the area.

The salmon are reared from eggs in darkened tanks, which are fed with pure river water, until, after six months, they are placed in outdoor tanks exposed to the light and the weather. When they are about a year old, they are transferred to seawater net cages suspended from floating platforms. They are fed on a specially balanced fish food, which contains a substance to colour their flesh, until they are approximately two years old. The whole process, therefore, takes three years. During that period the farmer receives no income so large companies, with financial strength and backing, tend to predominate. The mature fish are killed and sent to smokeries, retailers such as Marks and Spencer, processors or to foreign buyers. Marine Harvest exports salmon to Europe, America and Japan. Recently the producers have combined in a marketing organisation known as the Scottish Salmon Growers' Association.

The spin-off from fish farming is substantial. Boats, nets, cages and fish food are needed. Boats are made in Corpach near Fort William, nets in Kilbirnie, cages in Strathclyde and fish food in Bathgate and Invergordon. There is also downstream employment in transport and in gutting or packing plants. Marine Harvest has opened such a plant at Corpach, in which it hopes to employ 100 people. Fish farming is becoming a vast and vital industry in the Highlands, providing work in remote areas for young people who might otherwise have left home. Conservationists, however, have expressed concern about its operations.

Licences to anchor cages off the shore are not subject to local authority planning controls but are in the hands of the Crown Estate Commissioners, an unelected and largely unaccountable group of civil servants. In granting licences the Commissioners obviously enhance the Crown Estate income and, although they claim that, in considering applications, they strike a balance between profit and conservation management, some local politicians and the Scottish Scenic Trust are most unhappy about their decisions and the secrecy surrounding applications for sites. As a gesture, the Commissioners have introduced consultation procedures but these are not a substitute for control and the councils are not given enough time to study the plans. There is no doubt that, with such a rapidly expanding industry in a sensitive area, regulation and constant vigilance are necessary.

A highly toxic chemical called dichlorvos is used to destroy sea lice on the salmon. It can also kill lobsters, crabs, mussels and other shellfish and its effect on the health of fish farm workers is causing alarm among conservationists. The Marine

A silver harvest – farmed salmon ready for market.

Conservation Society have called for a ban on the use of the chemical and the Friends of the Earth have attacked it. In spite of its pledge at the North Sea Ministerial Conference in 1988 to adopt a 'precautionary' approach to the use of such chemicals, the Government has granted a product licence to the manufacturers and it is now used widely in Highland lochs.

Damage inflicted on the nets and fish by seals, cormorants and other predators has been estimated at £5 million annually. It is not surprising, therefore, that the workers shoot animals and birds which threaten the nets. Experiments have been conducted using ultrasonic seal scarers and they are employed on some of the farms but are not installed universally. Fish farmers could not have been blamed for rubbing their hands when a mysterious virus swept through the seal population in 1988. Obviously more research is required to discover acceptable methods of controlling predators and to ascertain

Lochaline to Fishnish ferry.

the long-term effects of fish farming on the environment. Research and control of the industry are vital if fish farming is to expand to benefit the whole community and the environment in which it is located.

Beyond the salmon cages in Loch Aline are the remains of Ardtornish Castle. Built in the fourteenth century, this was one of the strongholds of the Lords of the Isles. 'Good John' of the Isles, son of Angus Og, established himself in a position of greater power than any of his race since Somerled, controlling the Western Isles and a great part of the mainland between Knoydart and Kintyre. In the Irish annals he was given the title 'Ri Innse Gall' (King of the Isles). John put away his first wife, Amie MacRuari, who had brought him most of the mainland territory as her dowry, and married Margaret, the daughter of King Robert II. He died at Ardtornish in 1378. Just over 70 years later a Great Council of the chiefs of the Isles was convened at the castle to witness the granting of lands to MacLean of Ardtornish and, more significantly, to discuss the appointment of a commission to negotiate a treaty with Edward IV of England. The Treaty of Ardtornish and Westminster of 1462 would have given the whole of Scotland to the Islesmen. The Scottish Government, however, discovered the plot and the Lord of the Isles was punished for his subversion through forfeiture of his lands. The ruin of the castle, where the Great Council met, stands on the headland overlooking the Sound of Mull where the fleets of galleys used to pass, ferrying the Lords of the Isles between their possessions in Ulster, Islay and the Western Isles.

Today the car ferry to Mull crosses from Lochaline to Fishnish. Beyond the jetty there is a sand mine. Established during the War in 1940, it was the only source of pure silicon sand for optical and special glass for the armed forces. In 1952 it still employed 50 workers. Now there are only 17 but, as this represents 14% of the area's working population, the mine plays a crucial role in the local economy. The white sand is shipped to England, Sweden and Ireland.

Lochaline village was founded about 1830 by John Sinclair, who owned the Tobermory Distillery. Above the village Keil Church, built in 1898 on the site of an older place of worship, stands in a well maintained graveyard. In the grounds there are the remains of a medieval chapel and a Celtic cross in a prominent position overlooking the Sound of Mull. Some of the ancient burial slabs have been taken into the church to protect them from the weather – a privilege which should be extended to some of the decaying eighteenth-century stones in the graveyard. The original Christian settlement here was founded by Columba of Iona and it is said that his mother, Eithne, is buried somewhere in the district.

The B849 to Drimnin follows the shore, providing some remarkable views of the Sound of Mull. In February 1746, as the Jacobite Rising reached its tragic conclusion, the Duke of Cumberland issued an order commanding that Morvern was to be laid waste as a centre of rebellion. Captain Robert Duff sailed up the Sound in the sloops *Terror* and *Princess Anne* and burnt Ardtornish and Drimnin. Nearly 400 houses with barns full of corn and the cattle, horses, meal and other provisions were destroyed. One local man described the shore as 'one great ember'. Thousands of acres of woodland were reduced to smouldering stumps. Passing beneath the tall beeches and sycamores on the roadside today, it is difficult to imagine the devastation. Above the road hazel and alders thrive on the rich soil and, on the steep slopes, Enchanter's Nightshade, Dog's mercury, Woodruff and the rare Narrow-leaved Helleborine form part of the rich ground flora. On the shore the dark sand and flat, black rocks are reminders of the volcanic origins of the landscape. In the late spring banks of yellow iris and campion add colour to the rocks and shelduck glide past the rafts of bladderwrack. Near Glenmorvern a plantation of beech, lime and oak overhangs the road and the verges contain a profusion of wild orchids. The woodlands are listed as a Site of Special Scientific Interest and are regarded as an area of national importance. This designation, however, does not give the public right of access and visitors are expected to respect the rights of the proprietors.

At Fiunary the manse was once the home of Doctor John MacLeod, the 'high priest' of Morvern – he was over six feet and a half tall – and an ancestor of Lord MacLeod of Fiunary, the founder of the Iona Community. The first member of this remarkable family to preach in Fiunary was Norman MacLeod of Skye, who, as a staunch Presbyterian and supporter of the Hanoverian cause, must have been at odds with his Jacobite parishioners. Like many Highland ministers at that time, he was also a farmer and held Fiunary Farm as well as the manse. Most of the land is now part of Fiunary Forest, which stretches right over the hill to Loch Teacuis, but the manse is still held by Lord MacLeod. Beyond Fiunary, beside the road, there is an extraordinary archway worn through a volcanic dyke by the sea before it receded to its present level.

West of the dyke, Caisteal nan Con (Castle of Hounds) stands on a promontory overlooking a small bay. Said to have been the hunting lodge of the Lords of the Isles, it is built of local volcanic rock and had three floors. The ground around it is covered with sloe and mallow and there are signs of an aqueduct in the rubble. In the small bay the remains of a stone fish trap can be seen at low tide, built to supply the lodge with fresh fish. Above the castle Killundine farm is all that remains of the original estate of 4,400 acres, which was bought by the State just before the Second World War and gradually planted by the Forestry Commission. The gorges of Killundine and Mungosdail rivers, with their cover of wych elm, ash, scrub oak and birch, provide an environment in which several varieties of rare fern flourish.

On the Drimnin side of Amhainn Mhungasdail there are the

remains of an eighteenth-century millhouse and a kiln used to dry the grain for the neighbouring tenants before it was ground. 25 families were evicted from Mungosdail farm in 1824 by the new proprietrix, Miss Christina Stewart of Edinburgh. By that time, however, the mill was already a ruin, a fact which suggests that the population had started to decline before the evictions. In 1779 there were 85 people in Mungosdail; in 1841 there were 12. Miss Stewart also cleared 75 people from Unimore (Aonach Mor) on the west side of Loch Arienas so that she could let it and Mungosdail as a sheep farm. Sadly the remains of their houses are now engulfed in a sea of conifers. One of the victims, Mary Cameron, who reached Glasgow and found work in a cotton mill, described their departure:

> The day of the flitting came. The officers of the law came along with it and the shelter of a house, even for one night more, was not to be got . . . I thought my heart would rend. I would feel right if my tears would flow but no relief did I find. We sat for a time on Knock na Carn to take the last look at the place where we had been brought up. The houses were being already stripped. The bleat of the 'big sheep' was on the mountain. The whistle of the Lowland shepherd and the bark of his dogs were on the brae . . .'

Miss Stewart, however, did not clear Bonnavoulin but built a row of houses for her tenants by the shore. The shell of one of these is still there. Bonnavoulin is a most attractive settlement, curving round a small bay with several sheltered places for picnics and splendid views of Ardnamurchan and the Isle of Mull. The public road ends at Drimnin but there is a track leading to Auliston, a township from which 100 people were evicted in 1855. As part of his scheme to encourage small tenants, the Duke of Argyll had settled ex-soldiers from his fencible regiment here in 1788. The proprietrix in 1855 had a different approach. The ruins of the houses, with their round gables and dry stone walls, stand as a poignant reminder of the distress of the people and the callous disregard of it by Lady Gordon. An extraordinary atmosphere pervades the ruins, as if the people had just departed. One can almost smell the peat smoke and hear the cartwheels creaking and children crying. Some of the tenants evicted from Auliston settled on the Isle of

Sunset over Loch Sunart.

Oronsay in Loch Sunart only to be removed again in 1868. One of the descendants of these people became a leading figure in the Highland Land League. John MacDonald, a Glasgow clothier's shop assistant, was chosen as the Lochaline delegate to the Highland Land Law Reform Association (later the League) in 1883 after his regular correspondence supporting the crofters' cause in the *Oban Times*. MacDonald helped to prepare the statements of the Bonnavoulin people to the Royal Commission and presented them on their behalf.

Laudale

Returning to the A884 and the junction at Achagavel, the road winds over the hill towards Loch Sunart. As it reaches the loch, a very narrow, twisting road turns west towards Laudale Estate. Taking this route, the first building on the right is Liddesdale or, as it was called in 1733, Liedgesdale. The tall ruin on the shore was the Morvern Mining Company's store and probably the building which was converted to a tacksman's residence in 1752. The lead vein, which is at Lurga over in Glen Dubh, was discovered by Sir Alexander Murray of

Landale House and oakwoods.

Stanhope, who founded the company, to extract both lead and copper ore from the mine. A road was made to Lurga and some minerals were extracted but the operations were abandoned after a few years. Liddesdale is now a holiday house and most of the old estate has been afforested.

In a small bay beyond Liddesdale there is a fish farm belonging to Marine Harvest. The hillside above the bay has been designated as a Site of Special Scientific Interest because of the woodlands and the rare lichens. The woods, which are mainly birch with oak and gean on the burnsides, contain mosses, liverworts and lichens, which can thrive only in the cleanest air and in an oceanic climate. One of the lichens can be found at no other site in Britain.

Near Laudale gates, the road passes through the cattle pens of the old pier. Twenty years ago sheep and cattle from the hill farms and crofts in the area were loaded here and taken to Oban for sale. The public road ends just beyond the pier at the cattle grid on the Laudale boundary. There is, however, a track through the estate to Glencripesdale, where there is an exclusive hotel. Laudale is run as a sporting estate and, as the stags are fed on concentrates in the winter, they can be seen in the fields beside the road. The sheep were cleared off the estate about fourteen years ago and the stock of deer is

Strontian from the Landale Hills.

increasing rapidly. A walk on the hill behind the farm is most rewarding, with the opportunity to watch red deer in their natural habitat and there is a superb view of Loch Sunart from the precipice above. However, visitors intending to leave the road should remember that sportsmen may be stalking on the hill between August and February and that they should, therefore, consult the head stalker before entering the forest. The walk along the shore on a summer's evening, with the haunting boom of eider drakes and the still water stirred only by swallows as they dip to catch flies, is an incredibly restful experience.

Strontian

Strontian, like Liddesdale, was also founded on lead mining and, like that of Lurga, the vein was discovered by Sir Alexander Murray, who had feued the estate of Ardnamurchan and Sunart in the early eighteenth century. In about 1723 Murray granted the rights of extraction first to the Duke of Norfolk and then to the York Building Company. By 1733, 500 people, some of them from Ireland, were employed in the mines and the seams were described as 'among the richest of their kind in Europe'. In 1740, however, the mines were closed and the workers dismissed. In 1764 an unusual mineral, later called Strontianite, was discovered in the seams and operations recommenced. By 1871, however, all the mines were closed. The shafts and galleries are still there and, in the piles of spoil from the excavations near the Bellsgrove and Whitesmith mines, it is possible to find samples of Strontianite, lead ore and barytes. Bellsgrove also yields traces of the rare barium minerals Brewsterite and Harmotome; indeed Bellsgrove is the 'world type' locality for the former.

Above Strontian today, on the Polloch road, there is an extensive barytes mine run by an English firm. 12 men are employed by the company, which extracts and processes barytes for use as drilling mud in the offshore oil industry. Unfortunately the firm seems to lead a precarious existence, seriously affected by currency fluctuations and imports of cheap barytes from Morocco.

Strontian village itself offers a wide range of tourist facilities. Strontian Hotel was originally London House, a timber building constructed in London, dismantled and shipped to Strontian. Several craftsmen now work in the area including a musical instrument maker, who specialises in psalteries. The Forestry Commission has laid out an interesting forest walk on the west side of the village, where there are some majestic Silver Firs planted by Sir James Riddell, the proprietor of Ardnamurchan and Sunart, about 150 years ago and a row of elegant beeches. The new plantation contains some Scots Pine and young Silver Fir and, at the end of the path, there is a seat overlooking Loch Sunart.

At Scotstown a road turns east to the Loch Sunart National Nature Reserve and a Nature Trail through the oak woods on the banks of the Strontian River. These woodlands are regarded as one of the most intact collections of ancient broadleaved trees in Britain and, as in the Laudale Woods, rare lichens and liverworts thrive beneath the tree canopy. At one time these woods were coppiced for charcoal and the remains of the colliers' hearths can still be seen in the clearings. Mature beech and spruce and delicate larches line the track and, in the green hollows, Globeflowers and Melancholy Thistles reach towards the light.

The drive to Polloch is the most dramatic in the area. It is extremely steep in places and, being very narrow, is quite unsuitable for caravans. There is a Forestry Commission viewpoint at the summit with views over Loch Shiel. It is worth stopping there, as the road continues through a tunnel of mature spruce and larch offering only the occasional glimpse of the magnificent scenery. The road descends to Loch Doilet, where fishing permits can be obtained from the Forestry Office. Polloch is a small community, an example of the unfulfilled promise of unlimited employment held out by the Forestry Commission during its spate of purchases in the 1950s. Many of the timber houses, gifted by the Swedish Government after the War, are not permanently occupied. In 1950 there were 20 people employed in Glenheurich; in 1987 there were six.

There is a road right through to Glenfinnan from Polloch along the shores of Loch Shiel but, as this passes through the lands of Conaglen Estate, even the Forestry Commission has very limited access. The gates are locked, so it is not possible to drive beyond Polloch.

There are, however, several interesting walks and places of interest in the glen. On Eilean Fhianain (Saint Finan's Isle), named after a missionary who built a sanctuary there in the sixth century, there are the remains of an ancient chapel and burial ground. A bronze bell, said to have been brought from Ireland by Saint Finan and reputed to possess healing power, still sits on the rough stone altar. The sacred island became a burial place for the people on both sides of the loch. After the Reformation, however, Protestants were buried on the south side and Catholics on the north, in case, no doubt, the Reformed corpses would be corrupted by those of the old religion. Several old coffin roads converge on the pier at Achnanellan, one of them leading from Polloch round the shoulder of Torran nam Mial to the environmental centre at Achnanellan. Another turns west from the centre to Ardshealach at Acharacle skirting Claish Moss. This moss is a National Nature Reserve and is one of the finest examples of what is called a 'raised mire system' with shallow domes surrounded by a maze of pools. Fourteen different Sphagnum mosses have been identified here and, in the winter, a flock of

Greenland white-fronted geese settles on the flats. However, as
the Reserve is surrounded by land which is not owned by the
Nature Conservancy Council, it is advisable to contact the local
Warden to obtain a permit before arranging a visit. From
Polloch there is also a longer, more strenuous walk through
Glen Heurich to Glen Scaddle.

Returning to Strontian, the road to Salen passes
Ardnastaing. In the bay below this township a floating church
was anchored in 1846. The Disruption, which split the Church
of Scotland in 1843, was essentially over the issue of patronage – the right of a landowner to impose his chosen minister on
the parish. When 400 ministers, declaring their opposition to
this principle, walked out of the General Assembly to form the
Free Church, they were taking an extraordinary risk. Had their
congregations refused to follow them, they would have had no
means of support. In the Highlands, however, the people were
only too aware of the tyranny of the landed class and flocked to
the new church. A few proprietors, such as the Earl of
Breadalbane, supported them but many found the initiative
offensive and refused to grant sites for new places of worship.
Sir James Riddell, an Episcopalian and proprietor of
Ardnamurchan and Sunart, was one of the latter. The
congregation of Strontian, undeterred, had a floating church
built in Port Glasgow and anchored it in the bay at
Ardnastaing. Used till 1873, this unorthodox place of worship
was 78 feet long and seated 400 people.

Beyond Ardnastaing, just over Allt a Mhoullin (The Mill
Burn), a track leads up to Ranachan. Below the main road at
this point, the remarkable ruin of Ranachan Mill is hidden in
the trees. Two massive millstones lie half-buried in the rubble
and the old iron shaft, with its hexagonal driving head, is still
in place. Above the road a solid granite barn and stables testify
to the prosperity of the larger farms in the nineteenth century.
Ranachan originally consisted of two holdings, Ranachan Mor
and Ranachan Strone. After the First World War, when many
Highland estates changed hands, these farms were purchased
by the Department of Agriculture and, as an experiment, were
let as three holdings in 1923, the incoming tenants being
assisted to take over the livestock with Government loans.
Although they survived for a time, there is only one man in

Ranachan today. There is a splendid walk from the old sheep fank out to the hill behind the farm and, on the shore below, a hide overlooking a sea pool where otters fish among the weed.

Beyond Ranachan the settlement of Ardery is almost hidden in the trees. It does not appear in the 1841 Census nor in the estate papers but it is said that the manager of the Salen pirn mill lived here in the 1850s. This was also the home of Allan MacDonald, a massive Highlander, who, when attacked by a bull, seized it by the horns and broke its neck. Apparently his wife was a slighter person, weighing only 24 stone!

At Resipole there is a caravan and camping site right on the shore with pony trekking and other facilities. Resipole is an ancient holding, its first known occupier being Dugald Stewart, who died there in 1426 and was buried on Iona. There were five crofters there in 1829 but, by 1840, it was a single holding. In 1861 it was let to one of the Camerons of Fort William. The head of that remarkable family, the famous Cameron of Corriechoille, started as a herd boy and became one of the largest flockmasters in the west, at one time holding eleven farms with 60,000 sheep. He was one of the few native Highlanders who managed to participate and succeed in the new sheep regime.

The small village of Salen provides a safe and picturesque anchorage and contains a hotel and small boatyard. The road forks there for Kilchoan and Ardnamurchan.

Acharacle

The A861 leads north to Acharacle and eventually to Lochailort. Leaving Salen, it climbs through a pass with mature pines on one side and tranquil lochans edged with water lilies on the other. In 1838 more than 2,000 people lived in Acharacle, which contained 16 crofts with another 10 at Arivegaig. Some of the crofters held their sheep stock in a 'club', a system in which their arable land was held separately while the sheep were run as a single flock on their pasture. This was a structure through which native Highlanders might have participated in the sheep farming boom, but sadly it was rarely attempted and occasionally deliberately destroyed by the landlords. The Acharacle club still existed in 1883 with 300 sheep and eight shares but it did not survive the changes of the twentieth century.

North of Acharacle the B8044 forks left for Ardtoe. The minor road heading west leads to Arivegaig and Gortenfern and provides access to the beaches of Camas an Lighe. The public section, however, ends at the bridge over Allt Beithe, where there is a parking place and picnic point on the banks of the river. The foundations of this road were laid during the potato famine, when, in order to obtain meal for their starving families from the authorities, the men had to work on the road – a sort of nineteenth-century job training scheme. The track beyond the bridge leads round to Ockle with incredible views of Eigg and Rhum. The road to Ardtoe crosses Kentra Moss.

At Ardtoe there is a small white beach and a car park. The view from Carn Mor of the Isle of Skye and the Small Isles is quite unique and well worth the short walk from the beach. The Sea Fish Industry research station, where experiments in the rearing of turbot, halibut and shellfish are conducted, is near the car park. The road to Ardtoe is very narrow and not suitable for large vehicles. Yet, because of its popularity and picturesque setting, the bay tends to become rather overcrowded.

The road to Shielfoot winds along the River Shiel, passing the grounds of Shielfoot House. These used to contain a three-storey mansion, built by Charles D. Rudd in 1898 as his principal residence on the estate. Rudd had formed a partnership with Cecil Rhodes in Africa to form a company called Gold Fields of South Africa, which, in its first year, paid dividends of 97%. He is principally remembered for the 'Rudd Concession', through which the British South Africa Company obtained access to the mineral reserves of Zimbabwe. Part of the vast fortune which Rudd accumulated in Africa was invested in Ardnamurchan. He bought the western part of the estate in 1897 and built Glenborrodale Castle in 1902. Shielbridge estate was eventually purchased by a Glasgow syndicate interested mainly in its fishing rights and the mansion was demolished in the early 1950s. The outbuildings, the estate walls and the gardens are still there. Beyond these

Kentra Moss near Ardtoe.

grounds the township of Shielfoot lies in the shadow of a steep rock, on which the remains of an ancient fort are visible in the scrub.

Glenborrodale

Returning to Salen, the B8007 follows Loch Sunart westward, with a plantation, containing some old pines and magnificent beeches, above the road and the sea below it. There are some holiday houses in the beautiful bay of Camasinas but the first large settlement is at Laga Bay. The farm steadings here were built by Lord Trent, the son of the founder of Boots Pure Drug Company, who ran Laga as a dairy farm after he bought Ardnamurchan Estate in 1936. Laga Bay is now the headquarters of the McConnel salmon farming operations in the area; in fact more than 30% of the firm's annual output of 2,000 tonnes comes from the Loch Sunart farms. The great network of cages does detract from the beauty of Laga Bay but the employment provided by McConnel helps to keep young people in the area. It is possible to hire boats there to fish in the loch or to cruise along the shore.

The settlement beyond Laga is Glenborrodale. On the west side of the village, barely visible from the road, Glenborrodale Castle stands in about 100 acres of gardens and woodland. Built by Charles Rudd in 1902, it is an impressive piece of architecture. When the Riddell estate, which included Sunart and Ardnamurchan, was split up in 1853, the western end was sold to James Dalgleish, a Writer to the Signet in Edinburgh, who held it till 1897. Dalgleish had a house on the site of the castle but Rudd had it demolished to build a residence which would reflect his affluence. His castle is constructed of sandstone imported from Annan, Dumfriesshire, a material which does not help it to blend with the landscape. It took three years to complete the building, employing between 50 and 100 men. When Rudd died in 1916, the estate was sold to Sir Kenneth Clark, a thread manufacturer from Paisley and father of Lord Clark the art historian, then to Lord Trent. During Clark's time the castle was let occasionally to shooting tenants, such as Sir Thomas Sopwith, whose Sopwith Camel caused such havoc to the enemy during the First World War, and Sir Thomas Lipton. During the Second World War Ardnamurchan was a restricted area, Loch Sunart being used as a convoy assembly point, and the Castle became a naval base. It now belongs to Peter John de Savary, who runs it as an exclusive, 16-bedroom hotel, which is open from May to October. Mr de Savary's company, Land Leisure, also owns Aspinall's gaming club in London and the tourist complex at Land's End and he now owns a substantial part of Breakfast TV. The gardens are being tastefully restored and contain several exotic shrubs taken from Africa by Charles Rudd.

In Glen More there is an excellent natural history centre, run by the photographer Mike MacGregor, and a pottery. The exhibition in the centre was transferred to the Glasgow Garden Festival in 1988 to form the basis of the Ardnamurchan display but has been returned to Glen More. Beyond the centre there are several places to camp overlooking the sea.

The next bay, Camas na Geal, is the most beautiful inlet on the peninsula. The green arable land, surrounded on three sides by steep hillsides, curves round the sandy shore. Beside the road, high above the fields, there is a parking place from which a track leads down to the bay, where a row of sycamores

Glenborrodale Castle.

hangs over the path and shades a prehistoric cairn of massive slabs. Near the shore there are the remains of a chapel with two gravestones dated 1737, thought to be those of the Campbells of Ardslignish. Below the chapel there is an ancient standing stone with a primitive cross carved on the hard surface. On the far side of the bay there is the ruin of a fort situated above steep rock faces to give it protection. On the shore, which is, sadly, littered with plastic bags, bottles and other debris of the consumer society cast up by the tide, it is possible to find small amethysts and cairngorms.

Above Camas na Geal, on the side of Ben Hiant, the deserted township of Bourblaig, from which the people were cleared in 1828, lies in a hollow above the escarpment. John MacColl, a tenant of Tornamony in Camas na Geal, became the sole tenant of both Tornamony and Bourblaig by 1829. In 1807 Tornamony contained 13 families and Bourblaig 10. By 1840 MacColl also had Mingary, where he is said to have cleared the townships of Skinaid and Corryvulin, having four and 12 families respectively in 1829. Sir James Riddell, on MacColl's behalf, had no less than 39 families evicted to form the sheep farm of Mingary. MacColl, however, was blamed for this and was cursed by an old woman from Kilchoan, who prophesied that he would not live much longer and that no grass would grow on his grave. MacColl was buried in the old churchyard at Kilchoan and his grave is surrounded by iron railings. Nothing will grow on it, in spite of surreptitious attempts by his relatives to plant grass seed. As in Auliston on Morvern, an atmosphere of melancholy pervades the ruins of Bourblaig. High on the hillside, with a magnificent view across the loch, it is protected from the south-west by strange ridges formed by volcanic cone sheets. It can be found by locating a gate in the roadside fence in the green basin north of Camas na Geal and by following a farm track to the south-west.

Kilmory

The main road climbs round the shoulder of Beinn nan Losgann above Loch Mudle, crossing the old road joining Ardslignish and Camphouse. The road to Kilmory turns north beyond the summit of the hill. Kilmory is an extremely fertile glen with rich Mesozoic sediments down the middle of the strath. The western fork of the road beyond Braehouse leads to Achateny beach and Faskadale, where the landscape is quite different, with profuse birch and hazel scrub on one side and a vast peat moss on the other. The remains of an old thorn hedge grow beside the road, twisted and bent towards the east by the prevailing wind. There is a path down to Achateny beach, with a walk of 400 yards, about halfway to Faskadale. Faskadale itself lies at the north end of a huge gabbro ring, which stretches through Kilchoan right round to Sanna Bay. This was one of the rings formed by the volcanic centre near Achnaha. Faskadale, therefore, is not as fertile as Kilchoan. It is mainly a salmon station, where 'wild' fish are caught in nets off the shore. Before the Isle of Soay was evacuated in 1953 some of the islanders used to travel to Faskadale for the season. There is an old ice house near the shore, which traditionally filled with ice from the hill lochs carried by pack pony, but it is now used as a store.

The eastern fork of the road at Braehouse leads to Kilmory. The landscape is much more open here with broad stretches of arable land between outcrops of hard quartz dolerite. The old school, which was closed in 1961, stands on the east side of the road. In 1829 there were at least 15 families living in Kilmory with another eight tenants and four cottar families at Branault. Achateny by that time was already a single tenant farm let to James Thorburn, described by Riddell's adviser as 'the best man to farm in Ardnamurchan'. By the end of the century there were only eight crofters in Kilmory and one at Branault. Now there are only six crofts, held mainly by elderly people with no cattle, and very few children.

The schoolmaster in Kilmory between 1732 and 1739 was Alasdair mac Mhaighstir Alasdair, Alexander MacDonald, said by Hugh MacDiarmid to be by far the greatest Gaelic poet. Alasdair had married a girl from Dalness in Glen Etive, writing of her:

> Air Allt Ghartain ghlacas bradan,
> Ban-iasg ghasda lan-mhaiseach . . .
> (In Gartan burn I've caught a salmon
> A magnificent, full-beautiful woman-fish)

When he and his family arrived in Kilmory, there were 40 children in the district and Alasdair not only taught them English and Arithmetic but was responsible for their religious and moral development. He was employed by the Society in Scotland for the Propagation of Christian Knowledge (SSPCK), which was assisted by a grant from George II 'to be employed for the reformation of the Highlands and Islands and other places where popery and ignorance abound'. In its early years the SSPCK had forbidden the teaching of Latin and the use of Gaelic in schools. However, when it was discovered that children could recite long passages of the scriptures in English without understanding a word of it, the policy was abandoned and Alasdair produced their first 'Galick and English Vocabulary' in 1741. As a schoolmaster Alasdair also had responsibility for the morals of the adults and he occasionally admonished errant members of the community in his Gaelic verse, warning them, at one point, of the dangers of venereal disease, which was 'all over Ardnamurchan' and which had apparently been brought to the peninsula by the Strontian miners. He also castigated two old men who had taken to 'striopachas' (whoring) at the age of 70:

> The old bulls are as randy
> As well-equipped three year olds
> And, though good is the grass of the Corries,
> Seven times better is the grass of Faskadale.

Everyone in the community would have understood the allusion. The local minister also complained that his parishioners were inclined to indulge in 'profanation of the Lord's day, swearing, drinking, fornication, duelling, theft, burning houses in the night tyme and haughing cowes and horses . . .'. Evidently Alasdair was responsible for a community with a healthy disregard for prevailing mores.

Alasdair was brought up as an Episcopalian but, probably for financial reasons, became a Presbyterian. When the Prince landed in 1745, however, he joined the Jacobite army and became a Roman Catholic.

On the road to Ockle a small graveyard, surrounded by a drystone wall, stands in dignified isolation in a broad green hollow beside the burn. The church, now abandoned as a place of worship, is on the hill on the south bank so, at a funeral, mourners had to cross the small bridge to reach the graveyard. Within the cemetery the remains of an ancient chapel stands among the headstones. This building probably gave the settlement its name, Cille Mhoire or the Cell of Mary. In the ruins there is an old stone font, which, it is claimed, never runs dry. It was from Kilmory that word of the Prince's landing in August 1745 was relayed to London. The minister, a staunch Hanoverian, noticed that his congregation in Kilmory were particularly excited and, knowing them to be sympathetic to the Jacobite cause, trapped one of them into revealing the facts and sent the news to the factor at Mingary Castle. From there it went to Campbell of Airds and the Sheriff at Inveraray.

Following the road to the east, there is a magnificent view above Swordle, where the District Council have thoughtfully provided a seat. Sadly, it lacked either the vision or the resources to provide a small car park as well. The soil is remarkably fertile in the Swordle area, consisting of sandy shales and limestone between hillocks of quartz-dolerite. The array of wild flowers in late spring, therefore, is quite amazing, in spite of the sheep. In 1859 there were 29 households at Swordle; by 1861 only eight remained, one of which was that of John Ramage from Wiston, Lanarkshire, the sheep-farming tenant of Swordlemhor. Below the farm there is a splendid beach, facing north to Rhum and Eigg, and, further on, the settlement of Ockle. There the road comes to an abrupt end but a path leads round the shore to Gortenfern.

Kilchoan

Returning to the B8007 and descending to Kilchoan, the main centre of population in Ardnamurchan, the road passes the entrance to Mingary Farm and Castle. The latter is a most impressive building, strategically placed above a natural landing place, where the sharp edge of a flat volcanic sheet forms a deep channel. It has been built on a steep rock face overlooking the Sound of Mull and can be entered only from the north. At the moment the castle is unsafe and not open to the public. It is remarkably well preserved for a castle of its age but it is decaying rapidly and swift action is needed before it begins to collapse.

Its foundations were possibly laid during the thirteenth century. In 1493, after the fourth and last Lord of the Isles was forced to forfeit his lands, James IV came to Mingary to receive the submission of the Lord's vassals in the southern isles, returning two years later to accept the oath of allegiance of the northern chiefs. The castle, therefore, witnessed the collapse of the Lordship of the Isles, a great tragedy for Gaeldom. A contemporary bard wrote in Gaelic:

> It is no joy without Clan Donald,
> It is no strength to be without them,
> The best race in the round world,
> To them belongs every good man
> . . . For sorrow and for sadness
> I have forsaken wisdom and learning.
> On their account I have forgotten all things.
> It is no joy without Clan Donald.

Although the Lordship was a Viking foundation, it was fundamentally a Gaelic regime. It was governed by the Lord and a Great Council, which consisted of thanes, sub-thanes and freeholders and was responsible for the Lord's initiation ceremony. At its zenith the Lordship was a powerful kingdom, establishing a network of castles said to be 'the most remarkable collection of thirteenth century lord's strongholds to be found in any one region of Britain'. Mingary was a late addition to the collection. The Lords recruited not only warriors to their retinue but also sculptors, musicians and physicians. It was a sophisticated, if, in war, rather brutal, culture. Standing on the shore at Mingary, it is not difficult to imagine the great galleys, with more than twenty oarsmen, gliding into the bay with their sails furled and the warriors disembarking, clad in their long, quilted surcoats and helmets and armed with their massive two-handed swords.

After 1493, the collapse of the Lordship led to interminable disputes among the chiefs in the west. In 1517 Sir Donald MacDonald, in rebellion against the Crown and attempting to claim dominion over the Isles, expelled MacIan of Ardnamurchan from Mingary, razed the Castle and laid waste the surrounding townships. The Castle, however, was quickly rebuilt. In 1588, when a Spanish ship was forced into Tobermory Bay on Mull, Lachlan MacLean of Duart, promising to provide canvas and timber for the repairs, obtained the services of 100 Spanish soldiers to plunder the Small Isles and Ardnamurchan. They laid siege to the Castle for three weeks but could not overwhelm it and left it standing.

In the seventeenth century the Campbells gained control of the area and, because of their oppression of the Ardnamurchan people, provoked the last serious, but unsuccessful, rising against the Scottish Crown. The former lairds, the MacIans, virtually disappeared from the scene when the rebellion was suppressed. The Campbells were caught on the losing side in the Civil War, and the Castle was assaulted again and finally taken by Colkitto MacDonald in 1644. It was garrisoned during the Jacobite rising and inhabited till at least 1819. An Alexander MacDougall lived there between 1792 and 1819, entertaining, on one occasion, Sir James Riddell, the laird of Ardnamurchan. MacDougall emigrated to Canada, chartering three ships to carry his family and retainers and settled at Mingary on Flatt River.

Kilchoan is a picturesque crofting settlement set in a broad bay facing the hills of Mull and Morvern. The village contains a shop, a post office, petrol station, gallery and hotels – one of the latter, on the road to the lighthouse, is run by a native of Ardnamurchan and can produce the best cooking on the peninsula. The crofts of Kilchoan are scattered round the village but the township of Ormsaigbeg is laid out in small holdings along the western hillside. The latter is an example of the kind of crofting community envisaged by the 'improving' landlords, who deliberately restricted the amount of land given to each tenant to force him to work at what they considered to be more productive activities, such as fishing or kelp burning.

In the winter of 1836/37 crop failure threatened many Highland communities with starvation. Funds were raised in the cities to provide meal for the stricken districts of the north. In spite of these efforts, arrears of rent mounted and 20 families left Ardnamurchan and Sunart in September 1837 on the *Brilliant*. In those days emigration usually meant permanent separation from those who remained. There was little chance of a return journey. The pain of the little groups, who stood on the deck and watched Ben Hiant disappear behind the Morvern hills, is unimaginable. The population of Ardnamurchan fell from 1,514 in 1798 to 1,430 in 1838. In fact, comparing the number of births with the number of deaths, it should have risen by about 260, which suggests that about 350 left the parish during these years. More were to leave during the Great Famine of 1847/55, the population falling to 1,179 in 1849. By 1889 there were only 14 crofters in Ormsaigbeg and four in Kilchoan. Today, although there are 23 crofts in the former township, only four or five of them are worked. There are three larger crofts in Ormsaigmore and three or four in Kilchoan. The steady flow of emigration has weakened the community and the last war took its toll of the young men. Ormsaigbeg provided no fewer than 52 seamen between 1939 and 1945.

Above the village, behind the old manse, the ruins of a church stand on the hill. An eighteenth-century building, incorporating apparently an earlier twelfth- or thirteenth-century one, it has three arched windows and a slab-lintelled doorway. In the cemetery there are several ancient stones, which would benefit from some additional protection from the weather. One of these, a long, flat stone, is said to have been brought from Iona. John MacColl, the notorious tacksman, is buried here and John Patience, who was minister of the parish between 1804 and 1827. One of the ministers, Daniel MacLauchlan, was imprisoned in London in 1735, suspected of being the author of 'a vile, abominable and obscene pamphlet dedicated to a Noble Peer' – an essay, in fact, on 'Improving and Adding to the strength of Great Britain and Ireland by Fornication'.

Almost opposite the new church, a road leads down to the pier and the ferry to Tobermory. Unfortunately this is not a car ferry and, because Tobermory lies in Strathclyde Region and Kilchoan in Highland, it seems unlikely that the service will ever be improved. When the new Regions were formed in 1974, inhabitants of remote areas were assured that they would gain from incorporation in local authorities which possessed a stronger financial base. There is little evidence of such benefits in West Ardnamurchan. A permanent car ferry service would be of incalculable value to the whole peninsula.

The road leading to the lighthouse passes a beautiful hill loch covered with water lilies and winds north through black volcanic knolls and hazel scrub. At Achosnich the road swings sharply up the hill towards the west. Grigadale is the last farm before the lighthouse. Originally the lands of Grigadale were held by the monks of Iona under the Lords of Isles.

Beyond Grigadale lies the most westerly point of mainland Britain and Ardnamurchan light. This point marked the division between the different lines of Clan Donald from the time of Somerled to that of James VI. It is a wild place in a west wind, with the great swell crashing against the rocks and curling up round the lighthouse. On a quiet summer's evening, on the other hand, the sunset over Coll can contain all the extraordinary shadows and fires of a Turner painting. There is a car park near the lighthouse and one or two places to camp. Campers, however, should remember that, if a sea fog rolls in during the night, the fog horn, which, from a distance, is merely a plaintive drone, will blast out its warning like a great

Ardnamurchan Lighthouse, on the most westerly point of the British mainland.

organ, its bass notes reverberating almost palpably round the rocks. The short walk to the lighthouse should not be missed. On the thin soil, between the outcrops of gabbro, harebells, saxifrages and small yellow trefoils seem to crouch close to the ground for shelter. At sea, gannets plummet towards the waves to pluck invisible fish from the green depths. At night the beam of the light swings across the sky, as it has done since 1849, faithfully warning mariners of the treacherous rocks. In 1838 the Kilchoan minister had complained that there was no light to guide the increasing number of steamers which sailed between Glasgow and Skye. Eight years later Alan Stevenson, the father of Robert Louis, was asked to design one for this remote point. Red granite from the Ross of Mull was shipped to the site and each stone carefully shaped to form an arc. It cost almost £1,400 and was completed in 1849. It is possible to visit the tower by arrangement during the day and see the original lens mechanism. The walled gardens below the lighthouse – now mechanised – allowed the keepers to have fresh vegetables and potatoes before the road was improved.

A road forks off the B8007 at the telephone exchange near

Sanna crofts, Ardnamurchan.

Kilchoan, leading to one of the most popular beaches in the area. Sanna Bay, with its long dunes of white sand and fragile machair pasture, attracts visitors from all over the peninsula. There is a car park and even a telephone kiosk at the end of the road. Sanna was laid out in 20 crofts in 1851 with a stock of 20 cows and followers and 100 sheep. The crofters had to build houses for themselves and reclaim the land. Across the moss today, the ruins of Plocaig stand as a grim reminder of the evictions. Nine families lived here in 1861. In the whole of Sanna there were 12 crofts in 1889. Only one family lives there now. Sanna House, at the west end of the bay, was built by Miss M.E.M. Donaldson, the authoress of *Wandering in the Western Highlands*, in 1925. It was originally constructed in the traditional manner with a thatched roof but was destroyed by fire in 1947. It is now owned by an architect from Oban, who has modernised and extended the remains and uses it as a holiday house. Most of the houses in Sanna now fall into this category.

There are some splendid walks round Sanna. There is a track to the Glendrian caves, where fulmars wheel along the cliffs, and there is a path to Portuairk in the other direction. It does not take long to climb Meall Sanna, from which there is a wonderful view of the bay and, beyond the headland, the Small Isles. On the massive blocks of black gabbro, pools sparkle in the sun and form streams of extraordinary clarity in the crevices.

Sanna is the setting for the poignant reminiscences of Alasdair MacLean in his *Night Falls on Ardnamurchan*, who lived in one of the houses near the telephone kiosk. I remember asking a local worthy for his opinion of the book. 'A lot of bunkum,' he replied, dismissing what I regarded as a sensitive and erudite work in a few words. I discovered later, with some relief, that he could not read.

Ardgour (East)

Visitors returning from Ardnamurchan or Mull via Lochaline might consider following the A861 through Ardgour to Fort William instead of using Corran Ferry. Even for those staying in the Fort William area this route can provide a leisurely circular tour by crossing the ferry and turning northeast towards Loch Eil and Corpach.

Beyond Ardgour there is a cemetery with some eighteenth- and early nineteenth-century gravestones and a memorial to the MacLeans of Ardgour. An avenue of young rowans leads up to it from the roadside and an old fir tree hangs over the walls. Further east Conaglen House stands among some magnificent Sequoias on the banks of the Cona river. Owned by the Douglas Earls of Morton since the middle of the nineteenth century, this estate became a deer forest towards the end of the century, when Lord Morton, who was said to have had 'a mania for deer shooting', removed three crofters and a small farmer from Callop near Glenfinnan. Apparently one of the Garvans and Drumfearn on Loch Eil were also cleared but these removals seem to have preceded the formation of the forest. Conaglen is still a sporting estate, with excellent fishing and stalking as far as Loch Shiel, but it is no longer in the hands of the Mortons.

Beyond Conaglen the road passes through mature pines and

larches and a profusion of rhododendrons. Just as it emerges from some scrub oak woods, there is an extraordinary little house with sloping walls and a slate roof, its position on the roadside and its shape suggesting that it may have been a toll house. The first crofting township on this road is Trioslaig. A typical crofting settlement on the shore of Loch Linnhe, it contains 11 crofts, on which the old houses have been abandoned in favour of more comfortable dwellings.

As the road swings round the point opposite Caol, the Wiggins Teape Paper Mill comes into sight on the north side of Loch Eil. In 1980 the pulp section of the mill closed, leading to 460 redundancies. This was a terrible blow to the local economy, and the adverse effects of the closure are till felt in Corpach. For some time after this the timber felled for pulping in the West was shipped to Scandinavia, processed there and brought back to Scotland to be made into paper! The workforce and the local authority appealed to the Government for help but their pleas were ignored. A few years later it was pouring £1 million a day into the Falkland Islands. Shortly after the Corpach mill closed, a Finnish company opened an integrated newsprint mill at Shotton in North Wales, and a new mill has been built in Ayrshire by another Scandinavian firm. First the Highland glens were cleared of people to make way for sheep, then the sheep and shepherds were cleared to make way for trees, and finally, when the trees mature, scarcely any of the reward will return to the small communities of the north. If visitors pause to gaze across the still waters of Loch Eil towards the factory, perhaps they will see it as I do – a reminder of the fickle interest of alien companies whose predatory excursions into the Highlands leave little in their wake but demoralisation and decay.

Further along the shore there are several crofting townships. Achaphubail is the largest of these and, apart from the croft houses, contains a row of council houses and a school. Blathaich is the most attractive with a multitude of wild roses between the road and the shore, their delicate flowers contrasting with the dark water of the loch. Above the road, almost concealed in the hazel scrub, stand the ruins of abandoned houses, some of them with rounded corners and some with chimneys and dressed stone gables. The fallen

Corpach Paper Mill.

stones are covered in sphagnum moss, and squirrels leave hoards of hazel nuts on the hearths, once warmed by the peat fires of the people who tried to scrape a living from their small fields or by fishing in the loch. There is a little church, dated 1817, near the road, set in a beautiful natural meadow with a rich profusion of wild flowers and clovers. It is an attractive area with several good camping and picnic places on the shore.

Just beore Dubh Uisge (Black Water) there is a pleasant walk along the old road past a building which must have been a mill. There is a glacial knoll above the ruin, covered in pine, spruce and hazel. In the early summer the ground beneath the trees is a mass of bluebells and, on a fine day, with the sweet smell of resin, it is a delightful place for a rest. The gooseberry bushes beside the mill can add the perfect finishing touch to a picnic. The track continues over the hill to Corrlarach through a conifer plantation.

Beyond Dubh Uisge the road follows the shore to Garbhan (Garvan), where there is a large salmon farm and a splendid view of the Lochaber hills. At Drumasallie the single-track road ends and joins the A830. Just west of this junction, at the head of Loch Shiel, Prince Charles Edward Stewart raised his standard in August 1745, commencing a campaign which almost unseated the Hanoverian King but ended in the decimation of the Jacobite clans at Culloden. More myths have been generated by this rising than by any other event in Scottish history. It was not a Highland rebellion. Many Highlanders did not take part in it and some were forced to join it by threats of eviction or removal of their cattle. The Jacobite support came mainly from Appin, the Great Glen, Locheil, Lochaber, Moidart, Knoydart, Ardnamurchan and the Western Isles. The Reay, Sutherland and Assynt people were not 'out' and only one of the three Skye chiefs joined the Prince. At Culloden, the last great battle on British soil, there were Highlanders and Lowland Scots on both sides. However, the punishment inflicted on those who supported the Prince after the battle produced a bitterness in which mythology was bound to flourish. The Duke of Cumberland let loose his soldiers on the countryside. The wounded were slaughtered, homes were burned, and, worst of all, black cattle, on which the people relied to pay their rent, were stolen and driven in vast herds to the southern trysts. The Jacobite clansmen were thus deprived of their most valuable asset and the effect of that deprivation lasted for more than a century. The monument at Glenfinnan is as much a reminder of 'Butcher' Cumberland's atrocities as a memorial to the unrealised dreams of the Jacobites.

Further Reading

History

J. Bannerman, *The Beatons*. Edinburgh, 1986.

R. Black, *MacMhaighstir Alasdair – The Ardnamurchan Years*. Inverness, 1986.

D. Duff (ed.), *Queen Victoria's Highland Journals*. Exeter, 1980.

T. Devine, *The Great Highland Famine*. Edinburgh, 1988.

A. Fraser, *Inveraray – The Royal Burgh*. Edinburgh, 1977.

P. Gaskell, *Morvern Transformed*. Cambridge, 1968.

I. F. Grant, *Highland Folk Ways*. London, 1961.

A. R. B. Haldane, *The Drove Roads of Scotland*. Newton Abbot, 1973.

J. Hunter, *The Making of the Crofting Community*. Edinburgh, 1976.

H. MacDougall, *Island of Kerrera*. Local pub., n.d.

A. McLeary, *The Tobermory Treasure*. London, 1986.

W. Orr, *Deer Forests, Landlords and Crofters*. Edinburgh, 1982.

J. Prebble, *The Highland Clearances*. Penguin, 1963.

D. Wordsworth, *A Tour in Scotland*. Edinburgh, 1981 (reprint).

Geology

G. Y. Craig, *The Geology of Scotland*. Edinburgh, 1983.

C. D. Gribble (ed.), *Ardnamurchan – A Geological Guide*. Edinburgh, 1976.

R. Price, *Highland Landforms*. Inverness, 1976.

Natural History etc.

M. L. Anderson, *A History of Scottish Forestry*. London, 1967.

F. F. Darling, *West Highland Survey*. Oxford, 1955.

R. Faux, *The West – A Sailing Companion*. Edinburgh, 1982.

H. Fife, *The Tree Life of Argyll*. Gartocharn, 1981.

General

O. Brown and J. Whittaker, *A Walk Round Tobermory*. Oban, 1988.

M. Campbell, *Argyll, The Enduring Heartland*. London, 1977.

C. Hunter, *Oban, Kilmore and Kilbride*. Privately printed. 1984.

J. Macgregor, *West Highland Way*. BBC, 1985.

A. MacLean, *Night Falls on Ardnamurchan*. London, 1984.

P. A. MacNab, *The Isle of Mull*. Newton Abbot, 1970.

J. Mackechnie (ed.), *The Dewar Manuscripts*. Glasgow, 1963.

J. B. Stephenson, *Ford – a Village in the West Highlands*. Edinburgh, 1984.

Mairi MacDonald, West Highland series of local guides.

Index

223